Kirkyard Romanticism

Edinburgh Critical Studies in Romanticism
Series Editors: Ian Duncan and Penny Fielding

Available Titles

A Feminine Enlightenment: British Women Writers and the Philosophy of Progress, 1759–1820
JoEllen DeLucia

Reinventing Liberty: Nation, Commerce and the Historical Novel from Walpole to Scott
Fiona Price

The Politics of Romanticism: The Social Contract and Literature
Zoe Beenstock

Radical Romantics: Prophets, Pirates, and the Space beyond Nation
Talissa J. Ford

Literature and Medicine in the Nineteenth-century Periodical Press: Blackwood's Edinburgh Magazine, *1817–1858*
Megan Coyer

Discovering the Footsteps of Time: Geological Travel Writing in Scotland, 1700–1820
Tom Furniss

The Dissolution of Character in Late Romanticism
Jonas Cope

Commemorating Peterloo: Violence, Resilience and Claim-making during the Romantic Era
Edited by Michael Demson and Regina Hewitt

Dialectics of Improvement: Scottish Romanticism, 1786–1831
Gerard Lee McKeever

Literary Manuscript Culture in Romantic Britain
Michelle Levy

Scottish Romanticism and Collective Memory in the British Atlantic
Kenneth McNeil

Romantic Periodicals in the Twenty-first Century: Eleven Case Studies from Blackwood's Edinburgh Magazine
Edited by Nicholas Mason and Tom Mole

Godwin and the Book: Imagining Media, 1783–1836
J. Louise McCray

Thomas De Quincey: Romanticism in Translation
Brecht de Groote

Romantic Environmental Sensibility: Nature, Class and Empire
Edited by Ve-Yin Tee

Romantic Pasts: History, Fiction and Feeling in Britain, 1790–1850
Porscha Fermanis

British Romanticism and Denmark
Cian Duffy

The Lady's Magazine (1770–1832) and the Making of Literary History
Jennie Batchelor

Mary Wollstonecraft: Cosmopolitan
Laura Kirkley

Romanticism and Consciousness, Revisited
Edited by Richard Sha and Joel Faflak

Remediating the 1820s
Edited by Jon Mee and Matthew Sangster

Romanticism and the Poetics of Orientation
Joey S. Kim

Romantic Women's Writing and Sexual Transgression
Edited by Kathryn Ready and David Sigler

Seeking Justice: Literature, Law and Equity during the Age of Revolutions
Edited by Michael Demson and Regina Hewitt

Kirkyard Romanticism: Death, Modernity and Scottish Literature in the Nineteenth Century
Sarah Sharp

Visit our website at: www.edinburghuniversitypress.com/series/ECSR

Kirkyard Romanticism

Death, Modernity and Scottish Literature in the Nineteenth Century

Sarah Sharp

EDINBURGH
University Press

Edinburgh University Press is one of the leading university presses in the UK. We publish academic books and journals in our selected subject areas across the humanities and social sciences, combining cutting-edge scholarship with high editorial and production values to produce academic works of lasting importance. For more information visit our website: edinburghuniversitypress.com

© Sarah Sharp 2024

Published with the support of the University of Edinburgh Scholarly Publishing Initiatives Fund.

Edinburgh University Press Ltd
13 Infirmary Street
Edinburgh EH1 1LT

Typeset in 10.5/13pt Sabon LT Pro
by Cheshire Typesetting Ltd, Cuddington, Cheshire,

A CIP record for this book is available from the British Library

ISBN 978 1 4744 8341 4 (hardback)
ISBN 978 1 4744 8343 8 (webready PDF)
ISBN 978 1 4744 8344 5 (epub)

The right of Sarah Sharp to be identified as the author of this work has been asserted in accordance with the Copyright, Designs and Patents Act 1988, and the Copyright and Related Rights Regulations 2003 (SI No. 2498).

Contents

Acknowledgements — vi

Introduction: 'I was a "Young Mortality"' — 1
1. Intertextuality, Tradition and the Kirkyard Forefathers — 28
2. 'In the burial ground of his native parish': Romancing the Kirkyard — 51
3. The Suicide's Grave: Suicide, Civilisation and Community — 73
4. The Doctor and the Dead: Anatomy, Feeling and Genre — 103
5. 'Burking, Bill and Cholera': Death, Mobility and National Epidemic — 127
6. 'To lay our bones within the bosom of our native soil': The Kirkyard in the Age of Migrants — 151

Bibliography — 179
Index — 194

Acknowledgements

The initial development of this project would not have been possible without doctoral funding from the Wolfson Foundation's Postgraduate Scholarship in the Humanities. I am also indebted to the Leverhulme Foundation, the Irish Research Council and the Fulbright Commission whose postdoctoral funding facilitated the maturation and expansion of the project to a more ambitious and outward-looking book.

It has been the misfortune of this book to be researched and written during interesting times. There is not space here to fully express my gratitude to the many colleagues, family members and friends who have supported me and my project amidst international moves, professional mobility and a global pandemic but I am going to have a go.

I want to thank first my doctoral supervisor Penny Fielding whose calm and consistent faith in my capabilities has always surpassed my own. I would also like to acknowledge the equally unwavering support and kindness of my second supervisor, Bob Irvine. Beyond my doctorate, I have had the benefit of the professional mentorship of Liam McIlvanney, Porscha Fermanis and Anthony Jarrells. I hope they will all be able to trace the footprints of our conversations in the pages of this book.

The book has also benefited from the ideas and input of many colleagues and friends. I would like to thank the members of the Romantic Studies Association of Australasia Writing Group, Sophie Cooper, Lucy Hinnie, Bradford Bow and Timothy Baker, all of whom have provided essential feedback on drafts of this work. I have also benefited hugely from conversations with colleagues and friends, including Patrick Scott, Alison Lumsden, the University of Edinburgh doctoral cohort of 2013–16, and the SouthHem Postdoc team while developing my ideas.

Finally, I would like to say a heartfelt thank you to my parents, Andy and Kirsty, my sister, Catriona, and my partner, Mo. This is also your book in many ways, and I hope that I have done your support and love justice.

Introduction: 'I was a "Young Mortality"'

> called upon to say what is the most interesting series of objects in almost any country, I should, without hesitation reply – the spots where the dead are interred.[1]

In his January 1858 'Australian Sketch' for *Tait's Edinburgh Magazine*, the Scottish-Australian writer and politician Thomas McCombie opens by advocating the graveyard as a site of national interest. He proposes an alternative grand tour of gravesites, suggesting that the Roman catacombs and Westminster Abbey's Poets' Corner are preferable attractions to the British Museum and the Vatican. He uses this argument to introduce his own account of a newer set of national memorials: the bush graves of settler colonial Australia. McCombie's enthusiastic extolling of these 'most interesting … objects' is part of a wider cultural trend of his time where the burial sites of the dead became places of increasing cultural significance. From the eighteenth century, the grave site had taken on new importance as a place of real and literary pilgrimage across the anglophone world.[2] McCombie's sketch also participates in an already well-established bush-grave-themed subgenre of Australian writing and art, describing the burials of colonists in the Australian bush.[3] Both trends are indicative of a wider association between national culture and the commemoration of a collective 'national dead' in the nineteenth-century imagination.

However, McCombie cites a specifically Scottish precedent for his sketch. Early in his essay, McCombie makes a connection between the origins of his own interest in the grave site and the Edinburgh-published literature of the early nineteenth century. In particular, he sets up the rural graveyard scenes of Walter Scott and Caroline Bowles Southey, and the medical tales of Samuel Warren, as possible antecedents to his own bush grave sketch. He describes his childhood self as a '"Young Mortality", peering amongst odd-shaped, moss grown tombstones'.[4]

McCombie's influences are an unexpected coalition of writers: Scott, the 'most successful writer of his day' and populariser of the Scottish historical novel,[5] Bowles, an English writer and poet whose posthumous reputation has often been dominated by her brief marriage to the Poet Laureate Robert Southey,[6] and Warren, a Victorian lawyer and critically neglected novelist best known for his medical and legal fiction.[7] In McCombie's essay, they form an unexpected alliance that, I want to suggest, plants the seed for a new way of thinking about Romantic writing. McCombie's models – Bowles, Warren and Scott – all published their influential graveyard scenes with one Edinburgh-based publisher, William Blackwood, between 1816 and 1837.[8] Their texts were not unique within the publisher's oeuvre; over the first decades of the nineteenth century, the kirkyard reoccurred across numerous novels, stories, poems, sketches and essays by writers with ties to Edinburgh and Blackwood.

During the early decades of the nineteenth century the publisher was an important node in the literary networks of Romantic Edinburgh, nurturing the careers of some of the period's most prominent Scottish authors and poets including John Galt, John Wilson and James Hogg. A commercial and political rival to Walter Scott's Whig publisher Archibald Constable, Blackwood hosted one of the era's most important periodicals, *Blackwood's Edinburgh Magazine*, and originated a 'Blackwoodian school of Scottish fiction' that capitalised on the post-*Waverley* vogue for Scottish fiction.[9] This book draws together a group of texts from the pages of *Blackwood's*, the books published by William Blackwood and the works of authors with connections to the publisher that feature one recurring motif: the dead. Whether the dead lie peacefully in their graves, like the saintly peasants of John Wilson's *Lights and Shadows of Scottish Life* (1822), or rise eerily from them, like the terrified revenant of John Galt's 'The Buried Alive' (1821), in these texts the deathbed, the rituals of burial, and the burial site are invested with particular significance. This significance, I argue, is not coincidental but part of a collective 'kirkyard Romanticism' shared by this loose network of writers.

The kirkyard texts participate in a very nineteenth-century fascination with the dead and dying,[10] but are distinguished by a shared set of conventions, concerns and representational strategies due to their Scottish publication context and their focus on the local and regional. They respond to the increasing ubiquity of what Saree Makdisi terms 'a narrative of modernization as world history' by using the dead to engage with concepts (the local, the traditional, the historic and the emotional) that seemed to be missing from this narrative.[11] By placing a nationally representative dead in Britain's peripheral spaces, these texts imagine a role for Scotland as a repository for the values that maintain the cultural distinctiveness and colonial supremacy of the still newly formed British nation. Scotland becomes Britain's synecdoche and time capsule: at once central to and removed from the national body. The kirkyard thus operates as a Romantic motif, countering, complicating and contributing to the formation of the modern nation by turns.

McCombie's sketch is a productive place to begin this book, not only because it draws attention to the network of writers whose work participates in the creation of the kirkyard archetype, but also because it indicates the wider argument I want to make about the archetype's importance and reach. Kirkyard Romanticism, I argue, extends far beyond the initial cluster of Scottish authors writing regional fiction for Blackwood. Its footprints are visible in Scottish literature and in writing about England and the British colonies throughout the nineteenth century. My use of the term 'kirkyard', in this book, riffs on the 'kailyard': a designation that originally referred to a genre of late nineteenth-century Scottish regional fiction but that has come to operate as a term of critique for all the 'wrong ways of writing about Scotland'.[12] As I will explore later in this introduction, the endurance of 'kailyard' as a term of critique within Scottish letters is part of a wider problem with the way in which Scotland's literary nineteenth century has been interpreted and remembered. In this narrative, the Victorian era is one of stagnation and inward-looking parochialism that follows a golden age of Romantic innovation. This book uses the motif of the kirkyard to suggest a different way to read the literature of this period. I argue that kirkyard Romanticism is a continuous and resistant tradition that evades conventional periodisation. It represents one of the throughlines that connects Romantics like Scott and Hogg to later Scottish writers such as J. M. Barrie and John Buchan at the turn of the twentieth century.

From its early employment in the English writing of John Wilson and Caroline Southey Bowles, the regionalist nationalism of the kirkyard is also highly modular and easily transferred to different regions of the British world. I argue that the kirkyard's capacity to articulate subnational national identity makes it particularly suited to the nation-building efforts of Britain's settler colonies during the nineteenth century. Recognising the kirkyard motif within Scottish Romantic writing, then, offers a new key to understanding, not just the Scottish literary culture of the 1810s, 1820s and 1830s, but the continued use of this imagery in Scottish literature and wider anglophone writing. As I will argue, McCombie's Australian graves, simultaneously lost in, and defining, their landscape, are suggestive of the ways in which we might trace the long shadow of these literary gravestones across the nineteenth century and the English-speaking world.

Our Dead: Society, Nation and the 'Something More'

The kirkyard texts draw upon an already established use of the dead in contemporary political and literary writing. The print culture of the eighteenth century was crowded with graves.[13] Both the graveyard poetry of the mid-century and Enlightenment theories of sympathy used the dead to muse upon the relationship between the individual, society and the past.[14] Graves and deathbeds also featured regularly in the sentimental fiction of the second half of the century, functioning as catalysts for sympathetic outpourings of grief and as opportunities for political commentary.[15] Meanwhile, the horrors of the crypt both entertained readers and articulated incisive critiques of power in the burgeoning Gothic novel.[16] Writers like Edmund Burke and William Godwin invoked the dead to explore their own visions of society during and after the revolutionary crisis.[17] The English Romantics further drew upon these images in their writing to explore human connections.[18] The grave in British literature by the late 1810s functioned as a multi-layered symbol that could be used to many different ends and allowed almost unparalleled intertextual reference.

Scottish Romantics also developed several distinctive approaches to the dead. The representation of a depopulated, but grave-smattered and haunted, Highland landscape in James Macpherson's Ossian poems responds to the political and social aftermath of the 1745 Jacobite Rebellion and is followed by an increasing interest in Highland ghost stories.[19] Commemoration of the dead is a recurring theme in Scott's historical novels and poetry prior to *Old Mortality* as the dead often come to articulate the relationship between history and modernity.[20] James Hogg's use of the dead in his early Scottish tales begins long before his involvement in *Blackwood's* and, as will be explored later in this book, provided one of the most important precedents for the kirkyard Romanticism of his contemporaries and inheritors. Scottish literature responded to the literary interest in death in wider British literature and formulated its own motifs.

Work by scholars including Ian Duncan[21] and John Barrell[22] has identified the figure of 'the upright corpse' as an important symbol in works of Scottish Romantic writing, particularly those of James Hogg. In these readings the dead are uncanny figures whose unnatural incursions bring the past into the present of the story in disruptive and troubling ways.[23] While these readings tend to foreground the rising dead, Anthony Hasler contextualises Hogg's rising corpses as a response to the sentimental deathbed scenes featured in John Wilson's Scottish fiction.[24] My own argument in this book also suggests that the upright corpses and the peaceful graves of Scottish Romantic writing are participants in a single conversation. Douglas Gifford has described a 'tradition of Scottish historical and social fiction, with its indigenous themes, patterns and symbolism, and its own deconstructive agenda'.[25] While this book strays beyond the generic confines of Gifford's original argument, I want to suggest that kirkyard Romanticism is underwritten by the same pattern of intertextual reference and deconstruction. Within the works I examine, the unburied dead operate as the buried dead's deconstructive double.

The roots of this binary between the risen and the peaceful dead can, I argue, be traced to the anti-revolutionary political rhetoric of the Whig MP and political theorist Edmund Burke, and his influence on the conservativism of *Blackwood's Magazine*. Burke has been identified by numerous scholars as a fundamentally important progenitor of the form of conservative discourse adopted by *Blackwood's*.[26] This ideological debt, as Anthony Jarrells and Matt Salyer note, is reflected in *Blackwood's* content which often refers to or cites Burke.[27] During the early decades of the nineteenth century Burke's influence on the magazine was sustained and obvious.

Burke's response to the French Revolution, *Reflections on the Revolution in France* (1790), is often cited as a touchstone of post-Enlightenment British conservative thought. Responding to the pro-revolutionary sermon *A Discourse on the Love of Our Country* given by the dissenting minister Richard Price in November 1789, Burke inaugurates an alliance between conservative ideas of nationhood and the binary of disturbed and undisturbed grave that would underwrite the kirkyard texts of the nineteenth century. Writing amid the shattering and reshaping of political and social life of the age of revolutions, the *Reflections* enlist personal sympathy for the dead to nationalistic and anti-revolutionary ends.

In multiple publications, of which *Reflections* was perhaps the most important, Burke asserts that the fundamental nature of British society rests in the social structures that men have formed over generations. Burke famously conceptualises the nation as 'a permanent body composed of transitory parts': thus, although individuals die and are born, generations renew the overall structure, replacing one another and allowing a culture and social system to endure.[28] In this schema, the nation contains no permanent units but is itself permanent. This theory of social relations foregrounds the role of the dead in the development of human culture, Burke argues that:

> society is indeed a contract ... As the ends of such a partnership cannot be obtained in many generations, it becomes a partnership not only between those who are living, but between those who are living, those who are dead, and those who are to be born.[29]

He also imagines identification with the nation as an attachment built upon familial and local sympathies:

> To be attached to the subdivision, to love the little platoon we belong to in society, is the first principle (the germ as it were) of public affections. It is the first link in the series by which we proceed toward a love to our country and to mankind.'[30]

Sympathy for our 'little platoon' is represented both as the 'germ' of patriotic national identification and as a universal human response. Thus, patriotic identification with Burke's British state is characterised as an uncontroversial natural reaction based on more immediate and local ties. Burke's perspective on community and inheritance explains why death and the grave are such central metaphors in his writing. If our very nature is contained within the social structures that we have inherited from our ancestors, then the graveyard contains the building blocks of ourselves, and of our nation.

David Bromwich has commented that in Burke's writings posthumous rituals represent a form of self-preservation: 'in the same gesture by which we honour people and things that have survived in memory, we make a possible place for the survival of something of ourselves'.[31] In remembering the dead and placing them at the centre of our sense of social relations, we not only build a sense of identity in the here and now but in some way attempt to prepare a posthumous identity for ourselves.

This enduring social structure is, however, disrupted in instances of rapid, uncontrolled social change. Burke's critique of the French Revolution is that, in attempting to fundamentally alter how society is organised, the revolutionaries disturb the foundations of civilisation itself, discarding the progress that previous generations have already effected. In his 1796 *Letter to a Noble Lord*, Burke resumes his criticism of the French revolutionaries. Imagining the Revolution through the prism of Gothic imagery, Burke depicts the *sans-culottes* as grave robbers who risk calling up a dangerous spectre through the disrespect they display toward the dead:

> Neither sex nor age – nor the sanctuary of the tomb is sacred to them. They have so determined a hatred to all the privileged orders, that they deny even to the departed the sad immunities of the grave ... they unplumb the dead for bullets to assassinate the living. If all revolutionists were not proof against all caution, I should recommend it to their consideration, that no persons were ever known to history, either sacred or profane, to vex the sepulchre, and, by their sorceries, to call up the prophetic dead, with any other event, than the prediction of their own disastrous fate.[32]

Burke's depiction of the revolutionaries aligns the disturbed grave with political instability and national fragmentation, and thereby associates the intact grave with social harmony. In this image, each 'sepulchre' becomes a small national monument that serves to unite the nation with its history and the people with their ancestors. The destruction of these monuments represents a traumatic shattering of this relationship between past and present, a rending of the national social fabric.

In the context of the periodical wars of the early nineteenth century, Blackwood's conservative contributors present the dead in a similar way. Burke's anti-revolutionary conservatism combined well with the radical Toryism proposed by *Blackwood's*. In particular, Matt Salyer argues, the aesthetic and polemical aspects of Burke's political writings accord with the type of political rhetoric that defined the magazine, 'Burke's ideological slipperiness, which endlessly frustrated his late eighteenth- and early nineteenth-century critics, makes sense in the context of *Blackwood's* similarly poetic and contradictory Toryism.'[33] Burke's decently interred dead uphold an image of society that is familial, local, stratified and patriarchal, while the unburied and mistreated bodies of the Revolution represent the destruction of these values. The core ideas that Burke's dead stand for are also at the heart of the *Blackwood's* image of nation. This use of the dead in both cases draws upon the emotional and the aesthetic rather than the logical. Burke, like the *Blackwood's* commentators who followed him, relies on an assumed concept of shared common-sense British values. The emotive images of intact and damaged graves that he deploys at moments of key rhetorical importance are designed to be unquestionable and unassailable. To disinter a body is to fundamentally sunder bonds of heritage and sympathy; it is an image designed for almost universal emotional impact.

Faced with the fear of a British revolution, Burke uses the dead as a symbol that can demarcate an apparently unquestionable set of conservative national values. He is not alone in using the idea of a collective or national dead to grapple with political and social change during this period. The growing proliferation of the literary dead in the eighteenth century emerges alongside new ideas of collective identity.

By the eighteenth century the development of an increasingly commercial society was rapidly altering the structures that had informed Western European life in previous centuries. These forces disrupted existing social roles and changed the relationship between the individual and the collective. As the century progressed, political revolutions seemed poised to topple previously enduring systems of governance. It is amid this tumult, many historians and cultural theorists argue, that the modern nation-state takes shape. As Andrew Lincoln has noted, it is increasingly 'commonplace to think of nations as political constructions' and to date their emergence not to prehistory or medieval dynasties but to the advent of print culture and mass literacy.[34] In one of the most influential of these studies, *Imagined Communities*, Benedict Anderson argues that the modern nation is 'an imagined political community' and dates its emergence to the late eighteenth century.[35] As the power of the idea of a 'divinely-ordained, hierarchical dynastic realm' waned, Anderson argues, the modern nation emerged as a collectively authored work of fiction.[36]

As I will explore in greater detail in the next section of this introduction, this period has been consistently recognised as the one in which the modern British nation, and Scotland's place within it, was taking on a new shape. The political unions between England and Scotland in 1707 and then with Ireland in 1800 led to the formation of an essentially new state. These changing national borders brought with them a changing sense of British identity. Drawing on the work of scholars like Anderson, Linda Colley identifies the years between 1707 and 1837 as those in which the 'invention' of Britain took place.[37] Burke's nation is actually a very young and still highly contested political state – a situation that the idea of an enduring national dead seeks to mask.

At a time of rapid social change and instability, the grave became a central motif for those interested in the relationship between the individual and society in this new world. Historians including Phillipe Aries[38] and Thomas W. Laquer[39] suggest that Western cultural attitudes to the dead during the eighteenth and nineteenth centuries can act as an index to the shifting shape of a rapidly modernising society. In her 1995 book *Bearing the Dead*, Esther Schor also traces what she describes as a 'transition from the "natural" sympathies of the Enlightenment to the "political" sympathies of a revolutionary age' through the representation of mourning within British texts during the eighteenth and early nineteenth centuries.[40] In Schor's reading, the theories of sympathy of the eighteenth century seek to identify a moral consensus that binds commercial society together.[41] However, she identifies the revolutionary controversy of the 1790s as a moment that traumatically shattered the possibility that sympathy could ever function as a truly unifying social force.[42]

Her identification of the 1790s as a watershed moment has been reinforced by more recent studies of the topic. David McAllister notes that 'the dead as an anonymous social group, and the representation of their transmortal community with the living, assumed a new importance in the political and literary discourse of the 1790s'.[43]

The use of the dead in this specific historical moment, when national identity is both being constructed and threatened, chimes with a wider pattern recognised by scholars of nation in which the dead are recruited as national symbols. Anderson opens the first chapter of *Imagined Communities* with an image of the grave of the unknown soldier. He uses this figure to articulate the centrality of the relationship between the living and the dead in the formation of the new nations of the eighteenth century. Anderson suggests that nationalism, like religion, is inherently tied to the dead, as it promises a form of immortality. Nations 'always loom out of an immemorial past and, still more important, glide into a limitless future'.[44] Numerous nation theorists have recognised that the nation is imagined as a community containing both the living and the dead, in what McAllister terms 'a transmortal relationship'.[45] The invocation of a collective national dead draws not just on the way that the dead can articulate continuity but their broader capacity to produce emotional bonds. Katherine Verdery associates the dead's political role with the 'something more' that extends beyond the technical processes of the nation or state; they invoke 'feelings, the sacred, ideas of mortality, the non-rational'.[46] The dead as a collective can be co-opted to this cause due to their position as both universal and highly personal signifiers, their emotional resonance, and their simultaneous ties to national history and the domestic. They are effective symbols within a Romantic cultural nationalism that seeks to invest the nation-state with a power that is 'something more' than the arbitrary imposition of borders, institutions and treaties.

Verdery differentiates between what she terms the 'anonymous dead' and the 'named and famous dead' in these constructions of identity.[47] The famous dead, whether they are William Shakespeare, Princess Charlotte or Robert Burns, and the anonymous dead both take on nationally figurative roles in Romantic discourse. Paul Westover has foregrounded the role of the latter in Romantic cultural nationalism, taking particular interest in the proliferation of 'visits to authors' homes, haunts, and graves' real and imaginary during the period.[48] This book, though, like McAllister's and Anderson's, is concerned with the role of the 'anonymous' in national imagining. Just as Anderson's 'unknown soldier' can become a carrier for 'ghostly *national* imaginings' due to his anonymity, the dead who people the imagined kirkyards we will discuss are an archetypal mass of humble humanity who are at once everyone's ancestors and no one's.[49] The anonymity of the imagined soldier is, according to Anderson, what distinguishes the vision of the nation that these monuments represent from prior ideas of identity: 'the public ceremonial reverence accorded these monuments precisely *because* they are either deliberately empty or no one knows who lies inside them, has no true precedents in earlier times.'[50] Like the solitary and imaginary heroes of novels whom Anderson argues belong to the national 'collective body of readers', the soldier is an effective symbol of the modern nation because he unites the world of the individual with the fiction of the nation.[51] The anonymous dead are unencumbered by biographical specificity and instead offer a direct and unmediated connection to 'an immemorial past'.[52] They, therefore, allow for the articulation of the identity of the reading nation. In post-union Scotland these capabilities mean that the dead are particularly attractive signifiers for writers with an interest in shaping the contours of the emerging British nation and Scotland's place within it.

Romanticism and Modernity

If the eighteenth century was a time of rapid change for Scotland, it was also a historical moment when the idea of change itself was undergoing intensive examination. The rapid pace of material change was accompanied by an increasing desire to document and explain its processes. As Alex Benchimol and Gerard Lee McKeever note, the rapidly changing material environment of post-union Scotland acted as a catalyst for new modes of social theory.[53] Many of the most important figures of the Scottish Enlightenment were interested in cataloguing the nature of human society and accounting for the changes or developments they witnessed. Arthur Herman's attribution of the 'invention of the modern world' to the Scottish Enlightenment is hyperbolic, but can be used to think productively about the way that Scottish thinkers helped to shape what it meant to 'modernise' or experience 'modernity'.[54] In particular, the emergence of a stadial model of history in the work of thinkers like William Robertson and Adam Smith began to formalise the idea of human society as a linear development from barbarism to civilisation. History is imagined, in the work of these thinkers, as a forward progression that culminates in European, eighteenth-century modernity. As Katie Trumpener has observed, this process is presented as inexorable and impersonal: 'the Enlightenment model is evolutionary, emphasising the inevitability with which each developmental stage, each historical culture, is replaced by the next, more advanced one.'[55] These theories of human society contributed to the increasing dominance of what Peter J. Bowler terms 'the idea of continuous social progress' over other modes of understanding the relationship between past, present and future.[56] Disruptive forces that appeared to be revolutionising social relations at an unprecedented speed could be rationalised through a narrative of modernisation in which change was understood as positive and inexorable development or improvement.

The emergence of Romanticism is often linked to these processes and discourses. Almost from its inception, the term 'Romanticism' has been a contested one. As Duncan Wu has noted, 'although many definitions are suggested, none command universal agreement.'[57] British Romanticism, since its retrospective identification in the latter half of the nineteenth century, has been repeatedly revised to encompass a shifting canon of writers, time periods or a set of concepts.[58] While in the first half of the twentieth century Romanticism was imagined as a recognisable, uniform philosophy shared by a defined school of writers, increasingly the concept of a monolithic Romanticism has given way to a more pluralistic concept of 'Romanticisms'. This book is born in part of this move away from a Romanticism focused on a perceived 'Big Six' to a wider gallery of writers that includes, for example, voices from the four nations and the colonies.

This bigger, pluralised Romanticism is, within this book, understood in terms of its relationship with emerging modernity. The concepts of modernity and modernisation, gaining such traction in this period, have often been understood by scholars as the object with which Romanticism grapples. Michael Löwy and Robert Sayre propose an oppositional relationship between the two concepts: 'Romanticism represents a critique of modernity, that is, of modern capitalist civilization, in the name of values and ideals drawn from the past (the precapitalist, premodern past).'[59] In this account, the 'hegemonic' modernity of late eighteenth-century free market economics and industry in Europe inspires a countermovement in the form of Romanticism.[60] Saree Makdisi offers a similar understanding of Romanticism as a response to 'the narrative of a universal history – the world history of modernisation' and characterises Romantic texts as 'anti-histories of this process'.[61]

However, this relationship is rarely characterised as a simple opposition or binary. As Löwy and Sayre acknowledge, Romanticism is 'a modern critique of modernity' constituted by and participating in the process it critiques.[62] Thomas Pfau and Robert Mitchell suggest that part of the difficulty in defining Romanticism as a concept is this simultaneously oppositional and constitutional relationship:

> Romanticism's marked ambivalence and resistance to decisive conceptualization arises from the fact that it simultaneously extends the project of European modernity while offering itself as a sustained critical reflection on that very process.[63]

The Romantic here is understood to not just be constituted by the processes of modernity but as an active participant in the constitution of modernity as a concept.

This understanding of Romanticism as inextricable from modernity has been especially useful to scholars working within the field of Scottish Romantic Studies. Scotland's experience of Romanticism is fundamentally tied to the development of Scotland's distinctive relationship with nationhood over the eighteenth and nineteenth centuries and the complicity of ideas of modernity in this development. The Union of Parliaments in 1707 shifted the seat of power from Edinburgh to London. David McCrone famously termed Scotland after this point a 'stateless nation'.[64] In McCrone's account, post-union Scotland, due to its lack of a state apparatus, instantiates a unique or unusual version of the nation that develops differently from nation-states. However, Leith Davis argues that Scotland's status after the Union simply denaturalises the relationship between state and cultural identity, foregrounding the complexity of nationhood: 'Scotland displays only more prominently the tensions and ambiguities that result from trying to articulate any national identity.'[65]

In 1707 England was the more powerful partner in the British project due to its higher level of economic development. The union, to an extent, represented both opportunity, as Scots sought to 'modernise' their country using the newly acquired resources of the British state, and danger, as Scots reckoned with what Andrew Lincoln terms the 'economic and political homogenization that threatened the surviving autonomy of Scotland within the Union'.[66] Katie Trumpener situates the emergence of Scottish, Irish and Welsh cultural nationalisms as responses to this threat, resisting 'Enlightenment programs for economic transformation' and 'Enlightenment theories of historical periodization and historical progress'.[67]

Recent scholarship on Scottish Romanticism has increasingly understood the relationship between Enlightenment-inspired modernity and Romanticism as an exchange or conversation. Murray Pittock in his summary of the field notes that many of the defining works of Scottish Romanticism are 'in dialogue with the arguments of the Scottish Enlightenment, neither in outright opposition to them, or subservient to them'.[68] His suggestion that the two will in the future be understood to be 'interrelated to the point of being aspects of a single phenomenon'[69] is fulfilled in Gerard McKeever's *Dialectics of Improvement*, which places Scottish Romantic texts within an ongoing 'dialectic', spanning the long eighteenth century, that is itself a 'key component of the culture of modernity'.[70] Recent work foregrounds what Kenneth McNeil has termed 'a Scottish post-union, post-enlightenment Romanticism' that reckons with and participates in the formation of modern Britain.[71]

This understanding of Scottish Romanticism, as rooted in the negotiation of a subnational national identity and intertwined with the modern, is key to understanding the Romanticism of the kirkyard texts. The kirkyard is a figure through which writers engage in dialogue over the nature of nation and community amid rapid social and political change. Rather than representing a single static set of ideas, kirkyard Romanticism offers an important motif for authors seeking a Romantic vocabulary for modern nationhood. From its inception, it is subject to an ongoing process of negotiation and deconstruction, Gifford's 'deconstructive agenda', and this allows writers to engage with and challenge one another and the wider concept of modernity.[72]

A Kirkyard School of Fiction

The historical moment in which Bowles, Warren and Scott published their influential kirkyard fiction is one of remarkable productivity and prominence for Scottish letters. These texts belonged to a wider Scottish literary boom that saw the Edinburgh press gain new importance within British literature. Ian Duncan describes the decades between 1802 and 1832 as ones in which:

> Scottish publications and genres dominated a globalising English-language market and made Edinburgh a literary metropolis to rival London. The forms, discourses and institutions produced there shaped an imperial British culture that lasted throughout the century, long after Edinburgh's relapse to provincial status.[73]

This was the era when the works of Walter Scott dominated the anglophone literary marketplace and Edinburgh played host to two of Britain's most prominent periodicals, *The Edinburgh Review* and *Blackwood's Edinburgh Magazine*. The authors whom this book examines were participants in this golden age of Scottish writing. Clustering, at first, around *Blackwood's Edinburgh Magazine*, writers including John Wilson, James Hogg, John Galt and J. G. Lockhart helped to inaugurate some of the influential 'forms, discourses and institutions' that Duncan suggests would shape subsequent British culture.

Their affiliation with *Blackwood's* means that many of these authors have been considered members of a 'Blackwood Group' whose work participated in the reimagining of the magazine form.[74] While many of the texts this book discusses were published beyond the pages of *Blackwood's* and Blackwood, the magazine was a crucible and rallying point for their specific brand of Romantic cultural nationalism and the kirkyard motif it often employed. *Blackwood's Edinburgh Magazine* has been characterised as 'the most important literary-political journal' of its time.[75] In the early decades of the century it was able to act as the cradle of the kirkyard archetype both due to its innovative format and its particular political and cultural outlook.

Blackwood's pushed the limits of the magazine form by placing different categories of writing conversationally alongside one another. It also offered relative creative freedom to the writers who contributed to its pages. Joanne Shattock notes:

> the collaborative spirit in which William Blackwood ran the magazine, asserting his authority when necessary but giving Wilson, Lockhart, Maginn, Hogg, and others free rein when it suited his interests and those of the magazine ... The creation of a literary community and a love of conviviality and conversation were part of the Blackwood management style.[76]

This created a literary space where texts from across genres participated in conversations with one another, and where a motif like the kirkyard could evolve. *Blackwood's Edinburgh Magazine* in the early decades of the nineteenth century was a dynamic and contradictory literary space where content was often only united by the miscellany form. This sense of multivocality is perhaps typified in the *Noctes Ambrosianae*, a series of seventy-one fictionalised vignettes that were featured in the magazine between 1822 and 1835. A recurring and distinctive feature of the magazine, the *Noctes* were a series of topical, imaginary conversations between the alter egos of key contributors to the magazine, characters from literature and contemporary figures of note. The reported conversations between the characters often referenced the subjects discussed in other articles and tales within the magazine, with the discursive format allowing for what Mark Parker terms a 'dialogic critical style'.[77]

The magazine's distinctive aesthetic was tied to a wider political and cultural outlook seeded in the Edinburgh-based political rivalries of these decades. David Manderson describes how during the early years of the nineteenth century 'the *Edinburgh Review*, a Whig-leaning publication suffused with Enlightenment values and regarded more highly than any other for its critical opinions, held sway' in Britain.[78] *The Edinburgh Review* was published by Archibald Constable, Walter Scott's publisher, and edited by Francis Jeffrey. In a period of polarised political partisanship in Edinburgh, *The Edinburgh Review* promoted a Whig agenda that was committed to sustaining what Ian Duncan terms 'an oligarchic and republican ideal of citizenship based on civic virtue, developed in the moral philosophy of the Scottish Enlightenment'.[79] Alongside reviews, the *Edinburgh* published 'articles on economics, travel, science, medicine and education'.[80] Its content was generally informative rather than overtly entertaining. This combination of discerning criticism and liberal politics placed the *Edinburgh* at the forefront of the British periodical marketplace; Pottinger asserts that 'the *Edinburgh* became the arbiter of the literary scene'.[81]

William Blackwood recognised a gap in the market for a Tory magazine capable of competing with the *Edinburgh* and Constable's failing monthly, *The Scots Magazine*.[82] After Blackwood's failed first attempt at launching a competitor publication, *Blackwood's Edinburgh Magazine* burst onto the periodical market in October 1817, with an infamous first issue that featured libellous attacks on the Edinburgh literary establishment (in the form of the 'Chaldee Manuscript') and famous London-based Romantic poets like Keats and Shelley ('The Cockney School of Poetry'). *Blackwood's* was conceived as a Tory alternative to Constable's rival publications, and perhaps the defining feature of the new magazine from its first issue onwards was its adversarial agenda. The magazine's tendency to employ personalities in its reviews drew contributors into high-profile disagreements with other writers, most famously in the case of the war of words between J. G. Lockhart and the editor of *The London Magazine*, John Scott, that ended in a deadly duel.[83] However, an aggressive and often libellous reviewing style was not the only aspect of the magazine that was oppositional. The very form and style of writing that the magazine adopted was designed to contrast with that employed by its Whig rival, *The Edinburgh Review*. Manderson asserts that: 'against the *Edinburgh's* Whig politics it was Tory, against the *Edinburgh's* controlled, balanced and rational voice it was provocative and sensual, a celebration of the appetites.'[84] *Blackwood's* is to a certain extent defined by what it is not, whether that antagonism is directed at the Whiggish *Edinburgh Review*, the flagging *Scots Magazine* or the London-based *London Magazine* and 'Cockney poets'. Ian Duncan identifies a 'set of political, commercial, and generic antagonisms – Whig versus Tory, Blackwood versus Constable, review versus magazine, essay versus fiction, political economy versus national culture' – that inspire the specific ethos of *Blackwood's Magazine*.[85]

An article titled 'Is the *Edinburgh Review* a Religious and Patriotic Work?', published in *Blackwood's* in 1818 by major contributor John

Wilson, casts the *Edinburgh* as an irreligious and unpatriotic publication, implicitly suggesting the orthodox and patriotic aspirations of *Blackwood's*. Wilson accuses the *Edinburgh* of damaging religious belief in Britain by perpetuating Enlightenment-era scepticism, and of unpatriotic criticism of the British government during the Napoleonic Wars. The author launches an attack on 'the sceptical and too often infidel, character of the *Edinburgh Review*' that he argues has contributed to 'a shameful ignorance of the evidences of Christianity' that 'distinguishes secular men of education in Scotland'.[86] He also cites the *Edinburgh Review's* criticisms of the high rates of tax imposed during the Continental Wars as treasonous, terming its reviewers 'an angry, irritated, unpatriotic, despot-loving band of disappointed partisans, alike destitute of wisdom and of magnanimity'.[87] Wilson holds up the example of 'the great statesmen of the elder times of England's glory' as the antithesis of the Whig reviewers:

> In dark and perilous days, they counselled resistance unto the death; submission was a thought that had no existence; and there was no difficulty – no danger – no suffering, that was not to be surmounted, faced, and endured, rather than that the bright name of England should be dimmed, or one inch shorn from her dominion. But if we turn to the recorded counsels and prophecies of our modern Whigs, we shall hear nothing but of disaster.[88]

Wilson cites pre-Enlightenment heroism as the antithesis of the Whig approach to the nation. In making these criticisms of *The Edinburgh Review*, *Blackwood's* less describes the *Edinburgh* than defines itself. In finding fault with the 'sceptical', 'unpatriotic' *Edinburgh*, Wilson lays out the ground work for the ethos that would inform *Blackwood's* – one that was to be self-consciously patriotic, religious and grounded in history.

Central to this self-presentation was *Blackwood's* adoption of the specifically Scottish identity that would inform the kirkyard texts. The magazine employs an emotive form of cultural nationalism to place Scotland at the centre of its vision of the British nation. Mark Schoenfield describes how '*Blackwood's* represents its own politics as emerging from the historical condition of Scotland as the trace of the medieval within Britain and an historical pageantry of customs, traditions and monuments'.[89] The *Blackwood's* depiction of Scotland is designed specifically to counter the scepticism and lack of patriotism Wilson attributes to the *Edinburgh* by characterising Scotland as a repository for pre-Enlightenment British values. Despite Edinburgh's status as the avowed centre of the eighteenth-century Enlightenment and the rapid pace of contemporary urbanisation north of the border, *Blackwood's* characterises its origins as rooted in the traditions of an older Scotland still visible in rural, labouring-class culture. The Scotland of *Blackwood's Magazine's* short fiction draws upon the regionalism of Scott's Tales of My Landlord while eschewing the sweep of stadial history often apparent in his novels. This opposition to stadial historiography, Anthony Jarrells has argued, formed 'part of the magazine's general opposition to the political economic stance that both marked the previous generation of literati in Scotland, and continued to provide the philosophical underpinnings for the most dominant periodical voice of the period, the *Edinburgh Review*'.[90] The regional and traditional Scotland depicted within the magazine's fiction becomes a repository that resists the sweep of Enlightenment-derived modernity.

Alongside the Scottish fiction published within the magazine, William Blackwood's publishing house produced a characteristic type of regional novel.[91] Gillian Hughes describes how 'during the 1820s Blackwood promoted a surge of Edinburgh novel publication, producing works of "Scotch" fiction by authors associated with the magazine (including Gleig, Galt, Hamilton, Hogg, Lockhart, Moir, and Wilson) several of which had first been serialised there'.[92] Capitalising on the popularity of Scottish subjects in the wake of the phenomenal success of Scott's Waverley novels, Blackwood published a large number of novels by popular Scottish authors that focused on Scottish themes. Francis Jeffrey's 1823 article for the *Edinburgh Review* famously characterises a group of Blackwood-published novels written by key *Blackwood's* writers (John Galt's *Annals of the Parish*, *The Ayrshire Legatees*, *Sir Andrew Wylie*, *The Steamboat*, *The Entail* and *Ringan Gilhaize*; J. G. Lockhart's *Valerius*, *Adam Blair* and *Reginald Dalton*; and John Wilson's *Lights and Shadows of Scottish Life* and *The Trials of Margaret Lindsay*) as 'Secondary Scottish Novels'. Jeffrey describes these works as 'imitations of the inimitable novels', emphasising the influence of Scott on Blackwood's premier novelists, and characterising their work as derivative and opportunistic.[93]

Sarah Green's 1824 novel *Scotch Novel Reading; or, Modern Quackery, by a Cockney* also mocks the rash of Scottish writing overtaking the British marketplace in the early decades of the century. The novel attacks Walter Scott, but particularly homes in on his imitators. Duncan comments that in *Scotch Novel Reading* 'the blame for the blizzard lies less with Scott himself ... than with a proliferation of cheap knock-offs'.[94] Green's adoption of the title 'a Cockney' is clearly aimed at the *Blackwood's* authors, referencing Lockhart's high-profile attacks on the London literati in the 'Cockney School of Poetry' series. The novel charts the re-education and Romantic trials of Alice Fennel, a born 'Cockney' with a ridiculous mania for all things 'Scotch'. Juliet Shields has argued that the publication of the novel 'demonstrates that the "showers of Scotch novels" published during the first three decades of the nineteenth century constituted a literary phenomenon remarkable enough to warrant a three-volume warning against these novels' potentially pernicious effects on English readers'.[95] *Scotch Novel Reading* documents a moment in literary history when the market for novels appeared to be flooded with new Scottish writing. Jeffrey's dismissive review and Green's novel show that the *Blackwood's* group authors were at the forefront of this phenomenon, feeding the public's apparently insatiable appetite for Scottish tales.

The Scotch novel and the regional tale became the primary genres in which kirkyard Romanticism emerges. Authors including Hogg, Wilson, Lockhart, Galt, Moir, Warren and John Howison participate to a greater and lesser extent in the oppositional cultural nationalism of *Blackwood's*. The dead come to play an important role in this project due to the way that they offer a way to incorporate 'feelings, the sacred, ideas of mortality, the non-rational' into the modern imagined nation.[96] The kirkyard can thus operate as a straightforward critique of an Enlightenment-derived, Whig modernity associated with *The Edinburgh Review*.

However, as this book will explore, the kirkyard at other times facilitates or excuses modernity. The kirkyard authors develop their ideas within the same intellectual milieu as those of *The Edinburgh Review*, and to an extent cannot escape Enlightenment-derived ideas of the modern. One of the key arguments of this book is that many kirkyard texts are tacitly complicit in the processes of modernity due to their provision of a virtual space outside the flow of 'universal world history'.[97] Participants in modernisation can identify with and preserve the kirkyard nation in textual form even as they fundamentally alter its real-world mirror image. Many of the kirkyard texts identify and explore this problem, questioning the possibility of escape or transcendence that their fictional worlds might seem to offer.

Afterlives: The Kirkyard and the Scottish Nineteenth Century

The 1830s are consistently identified as the end of the Scottish Romantic era and see the death and dispersal of many key Scottish Romantics. The death of Scott in 1832 was followed by the death of Hogg in 1835. John Galt suffered a stroke in 1832 and died in 1839. J. G. Lockhart had left

Blackwood's and Edinburgh for the London-based *Quarterly Review* in 1825. Although he remained a *Blackwood's* contributor and published his *Life of Sir Walter Scott* in 1837, Lockhart was no longer an Edinburgh-based author or a central figure at the periodical. While John Wilson continued to play an important role at *Blackwood's* and in literary Edinburgh, holding the Chair of Moral Philosophy at the University of Edinburgh until 1851, the deaths and dispersal of these authors, who had reached literary fame alongside him, signal the apparent waning of late Scottish Romanticism as a cohesive movement. These years, in conventional periodisation, also saw the transition from the Regency to the Victorian era with the ascent of Queen Victoria to the throne. In a classic literary history of the century, this would be the point where one chapter would end and a new one begin.

The periodisation of English literature into sharply delineated Romantic and Victorian eras has led to a narrative in which Scottish literature fails to make the transition from one chapter to the next. The popular account of Scottish literature after Scott has often been one of decline. The period that saw the ascent of Scott, *The Edinburgh Review* and *Blackwood's*, in this narrative, was followed by one of comparative mediocrity and provinciality – what Michael Fry terms a 'ghastly literary phase'.[98] Andrew Nash has identified two schools of fiction traditionally associated with nineteenth-century Scottish writing: 'historical romance, typified by Robert Louis Stevenson, and nostalgic rural idylls epitomised by the so-called Kailyard fiction of J.M. Barrie and Ian Maclaren'.[99] This understanding of Scottish prose literature after Scott as one consisting of two separate, depoliticised traditions has led to a tendency to characterise the later sixty years of the nineteenth century as a period of national stagnation. Or, as Nash puts it, 'the ascent of Victoria, it seemed, signalled the descent of Scottish culture.'[100]

The idea of a lost literary nineteenth century has been increasingly challenged in recent work on the period. Many of these reconsiderations have foregrounded the way that Victorian Scottish literature did not follow the same generic and stylistic trajectory as English literature, and therefore has not been sufficiently accommodated within existing accounts of nineteenth-century British literary history. As Shields notes, one of the overriding narratives has been that 'Scotland lacked a vibrant Victorian literature because its writers eschewed realism'.[101] Scottish texts from the period have been contrasted with the great English realist novel and critiqued for their Romanticism, sentimentalism and parochialism. While English literature grappled with the rapidly changing realities of Victorian Britain, these accounts suggest, Scottish literature became increasingly escapist and unwilling to engage with modern life.

However, recent commentators note that this mode of approaching Scottish writing fails to consider how the move away from literary realism might be a type of response. Nash's account of Victorian Scottish literature is dedicated to tracing 'some of the ways that Scottish writers responded to major cultural and intellectual issues'.[102] Foregrounding the works of authors including Thomas Carlyle, George MacDonald, James Thomson and John Davidson, he argues that 'a distinctive quality of Scottish Victorianism is its preoccupation with the imaginative apprehension of reality'.[103] Kirstie Blair's work on Scottish Victorian working-class verse offers another way of approaching a period that has 'attracted very little critical attention' by reclaiming a group of texts generally excluded from mainstream accounts of Scottish literature.[104] She suggests that these poets 'are indeed imitative, parochial, provincial, romantic, sentimental, and escapist. These are not flaws. They are strategic positions adopted on cultural and political, as well as personal, grounds.'[105] Shields has also countered the myth of the 'lost century' in several publications, highlighting the seemingly toothless regional sketch's potential for cultural resistance[106] and suggesting that, in the work of authors like Margaret Oliphant, 'Scottish literature challenges the categories that organize the study of English literature'.[107] Most recently, Michael Shaw has identified the later decades of the nineteenth century as the site of a 'Scottish romance revival' that encapsulates writers traditionally associated with both historical and kailyard fiction. What these authors share, in Shaw's account, is a resistance to dominant realist literary modes and a concern with countering overarching narratives of cultural development, many of which are rooted in the Whig approach to history. Romance revival texts, he argues, often interrogate 'improvement' and 'challenge the civilised-barbarous boundary'.[108] In this way they participate in the same political conversations that this book has identified in their Romantic predecessors.

These arguments for the value of Victorian Scottish literature share a series of features with my own arguments for the cultural importance of kirkyard writing and support the final argument I want to make about the literary kirkyard's lasting impact in Scotland. Like Nash, Shaw, Shields and Blair, I see the derivativeness, sentimentalism and localism of the kirkyard texts, and much of the 'ghastly' Scottish literature that followed, as strategic and resistant.

The kirkyard texts can be understood, not just as late-born offspring of an eighteenth-century conflict, but as texts that belong to a long nineteenth-century of liberal and counter-liberal thought. Contemporaries of Butterworth's foundational Whig historian Henry Hallam, responding to that important Whig mouthpiece *The Edinburgh*

Review, the kirkyard authors write at a moment when Enlightenment historiography was transitioning into the 'Whig interpretation of history' that would dominate nineteenth-century thought.[109] As Megan Coyer has argued, if *The Edinburgh Review* 'contributed to what would become the liberal hegemony of Victorian society' then 'the network of writers surrounding *Blackwood's* developed the foundations for the critique of that hegemony'.[110] The kirkyard dead can therefore be read within a long nineteenth century where they function as a resource for writers responding to Victorian ideas of history, society and nation.

This book, through the codas to each chapter, argues for a continued tradition of resistant Scottish Romanticism by placing the deathbed scenes and graveyards of later-century Scottish writers in dialogue with the kirkyards of Wilson, Hogg, Galt and their peers. The kirkyard texts as a group offer a precedent for the resistant Romanticism of late-century Scottish texts. Placing Maclaren, Buchan, Stevenson and their contemporaries in relation to the kirkyard cohort supports a reading of them as vitally political participants in an ongoing dispute over the nature of history and nation. Following one motif through all these texts indicates a complicated, interdependent and thematically cohesive Scottish nineteenth century.

Beyond Scotland, this book also seeks to suggest an international application for the kirkyard motif. When Thomas McCombie cites Scott, Warren and Bowles in his Australian sketch, he suggests a second usage for the kirkyard, born of its strong unionist nationalism and complex relationship with temporality. A nationally symbolic dead in the *Blackwood's* tradition can effectively articulate a subnational national identity in colonial space. For McCombie, Scottish unionist nationalism is not just a talismanic tradition brought from home but a useful precedent for imagining an Australian identity that can exist within a British colonial one. As Katie Trumpener has highlighted, 'most accounts of Britain's literary empire' focus on 'a literature forged by the influence of English models on English colonists'.[111] Like Trumpener, I am interested in the modularity of Scottish cultural nationalism and its transportability to the 'stateless' nations of Britain's nineteenth-century settler colonies.[112] My study joins the work of scholars including Trumpener, Jason Rudy, Juliet Shields and Nikki Hessel, in proposing the usefulness of reading texts from the British Empire in relation to the Scottish tradition.[113]

The centrality of English literature to our modern understanding of the nineteenth-century anglophone canon means that we have been missing productive ways of reading both anglophone colonial writing and Scottish literature. Born out of one of the most culturally influential periodicals of the early nineteenth century, and present in the novels of authors whose work was ubiquitous enough to spawn protest writing, the kirkyard is one example of an originally Scottish mode of imagining the nation with far greater reach than has been previously acknowledged.

A Walk in the Kirkyard

In this book I explore the birth and development of the way of imagining Scotland that I term 'kirkyard Romanticism'. I argue that, within the writings of a coterie of largely Edinburgh-based and Blackwood-adjacent writers, the Scottish rural graveyard offers a literary space for mapping a Romantic vision of British national identity. Seeping from the pages of the publisher's flagship magazine into those of canonical Scottish novels, including Galt's *Annals of the Parish* and Hogg's *The Private Memoirs and Confessions of a Justified Sinner*, and of other contemporary periodicals, a particular idea of the national dead became increasingly important to how Scotland was imagined in literature. This kirkyard Romanticism inaugurated a series of tropes that would subsequently haunt representations of Scottish heritage and culture and would inform approaches to settler colonial identities in the wider British world.

Chapters 1 and 2 root kirkyard Romanticism in the books and magazine content generated by two of *Blackwood's Edinburgh Magazine*'s most important early contributors, J. G. Lockhart and John Wilson. In their writings of the 1810s and 1820s the two authors assemble an imagined national 'home' for British readers in the idealised Scottish village graveyard, drawing upon a range of literary forefathers including Friedrich Schlegel, William Wordsworth, Robert Burns and Walter Scott. Wilson and Lockhart's kirkyard is a space that is simultaneously preserved and endangered, at the heart of the nation and peripheral to it. The use of the dead to anchor the living nation also creates a temporal paradox whereby Scottish rural space is both the foundation of, and removed from, the imagined national community. Wilson and Lockhart use this motif to offer an alternative vision of the British nation that counters the homogenising, centralising and de-historicising impulses of liberal modernity.

However, as I explore in four subsequent chapters, kirkyard Romanticism is inherently dialogic and deconstructive. I identify a series of aspects of the imagined kirkyard that facilitate national community, temporal stasis, emotional attachment and geographical insularity, and explore how authors deconstruct and reimagine them. In Chapter 2 the burials of suicides in Galt's *Annals of the Parish* and Hogg's *The Private Memoirs and Confessions of a Justified Sinner* lay bare the temporal disjunctions inherent in both liberal historiography and the kirkyard approach to rural life and death. The chapter proceeds to a reading of Hogg's famous exhumation scene. I argue that placing Hogg's suicide's body within contemporary debates about suicide, and in dialogue with the kirkyard archetype, is essential to understanding the text's relationship with ideas of historical time. The third chapter looks at the representation of body snatching in examples of *Blackwood's* signature terror tales and sentimental regional tales. I argue that these two genres, through their provocation of reader identification, can facilitate the exploration of the role of emotion in the formation of imagined community. *Blackwood's* body-snatching tales are thus able to employ the conventions of genre to problematise the emotional detachment that underwrites scientific progress and rationality.

The final two chapters of the book use the dead to ponder Scotland's wider global relationships and the way that Scottish regional writing interfaces with British and colonial space. In Chapter 4 I examine the limited literary footprint of the 1832 cholera epidemic and suggest that the disturbed graves of the cholera dead offer a particularly fertile political metaphor for nation in the months leading up to the passage of the Great Reform Bill. In poetry and tales by Hogg and James Montgomery, epidemic disease sketches the increasing mobility and connectivity of Britain's population onto the national map. I expand the parameters of this mobility in the final chapter of the book, considering how kirkyard ideas surface in the colonial fiction and poetry of John Wilson, D. M. Moir, John Howison and John Galt. I examine the relationship between emptied wilderness and memory-rich kirkyard Scotland in these texts, arguing that these poles of representation facilitate, not anti-imperial critique, but an alternative Romantic imperialism.

Throughout this book I am also interested in the endurance and geographical dispersal of these ideas. Each chapter closes with a brief coda that traces how the influence of the kirkyard archetype expanded beyond its initial context across space and time. These later uses throw into relief the complexity of the original archetype and its flexibility, and gesture to a new way of reading Scotland's nineteenth century.

Across this book, 'kirkyard Romanticism', then, refers to a constellation of responses to modernity that place an imagined Scottish national dead at their heart. *Blackwood's Edinburgh Magazine*, and the publisher William Blackwood, are a crucible for this mode of imagining Romantic nationhood. However, the kirkyard motif is neither limited to this publication context nor does it limit the thematic concerns of writers who publish within these venues. This book identifies one thematic route through some of the most prominent texts of this literary moment. In doing so, it offers a new way to approach Scottish Romantic nationalism and its afterlives – drawing attention to the many Young Mortalities who wrote about the kirkyard dead in the years after 1816.

Notes

1. McCombie, 'Australian Sketches – No. V. The Bush-Graves of Australia', p. 9.
2. See Westover, *Necromanticism*, pp. 5–6.
3. See Webby, 'The Grave in the Bush'.
4. McCombie, 'Australian Sketches', p. 9.
5. Hewitt, 'Scott, Sir Walter (1771–1832), Poet and Novelist'.
6. Blain, *Caroline Southey Bowles*, p. 4.
7. Dunlop, 'Samuel Warren', p. 265.
8. Although the majority of Scott's novels were published with Archibald Constable, Scott's *Old Mortality* was published during his brief period as a Blackwood novelist.
9. Duncan, *Scott's Shadow*, p. 22.
10. See Jalland, *Death in the Victorian Family*.
11. Makdisi, *Romantic Imperialism*, p. 2.
12. Nash, *Kailyard and Scottish Literature*, p. 14.
13. Westover comments that, from the mid-century, 'the Gothic was merely one important manifestation of a broader cultural phenomenon, signalled by a huge body of writing on death, the places of the dead, and the relation of both to literary creation and long-term reception'. Westover, *Necromanticism*, p. 6.
14. See Parisot, *Graveyard Poetry*.
15. See Williams, 'Deathly Sentimentalism'.
16. See Shapira, *Inventing the Gothic Corpse*.
17. See Schor, *Bearing the Dead*; McAllister, *Imagining the Dead*.
18. See Fosso, *Buried Communities*, p. 9.
19. McGill, 'The Evolution of Haunted Space in Scotland', p. 23.
20. See, for example, the commemoration of Fergus McIvor through portraiture in *Waverley* which is discussed in Craig, *Out of History*, p. 39.
21. Duncan, *Scott's Shadow*.
22. Barrell, 'Putting down the Rising'.
23. Barrell, 'Putting down the Rising', p. 135; Duncan, *Scott's Shadow*, pp. 213–14.
24. Hasler, 'Introduction', p. xxiii.
25. Gifford, 'The Roots That Clutch', p. 18.
26. Morrison and Baldick comment that 'Blackwood's political rhetoric had its roots in Edmund Burke, but it was a good deal less discriminating and more vituperative'. Salyer has argued that the 'Blackwood's circle advocated a kind of "traditionary" Romanticism' which was heavily indebted to the writings of Edmund Burke. Morrison and Baldick, 'Introduction' to

Tales of Terror from Blackwood's Magazine, p. x. Salyer, '"Nae mortal man should be entrusted wi' sic an ingine"', p. 100.
27. Jarrells notes that 'there are numerous references to Burke in Maga's early numbers'. Salyer has argued that during the 1820s *Blackwood's* 'reviewers placed the Anglo-Irish orator at the centre of a great agon of British responses to the revolution' ('"Nae mortal man should be entrusted wi' sic an ingine"', p. 95). From 1833 the magazine ran a series of articles on the life and writings of Burke, and in 1840 Blackwood and Sons published George Croly's Memoir of the Political Life of Edmund Burke. Jarrells, 'Tales of the Colonies', p. 272. Salyer, '"Nae mortal man should be entrusted wi' sic an ingine"', p. 95.
28. Burke, *Reflections on the Revolution in France*, p. 120.
29. Ibid., p. 195.
30. Ibid., p. 47.
31. Ibid., p. 52.
32. Burke, *Letter to a Noble Lord*, p. 5.
33. Salyer, '"Nae mortal man should be entrusted wi' sic an ingine"', p. 107.
34. Lincoln, *Walter Scott and Modernity*, p. 30.
35. Anderson, *Imagined Communities*, pp. 6, 4.
36. Ibid., p. 7.
37. See Colley, *Britons*, p. 6.
38. Aries, *The Hour of Our Death*.
39. Laquer, *The Work of the Dead*.
40. Schor, *Bearing the Dead*, p. 75.
41. Ibid., p. 6.
42. Ibid., p. 75.
43. McAllister, *Imagining the Dead*, p. 30.
44. Anderson, *Imagined Communities*, p.12.
45. McAllister, *Imagining the Dead*, p. 30.
46. Verdery, *The Political Lives of Dead Bodies*, p. 25.
47. Ibid., pp. 20, 13.
48. Westover, *Necromanticism*, p.17.
49. Anderson, *Imagined Communities*, p.12.
50. Ibid., p. 9.
51. Ibid., p. 32.
52. Ibid., p. 11.
53. 'Scotland's experience during the period – particularly the material improvements that unevenly transformed the nation's socioeconomic circumstances – generated a keen sensitivity to these concerns.' Benchimol and McKeever, 'Introduction', in *Cultures of Improvement in Scottish Romanticism*, p. 3.
54. Herman, *How the Scots Invented the Modern*.
55. Trumpener, *Bardic Nationalism*, p. 29.
56. Bowler *The Invention of Progress*, p. 7.
57. Wu, 'Introduction', in *Romanticism: An Anthology*, p. xxxii.
58. See Haekel, 'Romanticism and Theory'.
59. Löwy and Sayre, *Romanticism against the Tide of Modernity*, p. 17.
60. Ibid., p. 18.
61. Makdisi, *Romantic Imperialism*, pp. 2–3.

62. Löwy and Sayre, *Romanticism against the Tide of Modernity*, p. 21.
63. Pfau and Mitchell, 'Romanticism and Modernity', p. 267.
64. McCrone, *Understanding Scotland*, p. 1.
65. Davis, *Acts of Union*, p. 11.
66. Lincoln, *Walter Scott and Modernity*, p. 14.
67. Trumpener, *Bardic Nationalism*, pp. xi, 23.
68. Pittock, 'Introduction: What is Scottish Romanticism?', p. 8.
69. Ibid., p. 9.
70. McKeever, *Dialectics of Improvement*, p. 2.
71. McNeil, *Scottish Romanticism and Collective Memory in the British Atlantic*, p. 4.
72. Gifford, 'The Roots That Clutch', p. 18.
73. Duncan, *Scott's Shadow*, p. xi.
74. See Douglas, *The Blackwood Group*; Hart, *The Scottish Novel*.
75. Morrsion and Roberts, '"A Character so various, and yet so indisputably its own"', p. 1.
76. Shattock, 'The Sense of Place and *Blackwood's (Edinburgh) Magazine*', p. 435.
77. Parker, *Literary Magazines and British Romanticism*, p. 132.
78. Manderson, 'The Hidden Highlander', p. 88.
79. Duncan, *Scott's Shadow*, p. 14.
80. Segerblad, *Transcending the Gothic*, p. 6.
81. Pottinger, *Heirs of Enlightenment*, p. 3.
82. Pottinger notes that 'John Murray had brought out the *Quarterly Review* in 1809 in direct opposition to the *Edinburgh Review* but it had not so far challenged the supremacy of Jeffrey's journal'. Pottinger, *Heirs of Enlightenment*, p. 168.
83. See Mole, '*Blackwood's* "Personalities"', pp. 89–99.
84. Manderson, 'The Hidden Highlander', p. 92.
85. Duncan, *Scott's Shadow*, p. 27.
86. Wilson, 'Is the Edinburgh Review a Religious and Patriotic Work?', p. 228.
87. Ibid., p. 232.
88. Ibid., p. 233.
89. Schoenfield, *British Periodicals and Romantic Identity*, p. 102.
90. Jarrells, *Tales of the Colonies*, p. 267.
91. It is important to note here that these two categories of writing were not entirely distinct from one another. Several *Blackwood's* authors first published novels in serial form within the magazine (see, for example, Galt's *The Ayrshire Legatees*), and series and tales were often gathered into books (see Moir's 'Mansie Wauch' stories).
92. Hughes, 'The Edinburgh of *Blackwood's Edinburgh Magazine* and James Hogg's Fiction', p. 179.
93. Jeffrey, 'Secondary Scottish Novels', p. 160.
94. Duncan, *Scott's Shadow*, p. 32.
95. Shields, 'From Family Roots to the Routes of Empire', p. 919.
96. Verdery, *The Political Lives of Dead Bodies*, p. 25.
97. See Makdisi, *Romantic Imperialism*, p. 2.
98. Fry, *A New Race of Men*, p. 364. Qtd in Blair, *Working Verse in Victorian Scotland*, p. 7.

99. Nash, 'Victorian Scottish Literature', p. 145.
100. Ibid.
101. Shields, 'Oliphant and Co.', p. 3.
102. Nash, 'Victorian Scottish Literature, p. 145.
103. Ibid., p. 145.
104. Blair, *Working Verse in Victorian Scotland*, p. 6.
105. Ibid., p. 8.
106. Shields, *Nation and Migration*, ch. 5.
107. Shields, 'Oliphant and Co.', p. 5.
108. Shaw, *The Fin-de-Siecle Scottish Revival*, p. 37.
109. Butterfield, *The Whig Interpretation of History*, p. 3.
110. Coyer, *Literature and Medicine in the Nineteenth-Century Periodical Press*, p. 9.
111. Trumpener, *Bardic Nationalism*, p. xiv.
112. See Sharp, 'Exporting the Cotter's Saturday Night'.
113. See Trumpener, *Bardic Nationalism*; Rudy, *Imagined Homelands*; Shields, *Nation and Migration*; Hessell, *Romantic Literature and the Colonised World*.

Chapter 1

Intertextuality, Tradition and the Kirkyard Forefathers

In a prose reimagining of Robert Burns's 'The Cotter's Saturday Night' (1786), the *Blackwood's Edinburgh Magazine* contributor John Wilson describes a nightmare scenario of radical revolution where the traditions and structures of rural Scottish life have been irreparably disrupted. 'The Radical's Saturday Night' (1819) holds a dark mirror up to the scenes of domestic piety and familial affection that characterise Burns's cottage poem. At the climax of the sketch, a cotter turned radical declaims to his distressed father that: 'a hole dug in the earth is a grave – but we have no laws, I believe, against burial-grounds – only we must not call them kirk-yards – for where now are the kirks? This has been a glorious day for Scotland.'[1] The nightmare of radical futurity presented here is one that discards the religious, familial and historical bonds that tie the nation together. The loss of the 'kirk-yard' for Wilson is symbolic of a wider cultural disintegration where ancestral and cultural memories are lost. Wilson imagines the kirkyard as a resting place for the nation's forefathers that must be preserved. He also, through this Burnsian homage, participates in the construction of a Scottish literary tradition where Burns is co-opted as his own literary forefather.

This chapter uses Wilson's sketch as a starting point from which to tell the story of the emergence of kirkyard Romanticism in the works of Wilson and his close colleague J. G. Lockhart. Wilson and Lockhart were two important early contributors to *Blackwood's Edinburgh Magazine* and, I argue, used that platform to assemble a distinctive form of Scottish Romantic nationalism, where the rural graveyard played an important symbolic role. This chapter chronologically charts the construction of a kirkyard archetype in Wilson's and Lockhart's early work for the publisher William Blackwood. I focus on the way that this image drew on, and enmeshed itself with, the writing of existing literary progenitors. I argue that this incorporation serves both to legitimate

Wilson and Lockhart's project and articulate the men's conservative understanding of culture and tradition.

Troubling Forefathers: John Wilson and J. G. Lockhart

At the core of this chapter, and the next, is an argument for the importance of two of Scottish Romanticism's more controversial figures: John Wilson and J. G. Lockhart. In the first decades of the nineteenth century Wilson's and Lockhart's reputations and careers were heavily associated with one another and with the publisher William Blackwood. Wilson and Lockhart played an important role in the development of the publisher's flagship periodical, *Blackwood's Edinburgh Magazine*, and published volumes of prose fiction, criticism, translations and biography with Blackwood. While both men contributed to William Blackwood's magazine under the editorship of Pringle and Cleghorn, they took on greater importance to the publication after its relaunch as *Blackwood's Edinburgh Magazine* in October 1817. John O. Hayden characterises them as 'the two most important contributors to *Blackwood's* before 1825', with both men writing extensively across a wide range of genres and topics in the magazine and authoring episodes of the magazine's *Noctes* series.[2] Both also had an important role in shaping the content of the magazine.[3] One of Britain's most influential periodicals, and one of the most important publication venues in setting the course for late Scottish Romanticism, was thus, between 1818 and 1825, suffused with the writing and ideas of both Lockhart and Wilson. Their voices were often, due to *Blackwood's* employment of anonymity and pseudonym, indistinguishable from the corporate voice of the magazine itself.

Wilson's and Lockhart's association with periodical writing forms part of the puzzle of their critical decline. As Kim Wheatley has noted, periodicals were 'long neglected' within Romantic Studies due to limiting definitions of Romanticism that prioritised the solitary Romantic genius and isolated Romantic works from a wider marketplace and historical context.[4] Periodical writing with its emphasis on collaboration, its ephemerality, and its undisguised relationship to a fickle and shifting marketplace seemed at odds with Romanticism as it was traditionally conceptualised. The ephemerality of magazines, reviews and newspapers has also made accessing this work difficult when compared to novels and poetic volumes. While expanding definitions of the Romantic, and increasing accessibility through digitisation, have led to greater scholarly engagement with Romantic periodicals, the landmarks of the British and Scottish Romantic canons remain novels and volumes of poetry. The fact that much of Wilson's and Lockhart's most notable work is contained within *Blackwood's Magazine* has played a role in their relative critical insignificance.

Blackwood's early role as enfant terrible of the periodical marketplace has also created specific problems for Lockhart's and Wilson's legacies. They were both known for their brutal reviewing style.[5] Their involvement in the scandals and conflict of early *Blackwood's*, like the furore that followed the publication of the Chaldee Manuscript, and the death of John Scott in a duel over the 'Cockney School' reviews, mean that they often emerge as antagonists in other Romantics' biographies. Duncan Wu's characterisation of Wilson and Lockhart, in his biography of William Hazlitt, as men who 'possessed the kind of cleverness that coexists with sadism and arrogance, qualities they possessed in spades' is representative of this wider pattern.[6] Evolving literary tastes have also played their part, as the sentimental register that both men sometimes employ in their fiction and poetry has fallen from favour.

More broadly, the highly conservative political and social vision that both men propagate in their work proved hard to accommodate within twentieth-century accounts of Scottish literature. The writers' disappearance from the canon can be understood by looking at how the current 'cultural story' of Scottish literature has been constructed.[7] In his account of the development of Scottish Literary Studies, Ronnie Jack highlights that a perceived need to differentiate Scottish literature from the wider field of English literature has shaped the Scottish canon. It has involved the privileging of certain 'distinctive' characteristics and values of the tradition (writing in Scots, writing unpretentiously, writing on Scottish themes, and writing from a democratic point of view). This has made it less likely that texts that diverge from these criteria will be included in curriculums and surveys of the field.[8]

Wilson and, to an extent, Lockhart have been hard to accommodate within this narrative. Their conservative, and often moralistic, vision of Scotland means they are troubling ancestors for a Scottish literature that has increasingly identified itself as distinctively 'democratic' and 'unpretentious'. While fellow Romantic conservatives Hogg, Scott and Galt have been more easily recuperated due to the nuance and ambiguity they bring to rural subjects, the close relationship between Wilson's and Lockhart's political polemic and rural literary writing makes their texts far less easily rehabilitated. Their writing, and their national vision, are unappetising perhaps because they indicate a more conservative origin story for some of the key themes and perspectives that have continued to characterise Scottish letters. While it would be hard to argue that Wilson or Lockhart had the impact of Walter Scott, they were arguably more important to the formation of ideas of Scotland in the nineteenth century than has generally been acknowledged. Although Andrew Noble's damning 1988 indictment of Wilson is wholly critical, its claim that 'Wilson was significantly responsible for setting back Scottish literature for over a century' attests to a cultural power that we ignore at our peril.[9]

In an 1850 essay on John Wilson, Thomas De Quincey suggests that within his writings the reader can trace an overarching approach to society:

> A philosophy of human nature like the philosophy of Shakespeare, and of Jeremy Taylor, and of Edmund Burke ... is scattered through the miscellaneous papers of Professor Wilson. It is a philosophy that cannot be presented in abstract forms, but hides itself as an incarnation in voluminous mazes of eloquence and poetic feeling.[10]

Form and content interconnect here. De Quincey recognises that scattered 'eloquence' and 'poetic feeling' are central to Wilson's rejection of a way of thinking and writing about humanity and society that is 'abstract', theoretical and utilitarian. Lockhart is also arguably an author engaged in a similar opposition to the theoretical; Francis Hart, in his examination of Lockhart's fictionalised account of literary Edinburgh, *Peter's Letters to His Kinfolk*, characterises him as both 'romantic biographer' and 'cultural theorist'.[11]

The idea that both men were engaged in the same cultural project is suggested in one of the most influential contemporary responses to their fiction. In his highly critical 1823 review 'Secondary Scottish Novels', Francis Jeffrey draws particular parallels between John Wilson's and J. G. Lockhart's Scottish fiction. He suggests that their novels might have been mistaken for the work of 'only one author' due to their shared sentimentalism, religiosity and subject matter: 'they enlarge, in a sort of pastoral, empathetic, and melodious style, on the virtues of our cottagers, and the apostolic sanctity of our ministers and elders, the delights of pure affection, and the comforts of the Bible.'[12] For both Wilson and Lockhart in the 1810s and early 1820s, Romantic ideas of nation found expression in the idealised and moralised Scottish countryside that Jeffrey describes. The dead are a motif in this project, articulating a conservative vision of the relationship between contemporary culture and the past.

Welcome to Gandercleugh: Scott's Tales of My Landlord and the Scottish Regional Tale

While Jeffrey's article helps to map the relationship between Wilson's and Lockhart's regional writing, its primary focus is on placing the Blackwood adjacent 'Secondary Scottish' novelists in relation to the most prominent Scottish Romanticist of their era, Walter Scott. Jeffrey's article famously characterises novels written by John Galt, Lockhart and Wilson as 'imitations of the inimitable novels', referring to the works of the still officially anonymous author of *Waverley*.[13] Following the commercial success of the early Waverley novels, the 'author unknown' was a literary sensation whose work popularised and redefined the Scottish historical novel.[14] The Scottish novels and tales of the early decades of the nineteenth century were thus written and read, as Duncan has argued, in 'Scott's Shadow'.[15] Jeffrey's article participates in this comparative reading, characterising Wilson's and Lockhart's books as works that draw upon 'the poetical, reflective, and pathetic' parts of Scott's legacy.[16] While Wilson's and Lockhart's novels and stories were to diverge from Scott's wider oeuvre in a number of stylistic and thematic ways, the opening scenes of *Old Mortality* proved foundational to both authors' use of the kirkyard motif. Scott's novel set a precedent for the way that death and a provincialised Scottish national identity were to become allied in the literary imagination.

In the opening pages of *Old Mortality* fictionalised editor Jedediah Cleishbotham, 'schoolmaster and Parish-clerk of Gandercleugh', asserts his Parish's position in the world:

> Gandercleugh is, as it were, the central part – the navel (*si fas sit dicere*) of this our native realm of Scotland; so that men, from every corner thereof, when travelling on their concernments of business, either towards our 'metropolis of law, by which I mean Edinburgh, or towards our metropolis and mart of gain, whereby I insinuate Glasgow, are frequently led to make Gandercleugh their abiding stage and place of rest for the night. And it must be acknowledged by the most sceptical, that I, who have sat in the leathern armchair, on the left-hand side of the fire, in the common-room of the Wallace Inn, winter and summer, for every evening in my life, during forty years bypast, (the Christian Sabbaths only excepted,) must have seen more of the manners and customs of various tribes and people, than if I had sought them out by my own painful travel and bodily labour.[17]

Gandercleugh, in Cleishbotham's worldview, typifies the nature of Scotland in a way that neither 'our metropolis of law' nor 'our metropolis and mart of gain' can. To sit by the fire of the Wallace Inn is to understand Scotland in a way that the mobile and metropolitan Scots of Glasgow and Edinburgh cannot. As Richard Cronin puts it, Scotland 'finds its true epitome in the entirely undistinguished village of Gandercleugh'.[18] Cleishbotham supports his own ability to comment on the nation at large by comically asserting that he has visited Edinburgh twice and Glasgow thrice. This defence of the provincial is a playful pen portrait of Scott's fictionalised editor, designed to amuse his increasingly urban and outward-looking readership. Cleishbotham is a figure apparently marooned at an inn fireside, his confidence in his own knowledge of the world evidence of his complete isolation from the rapid changes taking place around him. However, Cronin highlights the fact that by 1816 the publication of a Scott novel had an importance that extended far beyond Scotland. Gandercleugh, within the reading nation, did have the sort of importance that Cleishbotham attributes to it: '*Tales of my Landlord* was a British rather than a Scottish publishing event: Gandercleugh established itself in the closing months of 1816, not at all ironically but as a fact amply borne out by the volume's sales figures, as the "navel" of the whole United Kingdom.'[19]

Cleishbotham's panegyric on Gandercleugh introduces the second frame narrative of Scott's novel: the teacher Peter Pattieson's account of a meeting with the ancient Cameronian, Old Mortality, in Gandercleuch's abandoned cemetery. Pattieson describes his evening stroll to the quiet graveyard that lies 'up the narrow valley, and in a recess which seems scooped out of the side of the steep heathy bank'.[20] While upon Pattieson leaving the school his walk is interrupted by the life of the village – 'the first quarter of the mile, perhaps, I may be disturbed from my meditations, in order to return the scrape, or doffed bonnet, of such stragglers among my pupils as fish for trouts or minnows in the little brook, or seek rushes and wild-flowers by its margin' – this tableau of village life ceases as the school teacher approaches the old cemetery.[21] The cemetery space is removed from the life and flow of the community, and also from the realities of recent death. The children are 'fearful' of the site, and no new burials take place there, allowing the cemetery to become a picturesque part of the landscape:

> It is a spot which possesses all the solemnity of feeling attached to a burial ground, without exciting those of a more unpleasing description. Having been very little used for many years, the few hillocks which rise above the level plain are covered with the same short velvet turf. The monuments, of which there are not above seven or eight, are half sunk in the ground, and overgrown with moss. No newly erected tomb disturbs the sober serenity of our reflections by reminding us of recent calamity, and no rank-springing grass forces upon our imagination the recollection, that it owes its dark

> luxuriance to the foul and festering remnants of mortality which ferment beneath ... Those who sleep beneath are only connected with us by the reflection, that they have once been what we now are, and that, as their relics are now identified with their mother earth, ours shall, at some future period, undergo the same transformation.[22]

The burial ground provides a repository for a history that is no longer 'rank' or vital. The link between the living and the dead is only that of mortality. This sequestration of the past allows the peaceful bucolic village to exist in the present. The tombs of the knight, the bishop and the Covenanters are removed from the living reality of Scottish rural life, fading slowly back into obscurity along with the conflicts they represent.

This division of the living from the dead might appear to be disrupted by Old Morality's efforts to maintain the graves of the Covenanters, but this behaviour is not portrayed as indicative of a continued tradition. Old Mortality is himself old, a dying remnant of a dying tradition. He is a sort of last Covenanter, in the tradition of Scott's *Lay of the Last Minstrel* (1802), another final survivor of what Scott perceives to be a dying indigenous Scottish culture that must be recorded and preserved.[23] After his death, the local people believe that the graves he maintained are supernaturally preserved but Pattieson is quick to discard this belief as superstition: 'it is hardly necessary to say that this is fond imagination, and that, since the time of the pious pilgrim, the monuments that were the objects of his care are hastening, like all earthly memorials, into ruin or decay.'[24] Although the local people feed and revere Old Mortality during his pilgrimages, they do not take on his responsibilities after his death. The Covenanting past has become an object of cultural memory rather than a stimulus for action. Summarising the role that historic allegiances and enmities should play in modern Scotland, Pattieson famously closes the frame narrative by quoting John Home's *Douglas* (1756):[25]

> We may safely hope, that the souls of the brave and sincere on either side have long looked down with surprise and pity upon the ill-appreciated motives which caused their mutual hatred and hostility, while in this valley of darkness, blood and tears. Peace to their memory! Let us think of them as the heroine of our only Scottish tragedy entreats her lord to think of her departed sire:– 'O rake not up the ashes of our fathers! / Implacable resentment was their crime / And grievous has the expiation been.'[26]

The loyalties of the past in *Old Mortality* are, like the abandoned graveyard, to be laid aside and left to fade from view. Scottish culture, like the graveyard, is to become an aesthetic and antiquarian object denuded of political threat and relevance.

Old Mortality was conceived as one of a four-volume series titled Tales of My Landlord in which each volume was to contain a different Scottish regional tale. While planning the series, Scott made the decision to defect from his previous publisher, Archibald Constable, to Constable's rival, William Blackwood. By 1816, in the wake of the publication of *Waverley*, *Guy Mannering* and *The Antiquary*, Scott was arguably the single most successful English-language novelist of his day and his success had helped to place Edinburgh at the forefront of British publishing, outside of London.[27] His defection from Constable to Blackwood was a major victory for the ambitious publisher. However, William Blackwood's coup was to prove short-lived. Scott's tale of the South, *The Black Dwarf*, adhered to the agreed formula of a single-volume tale but his tale of the West, *Old Mortality*, took on a life of its own, filling the three further agreed volumes. On the publication of these two novels, Scott, dissatisfied with his new publisher, chose to return to publishing his work with Constable, and the subsequent Tales of My Landlord were published with him. For a fleeting moment, Scott had been a Blackwood author, but this moment was to have a powerful impact on the direction of the publishing house and Scottish rural fiction. In particular, the early graveyard scenes of *Old Mortality* were to plant the germ of a way of imagining Scotland, and its role in early nineteenth-century Britain. As Ian Duncan has argued, Scott's Tales of My Landlord 'opened a path for the characteristically "Blackwoodian fiction" that followed'.[28]

The dual interest in regionalism and history evinced in these opening graveyard chapters sets up a particular way of seeing the Scottish nation. Through the double framing of Old Mortality's account of the covenanting wars, their political import is neutralised and removed. The peaceful kirkyard operates as an emblem of a safely contained and purely cultural nationalism. However, where Scott, in his preface to *Old Mortality*, seems to advocate that we 'rake not up the ashes of our ancestors' and instead look reverentially at the mouldering tomb, the authors who were to follow in his footsteps complicate this relationship between the living and the dead, relocating the kirkyard from the neglected outskirts to the very heart of the national community.

Christopher North's *Saturday Night* and *Peter's Letters from the Country*: Assembling the Intertextual Kirkyard

Writing in the wake of *Old Mortality*, Lockhart and Wilson also sought to articulate the relationship between nation and history through the figure of the graveyard. However, their approach to the national dead was underwritten by a wide range of contemporary influences and predecessors beyond Scott. Both Lockhart's and Wilson's writing is heavily enmeshed in prior and contemporary literary culture, and characterised by an intertextuality that can border on derivativeness.[29] This magpie-like quotation formally rehearses their political and social ideals as conservative men of letters. The literary text is Edmund Burke's social body built upon prior precedent. Between 1817 and 1820 Lockhart and Wilson assembled an important counter-Enlightenment social vision through the invocation of a pantheon of textual forefathers in their poetry, fictionalised travelogues and articles. In conversation with both each other and a wider tradition, these writers gathered the range of ideas and images that would characterise the kirkyard fiction of the subsequent decades.

For the first issue of William Blackwood's magazine in April 1817, still under the editorship of Pringle and Cleghorn, Wilson anonymously authored an imitation of Goldsmith's 'Deserted Village'. Titled 'The Desolate Village', the poem transported the titular village from rural England to the Scottish lowlands.[30] In its application of the concerns and forms of the English georgic to Scottish pastoral space, and its focus on mortality, 'The Desolate Village' offers an early glimpse of the preoccupations that were to characterise Wilson's rural writing.[31]

Wilson's village is, like Goldsmith's, an idyllic rural space eerily denuded of its human population. However, where Goldsmith's Auburn had been depopulated due to enclosure, and the poem participates in a critique of agricultural improvement, Wilson's 'sweet Woodburn' has been decimated by epidemic disease. Wilson's recasting of the cause of the village's desolation depoliticises his poem: instead of a sign of rapid modernisation, the village's desertion is the result of an act of God.[32] Wilson is able to engage with the desolate Scottish village as a purely aesthetic object of cultural memory, free of associations with contemporary social change.

Looking back to the life of the village before its desolation, Wilson describes an idealised realm of 'happy shepherds', pious pastors and 'shoals of bright-haired elves'.[33] The past life of the village is an idealised and politically neutralised one; Wilson's poem jettisons the incisive social commentary of its antecedent in favour of pastoral fantasy. However, 'The Desolate Village' also identifies the twin roles of imagination and memory in shaping and obscuring this poetic image of the past: "'Tis a picture floating down the sky, / By fancy framed in years gone by, / And mellowing in decay!'[34] These lines acknowledge the fictionality of the historical vision of the preceding stanzas. The village of 'happy shepherds' is one shaped retrospectively by 'fancy' and 'mellowing' memory. The village's desolation makes it a playground, not just for the wild animals and plants which reclaim its streets, but for Wilson's imagination. Death is necessary to the creation of this realm of romanticised memory; only once the living community has vacated the streets and fields can the 'picture' be safely placed in its 'frame'. The village is thus transported from the living political world of the current to an aestheticised and imagined history. Wilson's self-conscious response to Goldsmith operates like the posthumous portrait of Fergus Mac-Ivor in Scott's *Waverley*, where Cairns Craig argues 'life in history has been turned into art'.[35] In Wilson's earliest rural poem for *Blackwood's* the Scottish lowland village experiences a living death: existing only in a seemingly permanent state of aestheticised decline.

Where Wilson's early poem co-opts the conventions of English pastoral and georgic poetry, Lockhart's approach to Scottish national identity was heavily informed by his engagement with European Romanticism. Phillip Flynn has noted the 'Burkean, Staëlean, Scheleglian'[36] nature of Lockhart's political sentiments as expressed in his writings on the ideas of Germaine de Staël and Friedrich Schlegel. In 1818 he published the first translation of Friedrich Schlegel's *Lectures on the History of Literature, Ancient and Modern* with William Blackwood. Lockhart's August 1818 essay 'Remarks on Schlegel's History of Literature' in *Blackwood's* lays out his application of Schlegel's ideas to contemporary Britain. The essay opens with a critique of the concept of historical progress and by its conclusion has laid responsibility for the prevalence of these ideas firmly at the feet of Enlightenment philosophy and the periodical press. Lockhart quotes extensively from Schlegel's Lectures emphasising the importance of national literature. This climaxes in an extended quotation from the philosopher's critique of contemporary English letters which he terms 'the most profound and important reflections'.[37] He subsequently provides his own commentary on the state of British literature, arguing that the abstraction of the Scottish Enlightenment has damaged the character of national literature: 'it is a melancholy fact, that a single generation of abstract reasoners is enough to vitiate the pedigree of national sentiment and association.'[38] Schlegel's Romanticism is thus co-opted to the cause of Lockhart's counter-Whig cultural nationalism. The influence of Schlegel can be identified across Lockhart's writing and is arguably essential to the codification of Scottish cultural nationalism in the kirkyard.[39]

Both Wilson and Lockhart seek to write their works into a Scottish national literary tradition of the type that Schlegel advocates. In the February 1819 issue of *Blackwood's* Wilson published an essay titled

'Some Observations on the Poetry of the Agricultural and that of the Pastoral Districts of Scotland, Illustrated by a Comparative View of the Genius of Burns and the Ettrick Shepherd' that sets out to define the legacies of Robert Burns and James Hogg. In this essay Wilson casts Burns and Hogg as key figures in the history of Scottish rural writing and sets out to distinguish between Burns's 'agricultural' poetics and Hogg's 'pastoral' poetics. Burns and Hogg are both invested with the authority of literary progenitors but only given a specific and limited function within the arena of Scottish letters.[40]

Wilson, in this essay, writes into a burgeoning field of conservative responses to Burns. Burns's adoption by conservative commentators can be traced back to Henry Mackenzie's famous characterisation of the poet as 'heaven-taught ploughman'[41] and Robert Heron's 1797 biography.[42] In particular, the rural pietism of Burns's cottage poem 'The Cotter's Saturday Night' furnished these conservative commentators with a palatable way of imagining Burns's legacy.[43] As Andrew Nash argues, 'Burns was appropriated, and in a very strong way, by forces eager to impose their own patterns of cultural authority.'[44] Just such a 'Tory Burns' was to occupy a central role in John Wilson's imagined countryside. Wilson draws upon the authority of the bard to construct his own rural myth.

James Hogg can also usefully be thought of as an important originator of the themes and concerns of Wilson and Lockhart's kirkyard. Hogg's career had begun in the early 1800s as a peasant poet and song collector, writing in the tradition of Burns, but by 1810 he was publishing original rural fiction in his weekly paper *The Spy*.[45] In an 1810 rural sketch in *The Spy*, 'Description of a Peasant's Funeral', Hogg's frame narrator, John Miller, describes a visit to a rural community to witness a burial. An idealised traditional gathering is presented, complete with quaint and illogical customs that are described and rationalised to the urban educated reader in anthropological terms, but this scene rapidly dissolves into one of near Gothic horror.[46] Hogg's story provides an early example of the construction and deconstruction of idealised rural life that would characterise kirkyard writing. In his 'Description of a Peasant's Funeral', Hogg was already experimenting with death and burial as a synecdoche for rural Scotland's relationship with history and the wider nation. Hogg's rural Scottish writing significantly predated and set a precedent for the construction of Wilson's vision of the national kirkyard. As he had with Burns, Wilson turns away from the subversive aspects of this project, defanging the horrors of Hogg's tale.

However, in 1819 Hogg, unlike Burns, was still an active, living participant in the construction of literary Scotland, continuing to publish innovative and often subversive rural stories, sketches and poems. Wilson's decision to cast him in the role of worthy progenitor alongside Burns, therefore, draws attention to a temporal incongruity that is central to Wilson's perspective on the rural. In Wilson's writing, the Scottish countryside, and those who inhabit it, are understood as remnants or traces of a past, or passing, era. Although Hogg is his contemporary, Wilson casts him as an ancestor whose literary output exists in a previous time. As Schoenfield has commented, 'Hogg's significance to *Blackwood's* ... is a precursor, a legitimating figure, and a mode of exploring the uniqueness of Scottish culture.'[47] As we will discuss in greater depth in the next chapter of this book, Hogg chafed against this status as living ancestor and this depiction of rural life as temporally belated.

Wilson further limits and neutralises Burns's and Hogg's influence and legacy in his essay through his attribution of specific roles to each poet based on their occupation. He suggests that Burns's function as agricultural poet is to catalogue 'the feelings and the passions of the heart of man' rather than the beauties of nature.[48] Hogg as a shepherd should limit himself to 'the days of old' and 'the Court of Faery', and is warned against attempting 'any long poem in which a variety of characters are to be displayed acting on the theatre of the world'.[49] Wilson does not attribute the ability to move beyond this circumscribed role to either writer, suggesting that the field in which 'peasant poets' can operate is limited.[50] The 'peasant poets' are deemed incapable of the type of generic flexibility that was the hallmark of the major writers within the *Blackwood's* cohort, nor are they endowed with comparable wit and urbanity. Ian Duncan and Douglas S. Mack suggest that:

> John Wilson (the leading figure of *Blackwood's*) tended to present Hogg (and Burns) as writers about pious peasants, peasants who keep up the good old traditions of the good old days, peasants presented by Wilson as the salt of the earth and the backbone of Britain.[51]

Wilson's attempted differentiation between the two writers, based on forms of rural labour, reveals his desire to limit the scope of their influence and isolate their rural writing from the world of modern letters.

While Wilson's selection of Hogg and Burns as key figures in a personal canon of Scottish precursors is key to understanding his subsequent output, his broader reflections on Scottish rural culture and Burns's popular poem 'The Cotter's Saturday Night' in 'Burns and the Ettrick Shepherd' provide a glimpse of the approach to the countryside that would be explored in 'The Radical's Saturday Night' and his later short fiction. In these comments, Wilson overtly moves towards a wider account of Scottish national identity. 'Burns and the Ettrick Shepherd' opens with some general thoughts on the character of Scotland's rural peasantry. Wilson argues that 'the lower orders of the Scotch seem always to have had deeper, calmer, purer, and more reflecting affections than those of any other people' and that this unique character 'is to be attributed to the spirit of their religion'.[52] In the politically tense months that led up to the Peterloo Massacre in August 1819, Wilson casts Scotland's lowland peasantry as a docile, model working class. Discounting the radical inheritance of Scottish Presbyterianism, Wilson suggests that it is their faith that makes the Scots law-abiding and submissive. This docility and piety means that Scotland's rural working class are differentiated from their English counterparts:

> Of England, and of the character of her population, high and low, we think with exultation and with pride. Some virtues they perhaps possess in greater perfection than any other people. But we believe, that the most philosophical Englishmen acknowledge that there is a depth of moral and religious feeling in the peasantry of Scotland, not to be found among the best part of their own population.[53]

The Scottish countryside is not merely an extension of the English countryside in Wilson's essay. Scottish cotters are set apart as a 'purer, simpler, more pious race'.[54] The Scottish Kirk is given a central role in the maintenance of superior political order and continuity in Scotland. This characterisation wilfully ignores both the Kirk's controversial history in relation to the Union, and the increasing division and disharmony between the Moderate and Evangelical parties within the contemporary Church.

In line with this approach to the 'Scottish peasant', in 'Burns and the Ettrick Shepherd', Wilson first identifies the version of Burns's legacy that was to characterise his own approach to rural life.[55] Denouncing the satirical and bawdy Burns evinced in works like 'Holy Willie's Prayer', Wilson identifies 'The Cotter's Saturday Night' as the pinnacle of Burns's career, and as a work that reveals the true Burns:

> 'The Cotter's Saturday Night' shews what he could have done – had he surveyed with a calm and untroubled eye, all the influences of our religion, carried as they are in the inmost heart of society by our simple and beautiful forms of worship – had marriage – baptism – that other more awful sacrament – death – and funeral – had these and the innumerable themes allied to them, sunk into the depths of his heart, and images of them reascended thence into living and imperishable light.[56]

Wilson's reading of Burns not only praises the 'Cotter' in line with MacKenzie's conservative tradition but lays out the 'Cotter'-inspired poems Wilson wishes Burns had written. Where the 'Cotter' focuses on worship and family, Wilson highlights the role that death and the funeral might have played in his alternative Burns canon, laying the groundwork for his own Scottish rural writings.

Wilson's work also evinces an ongoing fascination with the elder English Romantic William Wordsworth and the Lake School.[57] Wordsworth's own sustained engagement with rural subjects and the dead is well documented. In poems like 'We Are Seven' and in his 'Essays on Epitaphs', Wordsworth posits an image of the relationship between death and the community that shares many important features with Wilson's subsequent approach. Both poets share an interest in imagining interpersonal relationships between the living and the dead. These offer an alternative model of community beyond the commercial exchange of political economy.[58] Kurt Fosso has convincingly argued that, in his early writing, Wordsworth's idea of the mournful community is not compatible with ideas of the national. However, in his later work 'the basis for social cohesion has shifted from troubled mourning to shared tradition, history, and religion', a concern which is in greater harmony with Wilson's.[59]

Wilson's picturesque sketch series 'Letters from the Lakes' appeared in *Blackwood's* in 1819. In these sketches a Germanic visitor, Phillip Kempfherhausen, describes a visit to the English Lake District. Kempfherhausen encounters not just the beauties of the Lakes but some of the 'Great Men' who live there, including Robert Southey and Wordsworth. The fictionalised encounter with Wordsworth features in the March 1819 instalment and situates the poet and his Romantic Lakes within Wilson's idealised nation.[60] Before encountering the Wordsworth family, the narrator visits an Ambleside churchyard: he describes its tranquil beauty and relates the sentimental tale of a local maiden who recently died of consumption. The young woman is described, as so many of Wilson's kirkyard heroines would be, resigned to death, visiting the churchyard each day to look at her final resting place. Her family and community likewise display the 'perfect resignation' that is associated with the rural poor in Wilson's Scottish fiction. When Wordsworth makes his appearance in the sketch, he too is presented in the conventional terms of a kirkyard story. The poet is presented as a paragon of the traditional, rural values that Wilson himself champions, as David Higgins notes: 'he appears, in part, as a country gentleman immersed in a network of healthy, paternalistic social relations and is thus linked with *Blackwood's*' Tory ideology based on agrarian virtue, the maintenance of social distinctions, and religious orthodoxy.'[61] Wordsworth is thus incorporated into Wilson's kirkyard vision as a character and forefather.

Wilson's ambivalent attitude to literary forefathers, living and dead, is in evidence again here. Higgins argues that, 'despite its panegyrical tone, by breaching the boundaries between public and private in such a way the article represents a deliberate insult to Wordsworth and reveals Wilson's ambivalent feelings about his former friend.'[62] Kempfherhausen's descriptions of his meeting with Wordsworth include, not just descriptions of Wordsworth, his home and family, but a recollection of a fictionalised conversation in which Wordsworth lauds the philosophy of Friedrich and August Wilhelm Schlegel, champions Coleridge, and critiques the critics and politics of his age. Wilson practices a type of literary ventriloquism through the fictionalised Wordsworth just as he would with the Ettrick Shepherd in the *Noctes Ambrosianae*. Wilson's incorporation of Wordsworth into his personal canon, like his championing of Hogg and Burns in 'Burns and the Ettrick Shepherd', serves not just to celebrate the English Romantic but also to limit and co-opt his legacy. Like Burns and Hogg, Wordsworth is not just celebrated but reimagined to better reflect Wilson's own sensibilities. Arguably in 'Letters from the Lakes' Wordsworth is incarcerated within the rural idyll, outside time, history and, potentially, modern literature. He appears as a sage rather than a contemporary man of letters.

July 1819 saw the publication of J. G, Lockhart's *Peter's Letters to His Kinfolk*.[63] Originally conceived as a co-written book of Scottish sketches by Wilson and Lockhart, by the time of publication *Peter's Letters* had morphed into a fictionalised travelogue similar to the 'Letters from the Lakes'. Lockhart took primary responsibility for the text, although Wilson was still involved in the writing of the narrative and was acknowledged as co-writer by Lockhart in his *Life of Scott*.[64] The book describes, through letters, the imagined impressions of a Welshman, Peter Morris, as he travels through Edinburgh and Scotland. Morris's observations on the life and character of Scotland allow Lockhart to construct an account of contemporary Scottish life that is highly critical of Whig approaches to culture and nation.

Like Wilson in 'Burns and the Ettrick Shepherd', Lockhart is engaged in assembling a vision of national identity from the materials of recent literary history. The title is an homage to Walter Scott's 1816 Napoleonic travelogue *Paul's Letters to His Kinfolk* while the use of a Welsh focalising narrator is reminiscent of Tobias Smollett's *The Expedition of Humphry Clinker* (1771).[65] There are also meetings with important Scottish literary figures such as Hogg, Scott and Mackenzie and repeated references to the works of Burns. William Ruddick has noted that 'in *Peter's Letters* Burns, Scott and Dr Chalmers are given extended treatment as representatives of the new Scottish spirit in the literature of the folk, in intellectual (and especially historic) nationalism and in the embodiment of the national spirit in religion'.[66] This hagiography of alternative Tory national figureheads is offered as an antidote to a Whig literary ascendency, who are presented as lacking in national feeling. Morris expresses his abomination of 'the scope and tendency of the *Edinburgh Review*' whose authors he suggests 'reduce the high feeling of patriotism to a principle of arithmetical calculation of utility'.[67]

The final chapters of Volume 3 build towards a final set piece: an account of the customs surrounding the 'giving of the Sacrament' in a rural parish.[68] Lockhart's narrator travels to a village in the west of Scotland at the suggestion of a Scottish gentleman. Although Morris's first point of reference for the Eucharist gathering is Burns's 'The Holy Fair' (1785), the gentleman is quick to reject this characterisation of Scottish religious life, asserting that the poem 'altogether omitted to do any manner of justice' to the character of these events.[69] He instead points Morris to 'The Cotter's Saturday Night' just as Wilson had directed his readers in 'Burns and the Ettrick Shepherd'. Morris then accompanies a young minister to a Eucharist gathering and provides an almost anthropological survey of the customs of the local people. This minute observation of folk tradition is paired with a commentary that lauds the endurance of the historical social structures and cultural practices of Scottish life.

Morris is fascinated by the sight of the local people listening to a preacher in the kirkyard among the graves. After quoting Grey's 'Elegy on a Country Churchyard', Morris describes the faces of the parishioners, young and old, lauding their 'solemn devotion'.[70] This scene inspires a moralised reflection on national character and literature:

> it is in rustic assemblages like these that the true characteristics of every race of man are most palpably and conspicuously displayed, and it is there that we can best see in multiplied instances the natural germs of that which, under the influence of culture, assumes a prouder character and blossoms into the animating soul and spirit of a national literature.[71]

In a rhetorical move that advocates for the culturally nationalist project in which Wilson and Lockhart are already engaged, Morris calls for Scotland's 'men of genius' to express 'the mind and intellect of their nation' by responding to and recording these scenes.[72] In *Peter's Letters* the kirkyard thus becomes the seedbed for Lockhart's Schlegelian concept of national literature.

Later that year Wilson's essay 'The Radical's Saturday Night' represented his first foray into reimagining the 'Cotter' in line with these political and aesthetic ideas.[73] Wilson opens the essay by once again reiterating the merits of the 'Cotter'. He suggests that Burns's poem documents the reality of cottage life:

> The picture which Burns has drawn of that hallowed scene, is felt by every one who has a human heart – but they alone can see its beauty, who have visited the fireplaces of the Scottish peasantry, and joined in their family worship. They who have done so, see in the poem nothing but the simple truth – truth so purified, refined, and elevated by devotion, as to become the highest poetry.[74]

The reader is invited to claim allegiance with an imagined group of informed readers who have witnessed the 'true nature' of Scottish cottage life, and therefore Scotland. Wilson imagines the poem as a virtual invitation to visit the homes of Scotland's rural poor. The reader is invited to experience the vision of Scotland that Wilson wishes to propagate. Andrew Nash succinctly summarises the rhetorical work that Wilson undertakes in these passages: 'to Wilson it's obvious: read Burns and you understand peasant Scotland, and, because peasant Scotland is unique, you understand what is unique to Scotland.'[75] This slippage between literary object, history and national character is already apparent in Wilson's earlier essays and in the kirkyard scene of *Peter's Letters*. Literature is presented as the true barometer of national identity and culture.

The author then asserts his own authority to represent peasant life and by extension Scottish culture. Although not a peasant poet, Wilson casts himself as an observer who has on multiple occasions witnessed similar scenes:

> Many a Saturday night has the writer of this joined in that simple service: more than once, when death had just visited the cottage – but at all times, whether those of joy or affliction – there was the same solemn resignation to the divine will – the same unquestioning, humble, wise, submission – the same perfect peace, and even lofty happiness – nor did he ever see one shudder, nor hear one sob that seemed to signify despair.[76]

The subsequent visit to a family of cotters recaps the key motifs of Burns's 'Cotter's Saturday Night'. Returning to a cottage that he 'had often visited when a boy', the writer comes across the 'gray-headed patriarch', who had lived there when he was young, and the cotter's daughter, now a wife and mother.[77] This figure of the returning literary man foreshadows the character who would narrate the stories in Wilson's collection *Lights and Shadows*: a city professional with country roots, able to use his critical gaze to observe and document country life. Wilson inserts a polite conduit into the cottage whose knowledge of urban *and* country life allows him to translate for his readers.[78]

Just as in his earlier essay Wilson had confined the Ettrick Shepherd to a countryside of fairies and history, in 'The Radical's Saturday Night' he places the cotters in a sort of historical stasis: 'nothing had happened to them since I came to bid them farewell on that summer morning I left school.'[79] Excluding a marriage and the births of children, life in the cottage is a point of complete continuity compared to Wilson's narrator's own life 'led in foreign countries'.[80] The 'secluded' cottage exists outside of the flow of time, sheltered from narratives of progress and change.[81] The old man reads from the 'big ha' bible' and leads the family in psalms and prayers echoing the scenes of the 'Cotter'. Thirty-three years after the publication of Burns's original poem, a work that was already an exercise in nostalgia at its time of publication, Wilson writes to reassure the reader that little has changed in the cottage.[82]

These idealised scenes of continuity and stability are contrasted with the nightmare visions that Wilson suffers on retreating to the 'neatly furnished' guest bedroom of the cottage to sleep.[83] He falls asleep musing with 'purest delight' on his evening with the cotters, but 'though all these impressions were calm, peaceful, and blessed, yet was the dream itself which they occasioned distorted, hideous, and ghastly, as if hell itself were suddenly to glare out through a vision of heaven'.[84] Wilson's nightmare features a Gothic counter-image of the scenes around the 'big ha' bible'. In the dream sequence, Wilson stumbles from a storm into the cottage to find it utterly altered by the overturn of 'throne and altar'.[85] The domestic life of the cottagers has broken down and Wilson finds the cottage 'patriarch' abandoned by 'the dead ashes of a scanty fire' in a dilapidated house.[86] On the return of the cotter family it becomes clear that the younger generation are now radical revolutionaries and have consequently lost their faith and their veneration for their elderly father.

The narrative emphasises the relationship between the breakdown of the patriarchal family unit and the collapse of organised religion. The young cotters no longer believe in a heavenly Father and similarly have little interest in their earthly father. The collapse of religion, the monarchy and the family are interconnected in 'The Radical's Saturday Night'; Wilson, like Burke, portrays God, the King and the father as interchangeable symbols of patriarchal order. Wilson returns repeatedly to images of the destroyed kirk and its surrounding kirkyard to emphasise the break with tradition and ancestral understandings of family that an atheist radical revolution represents. The atheist son describes the destruction of the local kirk in terms that directly reference the revolutionary controversy of the 1790s:

we have levelled the old crazy building with the ground – the pews, and lofts, and rafters – the pulpit too, with its sounding-board, where the old hypocrite used to preach salvation to our souls – by the bones of Thomas Paine, they made a glorious bonfire! And turned all the church-yard as bright as day – the manse itself looked red in the blaze. Had the ghosts leapt from their graves, they might have fancied it hell-fire.[87]

In this fanciful speech the bones of Thomas Paine replace the name of God and the kirkyard is transformed into the pit of hell. This world-upside-down image is remarkably similar to the images used in Burke's anti-revolutionary writings of the 1790s. In particular, Wilson's focus on the mistreatment of the elderly father and the bones of his ancestors draws upon images of the destruction of the 'aged parent' in the *Reflections*, where national traditions and institutions are depicted as a Pelias-like figure destroyed by his revolutionary progeny.[88] The father protests against the destruction of the graveyard:

'James! You have scattered the stones of the house of God, over the grave of your mother. Where will you bury these bones when your old father dies?' holding up his hands as he spake, his withered hands clasped as it were in prayer or supplication.[89]

The father characterises the destruction of the church and the family lair as actions that will prevent him not just from worshipping God but from being laid to rest with his late wife. However, as we began to explore in the opening to this chapter, his son shows little interest in his plea:

A hole dug in the earth is a grave – but we have no laws, I believe, against burial-grounds – only we must not call them kirk-yards – for where now are the kirks? This has been a glorious day for Scotland. More than a thousand kirks have crumbled into ashes – and tomorrow, not a bell will be heard singing from Tintock to Cape Wrath![90]

This dismissal of the family grave is symbolic of a wider rejection of the specifically Scottish values of piety and subservience to authority that Wilson attributes to the cotters. The centrality of this destruction of kirk and kirkyard to Wilson's 'Radical's Saturday Night' emphasises the increasing importance of the graveyard within his rural writing. The kirkyard represents both religion and the patriarchal family in a single Burkean image; its destruction symbolises the destruction of a patriarchal order founded on Church, throne and the father's hearth-side chair.

On awakening from this nightmare of radical revolution, Wilson finds himself in the orderly cottage of the night before: 'in a moment I recollected that I was reposing in the dwelling of peace, innocence, and piety.'[91] He accompanies the family to church and is reassured by the worthy old minister that 'the RADICAL'S SATURDAY-NIGHT would never be in Scotland any thing more than – a dream.'[92] Wilson's confident conclusion casts the Scottish lowlands as the repository of British political stability. This political stability is founded upon a patriarchal model of cultural inheritance and a depoliticised version of Scottish Presbyterianism, concepts that are intertwined in the potent image of an undisturbed rural kirkyard.

Over the 1810s Lockhart and Wilson build a set of overlapping and interacting concerns around death, culture and nation. In their writing for *Blackwood's* and the publisher William Blackwood the kirkyard comes to represent an organic, stable relationship between past and present. The citation of existing literary precedents for the kirkyard symbol is both a co-option of the cultural authority of previous writers and an articulation of that intergenerational relationship. Wilson and Lockhart's essays, poems and travelogues don't just describe a past tradition but laboriously assemble their place within it through quotation and assimilation. In doing so they imagine culture as multivocal and founded in past precedent. Through these works, we can see the formation of an idea of Scotland that is stable, belated and emotive, and often expressed through the synecdoche of the kirkyard. The next chapter explores how these curated ideas inform both Wilson and Lockhart's rural fiction.

Notes

1. Wilson, 'Radical's Saturday Night', p. 261.
2. Hayden, *The Romantic Reviewers*, p. 61.
3. Lang Strout refers to Wilson, Lockhart and the publisher William Blackwood as an 'uneasy triumvirate' between 1818 and 1820. Wilson and Lockhart took on many of the responsibilities of literary editors but could be overridden by Blackwood who took on an increasingly active role. He argues that this 'probably continued' until Lockhart's move to the *Quarterly* in 1825. Lang Strout, *A Bibliography of Articles in Blackwood's Magazine*, p. 3. See also Richardson, 'John Gibson Lockhart and Blackwood's: Shaping the Romantic Periodical Press', in *Romanticism and Blackwood's Magazine*, p. 38; Morrison, 'Camraderie and Conflict', p. 59.
4. Wheatley, 'Introduction', *Romantic Periodicals and Print Culture*, p. 1.
5. Wilson's often ruthless and hyperbolic reviewing style has inspired accounts of him like Andrew Noble's who describe him as the 'reviewer and public prosecutor of English Romantic poetry on behalf of his snobbish, semi-literate readership'. His personal controversies with other high-profile Romantics like Wordsworth, De Quincey and Hogg are well documented and rarely show him in a positive light. Lochhead has noted of Lockhart's early role at *Blackwood's* that 'his pen wounded'. Noble, 'John Wilson

(Christopher North) and the Tory Hegemony', p. 136; Lochhead, *John Gibson Lockhart*, p. 1.
6. Wu, *William Hazlitt*, p. 257.
7. Carruthers, *Edinburgh Critical Guide to Scottish Literature*, p. 4.
8. Jack, 'Critical Introduction: Where Stands Scots Now?', in *The Mercat Anthology of Early Scottish Literature, 1375–1707*, p. xi.
9. Noble, 'John Wilson (Christopher North) and the Tory Hegemony', p. 149.
10. De Quincey, 'Professor Wilson', p. 301.
11. Hart, *Lockhart as Romantic Biographer*, p. 49.
12. Jeffrey, 'Secondary Scottish Novels', p. 161.
13. Ibid., pp. 160–1.
14. Ibid., p. 160.
15. Duncan, *Scott's Shadow*, p. xii.
16. Jeffrey, 'Secondary Scottish Novels', p. 161.
17. Scott, *Old Mortality*, p. 5.
18. Cronin, *Paper Pellets*, p. 83.
19. Ibid., p. 83.
20. Scott, *Old Mortality*, p. 26.
21. Ibid., p. 26.
22. Ibid., pp. 26–7.
23. Scott, *The Lay of the Last Minstrel*.
24. Scott, *Old Mortality*, p. 34.
25. Home, *Douglas*.
26. Scott, *Old Mortality*, p. 36.
27. Duncan, *Scott's Shadow*, pp. 21–2.
28. Ibid., p. 34.
29. 'for the intertextually inclined, Wilson offers an embarrassment of riches'. Noble, 'John Wilson (Christopher North) and the Tory Hegemony', p. 137.
30. Goldsmith, *The Deserted Village*.
31. Wilson, 'The Desolate Village'.
32. Chapter 4 discusses how both James Hogg and John Buchan present disease as a symptom of social ills. However, in Wilson's poem disease is wholly depoliticised.
33. Wilson, 'The Desolate Village', p. 70.
34. Ibid., p. 70.
35. Craig, *Out of History*, p. 39.
36. Flynn, 'Early "Blackwood's" and Scottish Identities', p. 49.
37. Lockhart, 'Remarks on Schlegel's History of Literature', p. 509.
38. Ibid., p. 500.
39. Wall has suggested that 'Lockhart's Germanic interests provided the galvanizing force behind Blackwood's attempt to formulate a coherent and distinct conception of Scottish national literature, within the framework of its staunch Toryism.' Wall, 'Looking for Literary Scotland', pp. 215–16.
40. Wilson, 'Some Observations', pp. 521–9.
41. Mackenzie, Unsigned essay in *Lounger*, 97 (9 December 1786), p. 70.
42. Heron, *A Memoir of the Life of the Late Robert Burns*.
43. This appropriation is discussed in ch. 7 of Nigel Leask *Robert Burns and Pastoral*.
44. Nash, 'The Cotter's Kailyard', p. 181.

45. Hughes, 'Introduction', in Hogg, *The Spy*, pp. xvii–l.
46. Hogg, *The Spy*, p. 123.
47. Schoenfield, *British Periodicals and Romantic Identity*, p. 205.
48. Ibid., p. 524.
49. Ibid., pp. 528–9.
50. Ibid., p. 521.
51. Duncan and Mack, 'Hogg, Galt, Scott and Their Milieu', p. 220.
52. Wilson, 'Burns and the Ettrick Shepherd', p. 521.
53. Ibid., p. 522.
54. Ibid., p. 523.
55. Ibid., p. 522.
56. Ibid., p. 526.
57. See Dundas, 'John Wilson to William Wordsworth (1802): A New Text'.
58. Fosso has commented that 'Wordsworth's prose and poetry frequently depict churchyards, ruins, and other death-imbued topographies as sites of … "spiritual community"'. Fosso, *Buried Communities*, p. 6.
59. Ibid., p. 25.
60. Wilson, 'Letters from the Lakes'.
61. Higgins, 'Blackwood's Edinburgh Magazine and the Construction of Wordsworth's Genius', p. 129.
62. Ibid., p. 129.
63. Lockhart, *Peter's Letters to His Kinfolk*, pp. i–iii.
64. Ruddick, 'Introduction', in Lockhart, *Peter's Letters to His Kinfolk*, p. xvi.
65. Smollett, *The Expedition of Humphry Clinker*.
66. Ruddick, 'Introduction', p. xii.
67. Lockhart, *Peter's Letters*, vol. 2, pp. 127, 138.
68. Ibid., vol. 3, p. 302.
69. Ibid., vol. 3, p. 302.
70. Ibid., vol. 3, p. 324.
71. Ibid., vol. 3, p. 326.
72. Ibid., vol. 3, p. 327.
73. Wilson, 'The Radical's Saturday Night'.
74. Ibid., p. 267.
75. Nash, 'The Cotter's Kailyard', p. 185.
76. Wilson, 'The Radical's Saturday Night', p. 258.
77. Ibid., p. 258.
78. This mediation is perhaps indicative of Wilson's wider concerns about sympathetic engagement and 'low life'. See Dundas, 'John Wilson to William Wordsworth (1802): a New Text'.
79. Wilson, 'Radical's Saturday Night', p. 258.
80. Ibid., p. 258.
81. Ibid., p. 259.
82. Sharp, 'Exporting the Cottar's Saturday Night', p. 82.
83. Wilson, 'The Radical's Saturday Night', p. 259.
84. Ibid., p. 259.
85. Ibid., p. 259.
86. Ibid., p. 259.
87. Ibid., p. 260.
88. Burke, *Reflections on the Revolution in France*, p. 194.

89. Wilson, 'The Radical's Saturday Night', p. 260.
90. Ibid., p. 261.
91. Ibid., p. 261.
92. Ibid., p. 262. A sentiment echoed in Lockhart's poem for the same issue 'The Clydesdale Yeoman's Return' where the eponymous yeoman vows to stand out against radical weavers in the name of 'God's blessed word- King George's Crown- and proud old Scotland's laws!' Lockhart, 'The Clydesdale Yeoman's Return', pp. 321–2.

Chapter 2

'In the burial ground of his native parish': Romancing the Kirkyard

In the eleventh tale of John Wilson's story collection *Lights and Shadows of Scottish Life* (1822), an elderly minister and his son take a walk in the local parish graveyard, traversing an idyllic landscape:

> The Kirk of Auchindown stands, with its burial ground, on a little green hill, surrounded by an irregular and straggling village, or rather about a hundred hamlets clustering round it, with their fields and gardens. A few of these gardens come close up to the churchyard-wall, and in spring time many of the fruit trees hang rich and beautiful over the adjacent graves. The voices and the laughter of the children at play on the green before the parish-school, or their composed murmur when at their various lessons together in the room, may be distinctly heard all over the burial ground – so may the song of the maidens going to the well; – while all round around the singing of birds is thick and hurried; and a small rivulet, as if brought there to be an emblem of passing time, glides away beneath the mossy wall, murmuring continually a dream like tune around the dwellings of the dead.[1]

On reaching a particular 'low monument', the minister stops to tell the pathetic tale of English twins who died of fever while under his care. The gravestone acts as a physical marker of memory, a site that facilitates a certain kind of reminiscence or storytelling. The minister goes to the beautiful graveside to describe a beautiful death.

However, the gravestone and its situation within the burial ground, on a green hill have already affected a type of storytelling before the minister starts his narrative. The graveyard's position at the heart of the living world of the village is indicated by the 'fruit-trees' from neighbouring gardens overhanging the graves, and the melodic sounds of the children who attend the nearby school, the local 'maidens going to the well', and the songbirds that can be heard among the graves. The twins' deaths are therefore represented within a timeless rural cycle of seedtime and harvest, youth and decline, and their graves are placed at the heart of a community where death and life coexist organically.

The stream that passes the graves acts as 'an emblem of time' uniting the living and the dead in this continuum. This minute description of the kirkyard locates it within Wilson's particular social vision even before the minister can begin to tell his story.

This detailed image of the burial ground is typical of a text that consistently seeks to represent what a 'good death' might look like. There is an unusually high incidence of death in the twenty-four stories that make up Wilson's *Lights and Shadows*; fourteen of the tales directly describe deaths while another three mention deaths that have already happened and a further three stories contain near-death experiences. Wilson's obvious investment in representing the dead has been commented on in previous examinations of the collection but, as yet, has not been thoroughly explored within his wider oeuvre.[2]

Wilson, as we traced in the previous chapter, had in the years leading up to the publication of the *Lights and Shadows* stories been engaged, alongside his colleague J.G. Lockhart, in the construction of an approach to Scottish history and culture that I term kirkyard Romanticism. In these texts Wilson and Lockhart assembled a canon of literary forefathers for their own culturally nationalist project. This chapter explores how both authors' deployed these ideas in their 'Secondary Scottish novels and other Scottish rural fiction during the 1820s.[3] Located at the heart of the traditional village, Wilson and Lockhart's kirkyard operates to articulate a vision of Scottish identity that responds to modernity through its focus on local space and its invocation of local, historical, and emotional ties. I argue that both writers used the kirkyard in their stories and novels to reinforce a distinctive and highly influential vision of Scotland's place within Britain.

While Wilson and Lockhart's national imaginary has its most obvious influence on contemporary Scottish regional writing, and we will be tracing this influence in several of the following chapters, this was not its only legacy. The store of images and ideas that they assembled could be adapted and applied to other geographical contexts and survived in Scottish letters into the next century. The final section of this chapter turns to two afterlives for the kirkyard: one that foregrounds its modularity, and another that showcases its longevity. First, I examine the series *Chapters on Churchyards*, published by Caroline Southey Bowles in *Blackwood's* from 1824, arguing that the kirkyard nationalism of Lockhart and Wilson represents an important missing link between Bowles's popular prose pastoral and the English poetic pastoral tradition it is often imagined within. I argue that Bowles's English churchyard also sets a precedent for the transportation of kirkyard nationalism across the ever-expanding English-speaking world of the nineteenth century.

I then turn to the 'kailyard' writers of the late nineteenth and early twentieth century, focusing particularly on the works of J. M. Barrie and Ian Maclaren. The rural writing of Romantic authors like Wilson and Lockhart has often been identified as a precursor to this body of prose literature. I examine the way that both Barrie and Maclaren use sentimental death and burial scenes to underpin their ideas of Scottish national character, arguing for a continuous tradition of kirkyard Romanticism that predates and outlives the kailyard moment.

That Other More Awful Sacrament: Wilson's Rural Fiction

The image of Scottish rural life as a bastion of conservative values presented in 'The Radical's Saturday Night' was one that would be at the heart of much of Wilson's subsequent fiction. From 1820 Wilson began to publish the series of moralising short stories in *Blackwood's* that would eventually be collected into the short-story collection *Lights and Shadows of Scottish Life* (1822).[4] Like the tale of 'The Twins' that opened this chapter, the stories are consistently sentimental. They are often set in unspecified lowland rural spaces and narrated by a distanced narrator like the one employed in 'The Radical's Saturday Night'. The *Lights and Shadows* collection was followed by two novels that also drew upon Wilson's kirkyard-centred national vision: *The Trials of Margaret Lyndsay* (1823) and *The Foresters* (1825).[5] Both novels combine the regional and the sentimental, adopting a similar set of strategies and concerns to the stories of *Lights and Shadows*. Wilson's rural fiction has often been identified as a precursor to the 'kailyard' writing of the turn of the century; Ian Campbell comments that 'the themes of Wilson's fictions ... startlingly prefigure familiar themes of the kailyard'.[6]

In these works Wilson sets out to write the texts he earlier regretted Burns had not written, turning his attention in particular to 'that other more awful sacrament – death – and funeral'.[7] Consequently, one of the most jarring features of Wilson's fiction to a modern reader is its unrelenting focus on death. Mack describes *Lights and Shadows of Scottish Life* as 'a collection of short stories in which the characters tend to shed tears copiously', while Tim Killick describes it as a collection of 'syrupy stories of benign Providence'.[8] Wilson's preoccupation with representing death carries into his long-form fiction. The eponymous Forester family of Wilson's 1825 novel are besieged by the deaths of friends, neighbours and family members, while the heroine of *Margaret Lyndsay* survives her entire extended family and rakish husband in the course of the novel. Wilson's focus on death is constant, unflinching and deliberate. A series of intertwined concepts and meanings cluster around the graveyard and the dead in these texts. They echo the ideas Wilson had put forth in his poetic and polemical writing and consolidate his approach to the Scottish national character. In particular, Wilson's kirkyard fictions reject ideas of liberal modernity, in the form of progress, mobility and rationality, by championing memory, resignation, cyclicality and emotion.

These intertwining moral values can be seen in the *Lights and Shadows* story 'The Elder's Funeral'. The narrator takes time to reflect on the place of the graveyard within the local community following the funeral of a pious and worthy elder of the Kirk:

> The Churchyard, to the inhabitants of a rural parish, is the place to which, as they grow older, all their thoughts and feelings turn. The young take a look of it every Sabbath-day, not always perhaps a careless look, but carry away from it, unconsciously, many salutary impressions. What is more pleasant than the meeting of a rural congregation in the churchyard before the minister appears? What is there to shudder at in lying down, sooner or later, in such a peaceful and sacred place, to be spoken of frequently on Sabbath among the groups of which we used to be one, and our low burial-spot to be visited, at such times, as long as there remains on earth any one to whom our face was dear![9]

Just as in the description of the 'burial ground, on a little green hill' that opened this chapter, time is imagined in this story as an organic cycle from cradle to grave with the kirkyard an ever present and 'salutary' influence on life in the village. The individual is located in a specific 'place' within both society and the material landscape but must stay there. The good death and gravesite are reserved for those who know their social place and remain within it. The unchanging but well-tended rural graveyard becomes a guarantor of immortality. Wilson's rural graveyard acts as a site where the memories of local people can be incorporated into a larger communal narrative, where the dead are 'spoken of frequently on Sabbath', never truly dead but simply 'lying down'. This description of Scottish rural life capitalises on the grave's capacity to articulate a Burkean vision of national continuity. The cycle of rural life and death guarantees the survival of the nation in a way that linear ideas of progress cannot.

This cycle is underwritten by traditional familial structures. The importance of the family is explored in numerous kirkyard reconciliation scenes in Wilson's fiction. In 'The Headstone' the act of burying their father reunites his two estranged sons. This reconciliation is imagined as one that reunites both living and dead members of the family:

'the brothers stood fervently, but composedly, grasping each other's hands, in the little hollow that lay between their mother, long since dead, and that of their father, whose shroud was haply not yet still from the fall of dust to dust.'[10] 'The Elder's Death-Bed' and 'The Elder's Funeral' similarly reunite a rebellious husband with his wife and child at the bedside of his dying father. Death in these stories is ideally an event that reunites and reconciles rather than divides. They implicitly suggest that we achieve something like immortality through the familial structures we create on Earth. Just as God offers spiritual immortality to the righteous Christian through the possibility of Heaven, the text also postulates the possibility of earthly posthumous survival through the ties of love and kinship.

In *Lights and Shadows* the greatest tragedy is therefore to be buried away from home, community, family and ancestors. The story of 'The Twins' that opened this chapter is given pathos by the division of father, mother and children in death: 'her husband lies buried near Grenada, in Spain; she lies in the chancel of the Cathedral in Salisbury, in England; and there sleep her twins in the little burial-ground of Auchindown, a Scottish parish.'[11] 'The Minister's Widow' charts a similar tragedy describing the response of a minister's widow in a small Scottish parish to the deaths of her three sons, all of whom die abroad serving as soldiers or sailors. The death of their socially and geographically static father follows the typical conventions of a good death: 'to the dying man death had lost all his terrors … Accordingly, when the hour was at hand in which he was to render up his spirit into the hand of God, he was like a grateful and wearied man falling into sleep.'[12] In contrast, the sons' deaths are explicitly tied by the narrator to their restlessness: 'they knew that there was a world lying at a distance that called upon them to leave the fields, and woods, and streams, and lochs of Castle-Holm; and, born and bred in peace as they had been, their restless hearts were yet all on fire, and they burned to join a life of danger, strife, and tumult.'[13] This need to escape the pastoral world of Castle-Holm proves to be fatal to the young men.

The sentimentality that is obvious in these plots and that previous scholars have identified as a feature of Wilson's rural fiction has a particular function, participating in the creation of emotional ties between the reader and his subject. Employing what Anthony Hasler identifies as 'a sentimental mode derived from Henry Mackenzie', Wilson encourages the reader to act as a sympathetic witness to the trials of his characters.[14]

The concept of Christian resignation to these trials dominates Wilson's fiction to the extent that contemporary commentators noted the relationship between these texts and religious educational writing. *The Edinburgh Magazine and Literary Miscellany*'s[15] 1823 review of

The Trials of Margaret Lyndsay compared Wilson's text to the most famous religious tract of the era, asserting that 'its greatest drawback is a certain methodistical air, which occasionally suggests to us the ideas of an overgrown tract – Leigh Richmond and the Dairyman's Daughter'.[16] As I have argued elsewhere, one of the reasons Wilson relies so heavily on deathbed scenes in his rural fiction is that this allows him to draw upon a tradition of evangelical and conservative didacticism in contemporary literature and print culture.[17] Wilson's fiction, drawing on previous Scottish domestic fiction including Elizabeth Hamilton's *The Cottagers of Glenburnie* (1808), incorporates the archetypal death scenes of popular religious publications into narratives where issues of memory and community reinforce a conservative political message. A good death, with the respectable burial that follows, serves to represent not just the dying party's religious adherence but also their adherence to the rules of a rural hierarchised society. Wilson co-opts Christian resignation to death to politically conservative ends. His protagonists confirm their own secular and spiritual immortality by accepting the will of God in the form of grief, physical suffering and destitution.

This allegiance of social and spiritual resignation can be seen in Wilson's novels where heroes and heroines are subjected to earthly trials. In his 1825 novel *The Foresters* the eponymous family are largely characterised by their ability to accept suffering and loss. The elderly patriarch Adam Forester is introduced to the reader as a man of superior morality through an extended description of the bereavement he has suffered. Adam has experienced the death not only of his beloved wife, Judith, but of five children. His ability to find contentment and joy in his final years despite this litany of losses indicates his morality 'all the past was peace – now that he could look not only without one single pang on the grave-stone of his Judith, and the other five dead ones, all of them long ago so tenderly beloved, but even with the profound satisfaction of expecting rest.'[18]

This ability to sustain faith through bereavement, and to accept mortality, is paired with a capacity to endure worldly suffering and hardship. When Adam dies and the family's beloved home is lost, due to the crimes of Adam's profligate son Abel, the family are able to humbly accept their fall in status.[19] Similarly, when Adam's other son, Michael, is struck by lightning and blinded, Michael is able to resign himself to his loss so that his neighbours 'bore testimony to Michael's worth and the piety of his resignation'.[20] The story's happy conclusion with Michael's daughter married to the suitable son of an English vicar, rather than the aristocratic Edward Ellis she had first loved, and Michael and his wife's quiet retreat to their cottage in Scotland, is a fairy-tale ending of social resignation as each character finds comfort and happiness in their proper social place.

The Trials of Margaret Lyndsay (1823), with its high death count and stoic heroine, also entwines ideas of religious and social resignation. It is Margaret Lyndsay's ability to resign herself to the tragic fates of her parents, siblings, uncle, sweetheart and husband, and to the economic hardship that accompanies these losses, that signal her moral rectitude and heroism. Her fate contrasts with that of her father, Walter, whose loss of religious faith and dissatisfaction with the social system leads him to the writings of Thomas Paine, imprisonment for high treason, adultery and eventual death. Margaret's faith in the mechanisms of Providence in this life, and the next, allows her to weather her 'trials'.

This virtuous resignation is attributed specifically to Margaret's Scottish Presbyterianism. Her stoicism is drawn not from the broadly Protestant doctrine of *sola fide* but based specifically on the Calvinist concept of predestination.[21] When Margaret and her mother reflect on the death of Margaret's sinful, Paineite father Walter they do so in specifically Presbyterian terms, not praying for his soul but believing in his predestined election:

> had they thought that the prayers of the living would change the doom of the dead, they would, indeed, have worn the floor with their knees; but, in spite of all those natural emotions that have made such a belief Holy in other religions, they knew that the decree had gone forth – and, from the pages of the Bible, they only ventured to draw a firm trust that he was one among the number of sinners that were saved.[22]

Due to their strong Calvinist faith, Margaret and her family are not just resigned to the death of Walter but to God's will in the afterlife. Walter's fate cannot be changed through any worldly action but has been pre-decreed by an all-powerful and all-knowing God.

Across John Wilson's rural writing his protagonists' fates in life, death and the afterlife are inalienable and predestined. This approach both draws upon and rearranges the central message of Scottish Presbyterianism. Just as the doctrine of predestination holds that fate in the afterlife is preordained, these texts suggest that our status on Earth is also the inalienable will of God. They suggest not only that humility, faith and resignation are the keys to the religious afterlife, but also that political agitation and social aspiration are antithetical to religious virtue. By writing a version of Scottish religiosity that ignores the democratic traditions and internal debates of Scottish Presbyterian faith, Wilson portrays the Kirk's doctrines as agents of political and social passivity.

The ongoing survival of this virtuous kirkyard is tenuous and endangered. The sense of a passing or disappearing world that previously animated 'The Desolate Village' lurks just beneath the surface in most of Wilson's Scottish stories and novels. In 'The Elder's Funeral' the narrator describes the way that the graveyard operates on his memory: 'each tombstone and grave over which I had often walked in boyhood, arose in my memory, as I looked steadfastly upon their long-forgotten inscriptions.'[23] The rural graveyard here acts as a memorial where the forgotten is remembered. How memory and time operate in this passage is emblematic of a wider trend across *Lights and Shadows*. Just as the narrator's return to the graveyard brings back forgotten memories from his boyhood, Wilson's stories describe the return of the modern urban Scot to his idealised rural origins. The graveyard depicted in the text is a site of memory both in the sense that it is a gathering point for the memories of local people but also, and perhaps more importantly, because it is a type of burial ground that was an increasingly unlikely resting place for the reader. With an increasingly mobile and urban population, the odds of being buried among one's ancestors, of one's grave being frequently visited by neighbours and friends, was soon to become a pastoral fantasy for many rather than a real possibility. The kirkyard that Wilson's narrator visits is, like the community he describes, perhaps a relic of a past or passing age.

However, the kirkyard, and the type of memory it represents, is also designed to function as a point of commonality and return for this increasingly diffuse and politically unpredictable population. Mack highlights that the representation of rural working-class life in *Lights and Shadows* is linked to the contemporary political climate, arguing that 'fears about radical and revolutionary agitation ... form part of the context in which *Lights and Shadows of Scottish Life* sets out its approving descriptions of a strikingly pious and docile Scottish peasantry, who are represented as being affectionately loyal and obedient to their social superiors.'[24] In *Lights and Shadows* the endangered world of the cottagers is tied to the dangers that assail Britain's social and political stability. The kirkyard is cast as a space that endures and to which the exile can return. This return is arguably possible, not just for sinners against Wilson's imagined rural social order, but also for his readership. In reading these texts they enact an imaginative return to the idealised parish kirkyard and ally themselves with the national cultural identity it represents. Remembering (or rather idealising, or even imagining) a shared, stable past like the one Wilson describes creates a sense of kinship across geographical space and social class. Readers are not supposed to expect to be buried in a graveyard like the one Wilson describes; rather the graveyard of the cottagers is a symbolic memorial to a common, imagined past. This is designed to create ties between Wilson's readers who can claim a form of ownership over a virtual ancestral space: one that not only unites them but represents a specific set of inherited values and ideas that can be carried from the imagined rural kirkyard into the rapidly modernising world. The kirkyard does not so much resist modernity as offer a brief respite from it by offering a virtual space of continuity and preservation. Safely conserved in the book, the kirkyard, and the nation it represents, endures without disrupting progress.

'The tomb of his father': J. G. Lockhart's *Adam Blair*

J. G. Lockhart published his novel of grief, adultery and tested faith, *Adam Blair*, with Blackwood in 1822. Like Wilson's rural fiction, *Adam Blair* has been recognised by modern critics as a proto-kailyard novel: Ian Campbell has written that the novel 'anticipates much in later nineteenth-century writing'.[25] This positioning of the text as one that anticipates future literary trends obscures the text's place within a group of contemporary Scottish texts. *Adam Blair* when viewed within the trajectory of Wilson's and Lockhart's regional Scottish writing of the 1820s is completely enmeshed in, and inseparable from, the ideas and concerns of kirkyard Romanticism.

Contemporary reviews were attuned to the importance of grief and death in *Adam Blair*. While characterising the novel as containing 'many things both absurd and revolting', Jeffrey picks out the early scenes describing the protagonist's grief on the loss of his wife to illustrate the 'spirit and richness in the writing'.[26] *The London Magazine*'s[27] reviewer, in a morally censorious summary of the novel, disapprovingly draws attention to Lockhart's employment of the kirkyard space in his account of adultery: 'if any meditations exist, they are the meditations of a couple of holy and young Scottish creatures, who make love in a moonlight churchyard, on the tombstone of the deceased and buried Mrs Blair.'[28]

From its earliest pages *Adam Blair* foregrounds death and burial within its plot. The opening chapters describe the final moments and the funeral of Isobel, the wife of the eponymous minister, Adam. The scenes that describe her death expand upon the deathbed and burial sequences featured in Wilson's fiction, sharing many traits but also challenging some of their basic assumptions through a greater emphasis on individual psychology. Having borne the deaths of three children, Mrs Blair, like Wilson's heroines, is depicted as having 'dried her tears and endeavoured as usual to attend to all the duties of her household'.[29] However, she soon begins to waste away. Her death scene is a private domestic one reminiscent of *Lights and Shadows*' sentimental death-beds. However, the minister's response to the scene is different to those of Wilson's stoic peasants:

> He drew near to the couch – grasped the cold hand, and cried, 'Oh God! Oh God!' – a shriek not a prayer; he closed the stiffening eyelids over the soft but ghastly orbs; kissed the brow, the cheek, the lips, the bosom, and then rushed down the stairs, and away out, bare-headed, into the fields, before any one could stop him, or ask whither he was going.[30]

This scene with its ecstatic grief and 'ghastly' corpse is more reminiscent of the Gothic subversion of Hogg's peasant's funeral. Adam's extreme private grief is subsequently further explored in a scene where the minister lies on the forest floor communing with the spirits of the dead. Where in Wilson's novel *The Foresters* the family are both privately and publicly dignified in their resignation, in *Adam Blair* readers are able to mark the contrast between public official mourning and the private devastation of the bereaved husband.

This focus on the contrast between private and public is continued throughout the novel and allows Lockhart to draw a more nuanced and troubling portrait of rural community and connection than Wilson. In the description of Isobel's funeral Lockhart echoes the kirkyard idylls of his contemporaries. The population of the parish gather to express their respect for the minister, in a scene reminiscent of the retirement scene which fellow *Blackwood's* contributor John Galt had used to open his novel *Annals of the Parish* the year before.[31] Lockhart depicts a pious community united in their desire to commemorate the dead: 'It was a touching spectacle to see the churchyard when the procession entered it. Old and young stood around unbonnetted, and few dry eyes were turned on Mr. Blair when he took his station at the head of the open grave.'[32] Following Blair's return to the manse, the parishioners gather to discuss the event, using the graves to position Isobel's death in local and familial history. The graveyard functions as a physical record of history that the villagers draw upon to make sense of present events. Isobel's grave is contextualised through reference to the graves of Adam Blair's notable ancestors:

> On the wall of the church, immediately adjoining a large marble tablet had been affixed, to record the pious labours of Mr. Blair's father, who had preceded him in the charge of that parish ... But there was a green headstone there, rudely fashioned, and most rudely sculptured, to which their fingers were pointed with feelings of yet loftier veneration. That stone marked the

spot where Mr. Blair's grandfather was laid – a simple peasant of the parish – one whose time on earth had been abridged in consequence of what he had done and suffered in days when God's chosen race, and the true patriots of our country, were hunted up and down like beasts of the field ... They who are acquainted with Scotland – above all, with the west of Scotland – cannot be ignorant of the reverence which is still cherished for the seed of the martyrs. Such feelings were more widely spread, and more intensely felt, in former times than, I am sorry to say, they are now.[33]

Lockhart represents the Presbyterian rebellion of the Covenanters during the killing time as the legacy on which the stable rural community that Blair inhabits is built. The novel is not set in the past, yet Lockhart describes the world where people feel 'intensely' about the legacy of the Covenanters as an endangered and fast-disappearing one. The effect is to create a rural space outside of linear time. The village is a repository for the Presbyterian past and the sense of community that this shared legacy engenders. That we as readers are invited to sympathise with the narrator's sorrow about the imminent extinction of this cultural memory suggests that it is an inheritance that the reader might choose to share.

However, this apparently benign image of community, legacy and kirkyard acquires a darker aspect as Blair's public image as a man of God diverges from his private conduct. Blair's connection with Charlotte Campbell, which will eventually lead to adultery, is first indicated in a moment of consolation between the two at Isobel's grave.[34] Later, following the sexual consummation of that connection, Blair's self-disgust is symbolised in a dark vision of the kirkyard at Cross-Meikle:

> At one moment it seemed to him as if the churchyard of Cross-Meikle were the scene of his torments. He saw the tomb of his father, with filthy things crawling up and down upon the face of the marble; while he himself lying prostate upon the grave of his wife, heard the poisonous breath of fiends whistling in his ear above her dust. He saw his living friends; old Maxwell was there, with fierce angry eyes. Little Sarah stood close by him pale and motionless; farther off, the whole of his congregation were crowded together about the door of the church, and he heard the voice of scornful curses muttered everywhere round about him, by lips that had never opened but to bless him.[35]

The graveyard space is transformed in this vision much as it was in Wilson's 'The Radical's Saturday Night'. However, where Wilson's dream vision is deliberately unreal and designed to emphasise the godliness of the actual peasants of Scotland, Lockhart's dark kirkyard offers a nightmare vision of the space without reassuring readers that this image is a delusion. The parishioners' conversations at Isobel's grave are transformed into the 'scornful curses' of a community whose expectations and moral imperatives have become a claustrophobic straitjacket for the young, lonely minister. The kirkyard maintains the symbolic weight it carried in Wilson's rural fiction but it can be benign or malevolent. The ties of community and lineage do not purely protect and nurture; in Lockhart's country parish they can also constrain and imprison.[36] Lockhart's novel registers an ambivalence towards the kirkyard national mythology that is largely absent from Wilson's fiction or even his own earlier, more polemical, writing.

An English Kirkyard: Caroline Bowles and the National Dead

From 1824 the poet Caroline Southey Bowles, already a regular contributor to the magazine, published the popular recurring prose sketches series Chapters on Churchyards in *Blackwood's*. The series was collected into a book of the same name in 1829 and then reissued in 1841 following Bowles's marriage to the Poet Laureate Robert Southey. In Bowles's series of first-person picturesque sketches an unnamed, female narrator visits English churchyards and their environs, often using these settings to engage with stories and vignettes drawn from English history. The scenes combine nostalgia for an idealised, regional past with strong English cultural nationalism. As Paul Westover writes in his analysis of the Chapters, 'England still has its forefathers in the hamlet, Bowles seems to say, and she invites readers to visit them.'[37] Westover situates Bowles's 'prose pastoral' sketches within a wider context of English writing on death and the grave: 'they remind us of the dead in poems like Wordsworth's *Excursion* and "The Brothers", and on a more fundamental level they reanimate the dead from the old-canon graveyard poems and especially Gray's *Elegy*.'[38] However, this analysis misses a crucial link in the chain between the poetic English pastoral tradition and Bowles's work: the prose sketches and tales of the *Blackwood's* kirkyard. Bowles's characterisation of the relationship between a local dead and the living nation is remarkably like the image of cultural identity that Wilson's *Lights and Shadows* sketches were also engaged in painting. In the Chapters the village churchyard, like the kirkyard before it, is portrayed as a repository for the nation's past: a space that operates to form a national community across time and locality. Bowles also positions herself as a Blackwood author by drawing on a library of shared reference points and a hagiography of shared literary forefathers. Bowles is writing into an existing tradition of Scottish texts.

Bowles's use of the national dead draws attention to the ongoing relationship between Scottish kirkyard texts and the English literary tradition. As I have previously suggested, while Wilson and Lockhart's kirkyard is often stridently Scottish and draws upon a lineage of Scottish literary ancestors, it also draws upon a wider anglophone tradition of writing about the dead. By the time Bowles writes her English tales she is drawing on a precedent already set by texts like the 'Letters from the Lakes' and *The Foresters*. However, the Chapters on Churchyards are not limited to a real, specified geographical location, like Wordsworth's Cumbria. Instead Bowles, like Wilson in *Lights and Shadows*, sets her tales and sketches in a series of 'every-villages' that are simultaneously intimately local and nationally representative.

In the series of sketches titled 'Broad Summerford', Bowles's narrator tells a story set in the fictional village, not as she remembers it, but as her grandmother described it to her as a child.[39] Like Wilson's narrators, Bowles's narrator remains unnamed, experiences a return to her past (in this case through storytelling and memory), and operates as a guide for the reader. The narrator's grandmother is a storyteller who can 'recall ... to earth' the 'bewigged and brocaded host' of her ancestors, forging a connection between her grandchild and family history.[40] In retelling her grandmother's story the narrator takes on this role for the reader connecting them through her own 'little platoon' to an imagined national past.

The grandmother describes a childhood convalescence with elderly relatives in the village of Broad Summerford. Although Bowles's story begins with a focus on the domestic economy of the rector, Mr Seale, and his sister, Mrs Helen, and a series of childhood mishaps and experiences that befall the visiting child, the sketch quickly turns to mortality and the churchyards of Bowles's title. Like Wilson's country folk, Mrs Helen is resigned to her eventual demise. She prepares and stores her grave clothes in the house, a 'primitive custom of her native land', and the shock of finding these graven clothes is presented as a formative experience for the visiting narrator.[41]

The focus of the third chapter of the series is on Mrs Helen's thwarted wish to die before her brother and her 'fond, although perhaps *irrational* desire, that the earthly remains of her beloved companion and her own might mingle together in the same grave'.[42] The chapter only briefly describes the churchyard, first when the funeral of Mr Seale gathers an emotional congregation to mourn his loss – 'there was not a dry eye among the many hundred persons assembled in and about the churchyard of Broad Summerford, on the day of Mr. Seale's funeral' – and then when a gravestone is placed over his and his loyal servant's body – 'he also gave directions respecting the memorial stone, which should mark out the place of their joint sepulchre; and it may be seen to this day under the shade of a broad maple, which stands in the east corner of Summerford churchyard.'[43] However, even when Mrs Helen leaves the manse to make way for the new rector, the churchyard of Broad Summerford maintains an important, if negative, presence. Mrs Helen's exile from the churchyard and the grave of her brother continues to form the central tragedy of the sentimental story. Taken together 'Broad Summerford' mirrors the images and rhetorical strategies of *Lights and Shadows*: a concern with familial and ancestral memory, an emphasis on earthly and spiritual resignation, an anxiety about travel and posthumous exile, and the veneration of rural and traditional culture.

In another series of chapters, a visit to the ancestral cemetery of the almost extinct English noble family, the De La Veres, and to their decaying mansion, Halliburn House, sets out the national scope of Bowles's project. The tombs of the De La Veres, featuring 'a knight in armour' who fought at 'Cressy' and two ruffed figures from 'Elizabeth's or James's era', take the narrator and the reader on a journey through English history.[44] Similarly, on entering Halliburn House, Bowles's narrator is transported again through the halls of national history as she wanders the 'museum of ancient relics'.[45] The decaying family and mansion allow for the aestheticisation of both English history and rural English life. Like Scotland's rural spaces in Lockhart's and Wilson's work, the traditions and values embodied in the English countryside are forever locked in aestheticised decline, forever on the verge of an imminent and inevitable decease.

Bowles's awareness of *Blackwood's* 'house style' and her desire to align her churchyards with the existing tradition of *Blackwood's* kirkyards are indicated several times in the Chapters. She paraphrases Burns's 'Cotter', placing her writing within an existing group of rural Scottish texts,[46] and opens one chapter with a disparaging reference to the famous controversy between *Blackwood's* and the 'Cockney School' poets that positions her firmly in the *Blackwood's* camp: 'I have no very poetical fancies about my last earthly resting-place – at least no COCKNEY poetical fancies.'[47] These references combine with her wider mirroring of the ideas and concerns that had characterised the *Blackwood's* kirkyard. Bowles's employment of the conventions of *Blackwood's* regional fiction operates to position her as an English woman within the Scottish magazine. In Chapters on Churchyards she applies the tools, used by Wilson, Lockhart and their compatriots in Scottish settings, to articulate her vision of England along similar lines.

What this demonstrates is not just the influence that early *Blackwood's* rural fiction had on contributors, and the ways in which the reproduction of a 'house style' distinguished William Blackwood's publications during this period, but also the portability of the type of national myth making that characterised the magazine's Scottish writing. The kirkyard emerged as a mode of imagining Scotland within Britain but its basic features could be used to serve other culturally nationalist projects. In turning its light upon the English churchyard, Bowles reveals the flexibility of Wilson and Lockhart's kirkyard archetype.

The Kirkyards of the Kailyard: The Dead in J. M. Barrie and Ian Maclaren

The term 'kailyard' entered parlance as a literary term in 1895 in an article by J. H. Millar. In 'The Literature of the Kailyard' Millar engages with three popular contemporary Scottish writers of parochial fiction, J. M. Barrie, Ian Maclaren and S. R. Crockett, critiquing their influence as one that has created a Scottish literary sphere where 'hardly the humblest rag is without its study of native life'.[48] As Samantha Walton notes, Millar uses the term 'kailyard', meaning 'cabbage patch or kitchen garden', to 'deride the provincial outlook' of these works.[49] Millar's original critique is focused on a specific group of contemporary texts, but the term rapidly became a moniker for a wider group of Scottish texts characterised by a focus on rural settings, Presbyterian religious orthodoxy, moralism and sentimentalism.

Due to these features, the term 'kailyard' was applied retrospectively to many of the kirkyard texts. As Andrew Nash has highlighted, by 1903 Millar describes Wilson's *Lights and Shadows* as 'pure kailyard'.[50] An 1897 review of Sir George Douglas's *The 'Blackwood' Group* in *The Saturday Review* also makes use of the term in relation to Wilson and his peers. The reviewer attributes the decision to publish Douglas's book to the contemporary vogue for kailyard literature and characterises the previous generation of Scottish writers as the 'kailyarders' 'rude forefathers':

> To have been pestered by the kailyarders who are irritatingly alive is surely no sufficient reason why we should be bored by the kailyarders who are irretrievably dead. Yet here in this volume we have the resurrectionist at work, digging in the clay-cold pages of 'Blackwood' and drawing forth the bones of poor old Kit North, with some other rude forefathers of the Kailyard clan. It is a gruesome business.[51]

Titled 'A Scot's Resurrectionist', the review's use of a resurrection metaphor plays on a wider association between kailyard writing and deathliness. The tendency of kailyard literature to overuse deathbed and burial scenes is consistently an object of comment from the earliest critical appraisals. Millar, in that first terminology-defining article, notes Ian Maclaren's 'diseased craving for the pathetic'.[52] Nash describes a humorous 1895 *Glasgow Herald* piece where a parodically fictionalised kailyard author comments of his own work that 'the death beds are a' just beautiful'.[53] In the following coda I argue that the consistent use of death and burial as motifs in kailyard writing demonstrates a continuous relationship with the genre's 'rude forefathers'. I propose that turning our attention away from the representative space of the kailyard to the kirkyard when thinking about the Scottish regional fiction of the late nineteenth century offers a new way to understand these texts and places them within a more continuous tradition.

To illustrate this, I foreground the treatment of the dead in three works by major kailyard writers J. M. Barrie's *A Window in Thrums* (1889) and Ian Maclaren's *Beside the Bonny Briar Bush* (1894) and *The Days of Auld Langsyne* (1895). Although J. M. Barrie is popularly remembered for the creation of Peter Pan, he was during his own lifetime celebrated as a writer of theatre and novels and as an essayist.[54] His early provincial fiction has been identified as the 'precursor' to the wider kailyard school.[55] The author and Free Kirk minister Ian Maclaren is another of the figures most frequently associated with the kailyard.[56] Although, as this coda will suggest, Barrie and Maclaren brought different approaches to their material, both writers' rural fiction shared key features. They both published books of short anecdotal stories narrated by an intimately informed, but educated and slightly removed, first-person narrator, and featuring a recurring cast of humble, local characters.

In both men's work death is allied with the character of the community and culture they describe. Scattered amid the more humorous anecdotes in Barrie's novel are numerous sentimental tales of death, grief and resignation. His protagonist, Jess McQumph, is a character ennobled by her fortitude in the face of the grief of child death. The story 'Dead This Twenty Years' adopts a similar sentimental register to many of Wilson's in its account of the death of the saintly infant Joey.[57] Jess's capacity to resign herself to this loss and her understanding of her trials within a strongly Presbyterian worldview are what mark her as the moral heart of the book. Similarly, her daughter Leeby's understanding that 'her duty' towards her disabled mother 'lay before her, straight as the burying-ground road' differentiates her from her wayward bother

Jamie.[58] Mentions of death and the churchyard recur throughout the book, building up a sense of a world where death is omnipresent in daily life and thought. Like Wilson before him, Barrie presents the Scottish rural community as a space where an organic relationship between life and death survives.

In the opening passages of 'A Scholar's Funeral',[59] Maclaren also seems to echo Wilson's alliance of Scottish character with that 'other more awful sacrament'. His narrator describes the temperament of the fictional parish of Drumtochty as one suited to the funereal: 'Drumtochty never acquitted itself with credit at a marriage, having no natural aptitude for gaiety, and being haunted with anxiety lest any "hicht" should end in a "howe", but the Parish had a genius for funerals.'[60] Drumtochty cannot celebrate hopefully due to the continued anticipation of, and resignation to, loss. The narrator relates a local anecdote about an English undertaker who compared the Drumtochty mourners favourably to his own clientele of 'chirpy little Southerners'.[61] The Drumtochty men 'in their Sabbath blacks' have both natural 'advantage in the face' and 'an instinct in the blood' for their role according to the narrator.[62] Here Maclaren suggests that the character of the race of men who inhabit the Glen is one particularly suited to the commemoration of the dead. Through the comparison with the English mourners, this 'genius' is implied to be a distinctively Scottish one.

This allegiance of Scottish character with death and mourning is paired, in both authors' work, with an approach to time where the reader is invited to return to a nostalgic recent past. The opening of Barrie's second book, *A Window in Thrums*, effects a moment of time travel as the narrator invites the reader into a 'humble abode' where he used to lodge 'during the summer holidays.'[63] The Thrums of Barrie's tales is cast at first as a place just accessible to living memory and in the process of passing away. The narrator is 'stiffer now' and counts himself among the 'three or four who can to-day stand on the brae and point out Jess's window.'[64] In setting the scene he contrasts the modern growing suburb to the 'poor row of dwellings' that preceded it and the 'worn boards and ragged walls' of the now empty house to the humble but 'prim' interior of the past.[65] The early parts of the chapter thus emphasise the changes that have been wrought on Scottish provincial life. However, this elegy for a lost rural world is, in the later part of the chapter, placed within a wider cycle of life:

> The world remains as young as ever ... Here again has been just such a day, and somewhere in Thrums there may be just such a couple, setting out for their home behind a horse with white ears instead of walking, but with the

same hopes and fears, and the same love light in their eyes. The world does not age. The Hearse passes over the Brae and up the straight burying-ground road, but still there is a cry for the christening robe.[66]

The tragedy of modernity is tempered by the reassurance that the fundamental nature of life and death in Thrums remains constant. The general shape of the lives the book will explore remains even as the lives of the book's protagonists, Jess, Hendry and their children, slip from memory. Thrums, and the values it will come to represent, survives.

Maclaren's opening to *Beside the Bonnie Brier Bush* also orientates the reader temporally between the present day and a previous world. This time the narrator's exclamation that 'the revolution reached our Parish years ago' refers specifically to the replacement of the 'auld Schule-house' with a 'treeless and comfortless' modern schoolhouse.[67] There is less sense that these changes can be understood as part of an organic cycle than in Barrie's collection. Although 'to this day some famous man will come and stand in the deserted playground for a space', there is no suggestion that this will continue to be the case for the young boys and girls who attend the new 'well regulated' inorganic institution. Memory is all that remains of that old world. These opening scenes map the past upon the present and temporally locate the narrator and reader in relation to the world of the story. They effect a type of time travel that reveals the impact of modernity on the two authors' fictional worlds. While Barrie's Thrums endures in spirit due to the cyclical nature of folk time, Maclaren's Drumtochty is endangered, perhaps even already lost.

However, the authors' positions seem to flip in tales where long-absent characters return to the parish. Barrie's *A Window on Thrums* and Maclaren's *The Days of Auld Lang Syne* feature twin scenes of return. In both books characters come back to the parish after periods of absence and visit their old homes and the graves of their departed family members. These visits also focus on the inevitability of change and the relationship between modernity and the rural Scottish world. The landmarks of cottage and village school are joined by the village kirkyard as sites that register time's changes.

A Window in Thrums ends with the return of Jamie McQumpha to the village following a period of absence in London. Jamie finds that he has returned too late. The home of his family is relet and his family have died. The story's narration does not give the reader access to Jamie's thoughts and experiences; instead, his return is described only through the reports of the various villagers who sight him as he makes his pilgrimage. Jamie returns both to the humble cottage of the first chapter and the kirkyard: 'we learnt afterwards from the gravedigger that some one spent great part of that night in the graveyard, and we believe it to have been Jamie.'[68] Although several villagers invite him into their homes, Jamie chooses a voluntary exile.[69] Unlike the prodigal sons of Wilson's fiction, Jamie is estranged from his origins and from the reader in this final tale. There is no possibility of readmittance and reunion in Barrie's novel. Thrums is a paradise lost.

The final chapter of *The Days of Auld Lang Syne*, 'Oor Lang Hame', also describes the return of a lost or wayward son when Charlie Grant returns from America. The twin images of abandoned hearth and village kirkyard are also key to Charlie's journey. He first encounters the now empty home of his grandmother Mary where he is distressed by the contrast between past life and present dilapidation. This is followed by a visit to the kirkyard where the tragic fates of numerous characters are revealed to both Charlie and the reader. In these two scenes time has swept through the parish, leaving Charlie, like Barrie's Jamie, with no place of return. However, the kirkyard becomes a site of reconciliation when an encounter at the graves with the elderly farmer Drumsheugh leads to an invitation back into the warmth of the communal hearth: 'Na, na, gin there be a cauld hearth in yir auld hame, there's a warm corner in ma hoose.'[70]

This moment of return might be understood as a moment manufactured to encourage audience self-recognition for a section Maclaren's readership. Thomas Knowles has highlighted the popularity of kailyard fiction in America and his belief that kailyard authors 'wrote consciously ... for a non-Scottish audience.'[71] He notes how kailyard publishers advertised these works as 'gifts for banished Scots yearning for the native hearth'.[72] The kailyard authors themselves were transatlantic commodities, McLaren died during speaking tour in Mount Pleasant, Iowa. The kailyard is an export product aimed less at a Scottish market than at a wider British and global one. These scenes of return can be read in this context as expressions of the anxieties and fantasies of a readership adapting to an age of mass migrations.

This is perhaps what has been fundamentally misunderstood about nineteenth-century Scottish writing and parochialism. The focus on the local in texts like those of Wilson, Lockhart, Barrie and Maclaren is inherently outward-looking: a national and international localism. Provincial fiction is not solely provincial; through mobility and transferability it is arguably more widely accessible than the metropolitan. Or, to put it more simply, there is only one London but the inhabitants of many towns and villages in many regions of the world can buy into the fantasy of Thrums or Drumtochty.

Scottish provincial fiction offers an opportunity for imaginative homecoming, not just for diasporic Scots, but also for the many English-speaking readers experiencing mobility, due to the twin forces of industrialisation and globalisation, during this period. The imagined Scottish village, preserved and enduring in a rapidly changing world, offers a virtual opportunity to claim home. Over the nineteenth century texts like these build an association between rural Scotland and a timeless bucolic past in the anglophone imagination. The frozen temporality, emotional resonance and seeming stasis of these imagined spaces do not necessarily protest against modernity; in fact, their existence can give readers a shared sense of virtual belonging that negates and justifies their participation in its processes. The book becomes the hearth and grave that the reader can return to.

Notes

1. Wilson, *Lights and Shadows of Scottish Life*, p. 147.
2. See Hasler, 'Introduction', in Hogg, *The Three Perils of Women*.
3. Jeffrey, 'Secondary Scottish Novels', p. 160.
4. Wilson, *Lights and Shadows of Scottish Life*.
5. Wilson, *The Trials of Margaret Lyndsay*; Wilson, *The Foresters*.
6. Campbell, *Kailyard*, p. 40.
7. Wilson, 'Burns and the Ettrick Shepherd', p. 526.
8. Mack, 'John Wilson, James Hogg, "Christopher North" and "The Ettrick Shepherd"', p. 11; Mack, 'Lights and Shadows of Scottish Life', p. 15; Killick, *Short Fiction in the Early Nineteenth Century*, p. 150.
9. Wilson, *Lights and Shadows*, p. 144.
10. Ibid., p. 60.
11. Ibid., p. 160.
12. Ibid., p. 85.
13. Ibid., p. 87.
14. Hasler, 'Introduction', p. xviii.
15. The retitled *Scots Magazine* published by Archibald Constable.
16. 'Scottish Novels of the Second Class', p. 7.
17. See Sharp, 'A Death in the Cottage'.
18. Wilson, *Foresters*, p. 11.
19. Ibid., p. 60.
20. Ibid., p. 118.
21. This is the concept that salvation can be secured by 'faith alone' and distinguishes reformed theology from Catholicism where 'the Reformed and Lutheran churches said that Rome essentially required faith and works for justification'. See Allen, *Reformed Theology*, p. 77.
22. Wilson, *Margaret Lyndsay*, p. 163.
23. Wilson, *Lights and Shadows*, p. 142.
24. Mack, *Scottish Fiction and the British Empire*, p. 21.
25. Campbell, 'Introduction', *Adam Blair*, p. xvi.

26. Jeffrey, 'Secondary Scottish Novels', p. 133.
27. *The London Magazine* was founded in 1820 and was a rival of *Blackwood's* in the 1820s. Conflict between the magazines led to the now infamous death of editor John Scott.
28. 'Some Passages in the Life of Mr Adam Blair, Minister of the Gospel at Cross Meikle', pp. 385.
29. Lockhart, *Adam Blair*, p. 1.
30. Ibid., p. 4.
31. This will be discussed further in Chapter 3.
32. Lockhart, *Adam Blair*, p. 11.
33. Ibid., p. 12.
34. Ibid., p. 50.
35. Ibid., pp. 113–14.
36. This concept of a rural community as vitally malevolent is also a defining feature of James Hogg's short fiction. See Sharp, 'Hogg's Murder of Ravens'.
37. Westover, 'At Home in the Churchyard', p. 81.
38. Ibid., p. 81.
39. Bowles, *Chapters on Churchyards*, p. 121.
40. Ibid., p. 122.
41. Ibid., p. 156.
42. Ibid., p. 157.
43. Ibid., pp. 159, 161.
44. Ibid., p. 67.
45. Ibid., p. 88.
46. 'many a truant, and many a "toddlin' wee thing"', ibid., p. 18.
47. Ibid., p. 99.
48. Millar, 'Literature of the Kailyard', p. 394.
49. Walton, 'Scottish Modernism, Kailyard Fiction and the Woman at Home', p. 141.
50. Nash, *Kailyard and Scottish Literature*, p. 13.
51. 'A Scots Resurrectionist', p. 403.
52. Millar, 'Literature of the Kailyard', p. 385.
53. Qtd in Nash, *Kailyard and Scottish Literature*, p. 39.
54. Valentina Bold and Andrew Nash, 'Introduction', p. vii.
55. Nash, *Kailyard and Scottish Literature*, p. 40.
56. Nash notes that 'Beside the Bonny Briar Bush is the quintessential work of the kailyard'. Nash, 'Introduction', *Beside the Bonnie Brier Bush*, p. ix.
57. Barrie, *A Window in Thrums*, p. 48.
58. Ibid., p. 171.
59. A story that is the culmination of a plot similar to that of Wilson's *Lights and Shadows* story 'The Poor Scholar'.
60. Maclaren, *Beside the Bonnie Brier Bush*, p. 21.
61. Ibid., p. 21.
62. Ibid., p. 21.
63. Barrie, *A Window in Thrums*, p. 2.
64. Ibid., pp. 3, 7.
65. Ibid., pp. 1, 2.
66. Ibid., pp. 8–9.

67. Maclaren, *Beside the Bonnie Brier Bush*, p. 3.
68. Barrie, *A Window in Thrums*, p. 215.
69. Ibid.
70. Maclaren, *The Days of Auld Lang Syne*, p. 197.
71. Knowles, *Ideology, Art, and Commerce*, p. 87.
72. Ibid., p. 79.

Chapter 3

The Suicide's Grave: Suicide, Civilisation and Community

James Hogg's novel *The Private Memoirs and Confessions of a Justified Sinner* (1824) concludes with the disinterment of a suicide's corpse by a party of bounty-hunting city antiquaries.[1] Inspired by an account of the exhumation of a miraculously preserved corpse in *Blackwood's*, an account that had really appeared in the magazine under the title 'A Scots Mummy' in 1823, the men travel to the site described in the letter but discover the forepart of the body already disturbed and damaged with 'merely the appearance of flesh not the substance'.[2] Continuing to dig they uncover the leg and feet which are at first 'perfect and entire' but in the process of their uncovering are 'all shaken into pieces'.[3] In the suicide's pocket the grave robbers find a printed tract containing a strange first-hand account of supernatural doubling and fratricide. The reader retrospectively recognises the tract's contents as the account that has constituted one-half of the novel they've just read. This frame narrative throws the already uncertain timeline of the novel into further chaos. The final account of the suicide's grave cannot be aligned with the previously published *Blackwood's* tale, or indeed with the descriptions contained in the two previous accounts that make up the novel. Attempting to conform these different accounts to a linear narrative only emphasises their incoherence and instability. Each exhumation further alters and damages the substance of the narrative.

The scene at the suicide's grave has become one of the most discussed and reinterpreted grave scenes in Scottish literary studies.[4] This chapter re-examines the infamous suicide's grave in light of contemporary attitudes to suicide and to burial. I argue that the scene participates both in the turn to the nationally figurative grave that characterised the kirkyard texts of the last chapter and in the contemporary medical and legal conversations that sought to understand and categorise suicide.

The 'Suicide's Grave' scene with its self-murder, isolated grave, iconoclastic exhumation, and disturbed and putrefying flesh provides a troubling counter-image to the kirkyards of the previous chapter. The kirkyard, as it was envisioned in the Scottish writings of John Wilson and J. G. Lockhart, is a cypher for the way that Scottish rural spaces preserve British society's relationship with the past. This idea of a space outside linear time is one that recurs across Romantic writing and is informed by Enlightenment ideas of historical development. James Chandler describes how geography could be overwritten by temporality in Enlightenment accounts of history.[5] He describes the dual temporality of post-Enlightenment historiography where space is imagined as simultaneously temporally contiguous and divided. Enlightenment theoretical or conjectural histories, a group of writings that were retrospectively identified by Dugald Stewart in his account of the life and writings of Adam Smith in 1793, utilise information about contemporary 'primitive' societies in order to hypothesise about the nature of the prehistoric European past.[6] They assume a universal path of development, or stadial history, where human societies pass through a series of developmental stages from 'savagery' to 'civilisation'. This 'universal world history', as Saree Makdisi terms it, imposes a narrative of development on time and a culturally contingent definition of development on different geographical locations and cultures.[7] Barbarous and civilised societies in this conception exist at the same time but also in different 'ages'. The journey from developed Glasgow to undeveloped Glencoe takes place on one day but also functions as a type of time travel as the modern man journeys back into an uncivilised past. The idea that different ages can exist simultaneously with one another can offer the possibility of escape or preservation to the Romantic artist seeking shelter from the 'tide of modernity'.[8] Makdisi uses Wordsworth's term 'spots of time' to describe the 'self-enclosed and self-referential enclaves of the anti-modern' that Romanticists develop, describing how they 'articulate a (futile) desire to preserve such sites of difference and otherness, to register opposition to a homogenizing system by upholding certain sites as differential loci of space and time'.[9]

For Wilson and Lockhart, the kirkyard world of traditional Scottish rural life becomes just such a spot of time – an imagined bubble in which the values and traditions of recent history can be preserved, removed from the political and social pressures of the contemporary nation. That this imagined bubble is a soap bubble, liable to collapse on contact with the present inhabited by the reader, is implicitly acknowledged in texts like Wilson's 'The Desolate Village', with its focus on the fictionality of memory, and in Lockhart's doubtful, Gothic-inflected *Adam Blair*. The problem of Romantic history is not so much solved as placed to one side through the creation of a textual time capsule. The rural Scotland of kirkyard fiction is always just within living memory – a place of escape that lives only within the mind and the page. This time capsule simultaneously preserves and limits. By removing kirkyard locations from the flow of linear time and into a purely textual world, kirkyard fiction denies coeval status to rural Scotland and its inhabitants.

This chapter is interested in the way that two of Scottish Romanticism's most canonical novels, John Galt's *Annals of the Parish* (1821) and James Hogg's *Memoirs and Confessions of a Justified Sinner* (1824), grapple with the problem of Romantic temporality. Galt and Hogg were both authors with connections to Blackwood whose work had been recognised by contemporaries among the 'Scots novels' and tales of the kirkyard writers.[10] Both write their most enduring novels not only in the shadow of Scott but, as I'll explore in this chapter, with an eye upon this group of texts.[11] *Annals* and *Confessions* are both geographically placed within the kirkyard landscapes of lowland Scotland and both engage extensively with death and the grave. Both texts also foreground the creation of historical narrative. Galt's narrator, the Reverend Balwhidder, adopts the role of village chronicler, attempting to offer a chronological and authoritative account of rural history – a theoretical history that echoes and interrogates the methods of Enlightenment social theory. Hogg's use of unreliable narrators and shifting frame narratives meanwhile dissolves history back into folklore and myth.[12] When both texts depict suicide, they do so, I argue, because the suicide's body in contemporary culture is imagined as both temporally belated and modern: a leaving from the past and an emblem of the violence of progress. The figure of the self-murderer's body thus allows both authors to engage with and disrupt the temporal structures of both 'universal world history' and the Romantic kirkyard.

The chapter begins with a discussion of contemporary ideas of suicide. In early nineteenth-century discourse, the deaths and burials of suicides were simultaneously characterised as symptoms of the march of civilisation and symbols of primitivity. John Galt's novel *Annals of the Parish*, I argue, complicates both these narratives by depicting three very different suicides in a rural Scottish parish. His decision to foreground the minister Rev. Balwhidder's role as narrator and historian in these moments also problematises the idea of historical progress. The chapter then returns to Hogg's most famous novel by foregrounding the role of the suicide in the author's symbolic scheme. I focus on the letter 'A Scots Mummy', which Hogg first published in *Blackwood's* in June 1823 and then in an abridged form as part of his novel just over a year later. Hogg deliberately uses the figure of the suicide's grave and corpse across both texts to radically critique the Blackwoodian approach to rural Scottish culture. In clustering meaning-making around the perturbing figure of an outcast, unidentified and exhumed body, Hogg subverts the inclusive and immutable kirkyard. This critique is rooted, like Galt's, in the way in which the suicide's body operates symbolically within historical narratives of progress and improvement. When Hogg wrote about his 'Scots mummy', he did so in the context of a conversation about suicide that was taking place both within and beyond the pages of *Blackwood's*, as contemporary commentators attempted to situate the suicide's grave within the modern nation.

I then trace the echoes of this conversation in George Douglas Brown's 'anti-kailyard' novel *The House with the Green Shutters* (1901). Like Galt and Hogg, Douglas Brown subverts the static kirkyard through the location of suicide within the lowland countryside. The spectacular murder-suicide of the Gourlay family at the conclusion of the novel effectively explodes the idealisation of community memory in Scottish rural fiction while also continuing to invoke the emotive focus on death that made kirkyard writing an effective carrier for social and cultural critique.

Burying the Past and Treating Modernity: Imagining Suicide and Society in the 1820s

Quoting the biographies of Byron and Goethe, A. Alvarez famously argued that 'the Romantics thought of suicide when they went to bed at night, and thought of it again in the morning when they shaved'.[13] While this assertion of the centrality of suicide in the mental landscapes of Romantic-era writers is something of an overstatement, the figure of 'the suicide' did gain an increasing ubiquity in the literature of the late eighteenth and early nineteenth centuries. British representations of suicide drew not only on pre-existing religious and supernatural conceptions of self-harm but also took part in contemporary discussions of urbanisation, class conflict and nationhood. The latter half of the eighteenth century saw increasing concern that suicide was becoming an urgent social problem in Britain. Anxieties about textual contagion and urban degeneration found their outlet in texts that diagnosed a national suicide epidemic. Meanwhile, traditional burial sanctions used in cases of suicide were under growing scrutiny as they became associated with a barbaric and superstitious past. Talking about suicide thus also meant talking about the rapid changes taking place in British society. Portrayals of suicide as a struggle with the complexities and pressures of modern life clashed, and sometimes mixed, with a desire to reject traditional approaches to self-murder. Thinking about suicide became tied to thinking about society in broadly historiographical terms.

A major shift in sanctions against English suicides came into law in 1823 and precipitated Britain-wide conversations about the interment of suicides. Prior to the introduction of the 1823 Burial Act, approaches to the interment of those believed to have ended their own lives varied between the Scottish and English legal systems. In both systems a suicide faced the posthumous punishment of being denied burial in a churchyard and/or the forfeiture of their possessions to the Crown. In England, a body might be staked or buried at crossroads, while corpse dragging or gibbeting were more common in Scotland.[14] However, suspected suicides were increasingly identified as *non compos mentis* in enquiries into their deaths by the early nineteenth century, a verdict that meant that burial sanctions need not be imposed. The law had not changed but the ways in which it was enforced had been fundamentally altered. Dissatisfaction with sanctions against the dead in England grew in strength over the early decades of the nineteenth century until the 1823 Burial Act finally removed crossroads burial from English suicide legislation.[15] Contemporary accounts of the last crossroads burial of a suicide in London in 1823 describe it as 'an odious and disgusting ceremony' and 'an act of malignant and brutal folly'.[16] The emphasis on disgust and brutality in these reactions indicates that disapproval of sanctions against the dead was tied to perceptions of 'civilised' behaviour. Punishing suicides was increasingly represented as an archaism in contemporary discourse, a 'disgusting' survival from a less civilised time.

These discussions turned sanctions against the bodies of suicides into a particularly historiographically inflected concept. In thinking about the punishment of suicides' bodies writers and commentators could also think about the relationship between past and present, between civilisation and the 'disgusting' barbarity that preceded it. The suicide's grave in this context becomes a place where the troubling aspects of the past can, to some extent, penetrate the present, revealing their continued relevance and survival.

While the suicide's grave became a symbol of the past in contemporary discourse, in conversations about the disordered mind the act of suicide was increasingly characterised as a symptom of rapid modernisation. During the eighteenth century Britain had developed an unenviable reputation abroad as 'the European centre of suicide'.[17] Contemporary commentators used the term 'English Malady' to describe the perceived higher incidence of suicide across Britain. Although the number of suicides from the early nineteenth century through to the end of Victoria's reign did not significantly change, the perceived epidemic was characterised as a symptom of British industrial development.[18] The 'England' of the English Malady was therefore synonymous with urban, developed Britain, including Scotland, rather than England as a finite geographical nation. Peripheral, less developed areas of Britain, like the Highlands and Welsh mountains, were understood to be unaffected by the epidemic.

Within eighteenth- and nineteenth-century British thought urbanisation and high rates of suicide and violence became increasingly intertwined, as the cities came to be associated with a perceived moral decay within society. Urban life was pathologised and the countryside was transformed into a nostalgic image of a healthier and more socially connected time.[19] Suicide's association with the city was thus what Kelly McGuire terms 'a lament for a bygone era', a medical belief that reflected a perceived cultural change.[20] In his 1733 medical treatise *The English Malady; or, a treatise of Nervous Diseases of all kinds*, George Cheyne puts forward an argument that evinces nostalgia for a 'simpler' mode of living. He identifies a series of different factors that caused the apparent national epidemic of self-murder, many of which might be thought of as features of modernisation or, in eighteenth-century terms, 'civilisation'. These include the 'Humour of living in great, populous and consequently unhealthy towns', climate and diet.[21] Cheyne's interpretation of the causes of the 'English Malady' are, as Nigel Wood has since commented, rooted in a sense that society, in the journey towards modernity, has lost beneficial features: 'the problems that Cheyne identifies are prevalent in advanced societies, and this leads to the paradox that the search for physical security has led to psychic insecurity.'[22]

Theorists also often argued that 'peasants' and 'savages' were immune to suicidal urges. Andrew Halliday's 1828 book *A General View of the Present State of Lunatics and Lunatic Asylums in Great Britain and Ireland* argues that 'savages', 'slaves' and the residents of Britain's own 'wild' periphery experience a lower prevalence of 'insanity':

> [W]e seldom meet with insanity among the savage tribes of men ... Among the slaves in the West Indies it very rarely occurs and ... the contented peasantry of the Welsh mountains, the Western Hebrides, and the wilds of Ireland are almost free from this complaint.[23]

The pioneering Scottish doctor W. A. F. Brown supported this belief, arguing in 1837 that 'the more primitive and illiterate the district, the smaller the proportion' of that population would commit suicide.[24] Madness is synonymous with the stage of civilisation experienced by the residents of urban Britain. The colonies and peripheries are cast as ruder, simpler spaces where mental health is preserved. These ideas increasingly underwrote new approaches to caring for the mentally ill.

When the 'moral treatment' was piloted at the York Retreat in 1797, William Tuke's approach was heavily informed by the idea that the 'removal of the insane from urban to rural settings provided powerful therapeutic benefits'.[25]

Suicide is, then, implicated in two contemporary conversations about the impact of development on society. The years leading up to the 1823 Burial Act coincide with the emergence of Blackwoodian regional fiction, and suicides are key to the plots of two prominent examples of these texts. The suicide's grave's uncertain position as both tragedy of modernity and relic of the pre-modern make it a particularly useful figure within what are arguably both John Galt's and James Hogg's most enduring works of rural fiction.

Death Comes to Dalmailing: A Theoretical History of Suicide in Galt's *Annals of the Parish*

Although reportedly conceived in 1813, John Galt's *Annals of the Parish* were not published until 1821 and thus entered the public arena at a time when the *Blackwoodian* tale of local life was at the peak of its popularity.[26] Galt was an Ayrshire writer and merchant who first contributed to *Blackwood's* in 1819. During the 1820s he published multiple volumes of Scottish fiction with the publisher.[27] *Annals* was published as a single volume by Blackwood in the wake of the success of Galt's first serialised novel, *The Ayrshire Legatees* (1820), in the magazine and alongside the ongoing serialisation of his next *Blackwood's* novel, *The Steamboat* (1821). Galt associated the novel with these other two texts, proposing to William Blackwood that the three might be issued as books alongside one another in a series titled 'Tales of the West'.[28] Contemporary reviewers recognised the novel as part of a Blackwoodian oeuvre of writing; Francis Jeffrey included it in the 'Secondary Scottish Novels' review in 1823.[29] The text was also developed in close correspondence with the publisher William Blackwood. R. P. Irvine has documented the significant editorial interventions that Blackwood made during its inception, noting that 'it is clear ... that the novel published as *Annals of the Parish* is substantially the product of collaboration between the two men in late 1820 and early 1821.'[30] In spite of 'often an uneasy' relationship with the magazine's editors, *Blackwood's* and the publisher William Blackwood played an important role in Galt's development as a writer during the 1820s.[31] We can therefore think of *Annals* as a text that is written and developed, not just in the shadow of Scott, but in close proximity to another influential model of Scottish rural writing.

However, *Annals* diverges from the path taken by founding kirkyarders John Wilson and J. G. Lockhart through its adoption of the conventions of conjectural or theoretical history.[32] Focusing on the life of a rural Ayrshire parish between 1760 and 1810, the novel tracks the social and economic changes experienced by the local community. In her summary of his work, Regina Hewitt describes how Galt utilised the Enlightenment genre of conjectural history as a template for fictional works like *Annals* and its sister work, *The Provost*: 'Galt self-consciously wrote fiction, drama, and biography based on his observations of lived and recorded behaviour, elaborating on his "models" in ways associated with the "theoretical" or "conjectural" methods of Scottish Enlightenment historiographers.'[33] Galt himself commented of his Scottish fictions that 'they would be properly characterised ... as theoretical histories than either novels or romances.'[34] This approach to history represents the antithesis of the historical vision articulated in kirkyard fiction. Galt's mingling of the archetypal Whig form of conjectural history with the setting and concerns of *Blackwood's* regional tale represents a clash of rival approaches. The forward motion of stadial history confronts the timeless rural idyll.

Studies of *Annals* tend to examine the novel in terms of its relation to the progress plot, tracing how Galt's narrative critiques or advocates historical change.[35] This scholarship often highlights Galt's ambivalence and resistance to any form of overarching plot, his desire to resist even the disembodied progressive narrative of stadial history. As Anthony Jarrells comments, 'whatever the degree of plottedness that features in Enlightenment conjectural history, Galt seems to have recognised other possibilities in the form.'[36] In *Scott's Shadow*, Ian Duncan participates in this critical tradition in his analysis of the novel, highlighting a dramatic suicide in the final chapters of the novel as a key turning point in Galt's representation of historical progress.[37] In Duncan's argument, the deaths of Mr Dwining and his wife in the final chapters of the novel are exemplars of the influence of globalising forces on local and domestic spaces.[38] Suicide in this reading is a symptom of modern social separation: an event that foregrounds the casualties of the forward momentum of history.

This argument, however, isolates the Dwinings' deaths from other instances of suicide within the text. There are three narratives where characters end their own lives, or are suspected to have ended their own lives, across the novel. Looking at these episodes together, the variation in circumstance and mode of narration are indicative of an ambivalent attitude to progress and its impact on community connections. Through the representation of the deaths of Nanse Birrell, Meg Guffaw and the

Dwinings, Galt interrogates ideas of both human development and social degeneration, painting a complicated picture of a changing society. He also foregrounds the role of the author in imposing a narrative on that history. The burials of suicides come to represent neither the brutality of traditional custom nor the tragedy of modern social isolation.

Galt's novel opens at its own conclusion; in the opening chapter the Reverend Micah Balwhidder gives an account of his last sermon in the parish kirk of Dalmailing where he has ministered for fifty years.[39] Facing his congregation for the last time the minister gives a sermon that describes the relationship between the living community of the Ayrshire village, their ancestors and God.[40] The minister exhorts the young people to look to the example of their parents and the Covenanting rebels of the seventeenth century. He suggests that the historical legacy of the Covenanters should be a rural society that values moderate prosperity and peace. Balwhidder's generation, he argues, 'bore in mind the tribulation and persecution of their forefathers for righteousness' sake, and were thankful for the quiet and protection of the government in their day and generation'.[41] While acknowledging the radical inheritance of a Covenanting tradition in the rural west of Scotland, Balwhidder attempts to neutralise its application to secular politics in the aftermath of an age of revolution. Balwhidder's expanding rural parish with 'the tree growing, and the plough going' is the reward that follows the strife of earlier generations.[42] Like a tree 'growing', change in the parish is understood as an organic, desirable and gradual process.

Having held up the example of their 'plain, honest and devout' parents and ancestors to the young residents of the village, Balwhidder turns to his own generation:

> As for you, my old companions, many changes have we seen in our day, but the changes we ourselves are soon to undergo will be the greatest of all. We have seen our bairns grow to manhood – we have seen the beauty of youth pass away – we have felt our backs become unable for the burthen, and our right hand forget its cunning. – Our eyes have become dim, and our heads grey – we are now tottering with short and feckless steps towards the grave; ... Our work is done–we are weary and worn out and in need of rest – may the rest of the blessed be our portion! – and, in the sleep which we all must sleep, beneath the cold blanket of the kirkyard grass, and on the clay pillow where we must shortly lay our heads, may we have pleasant dreams, till we are awakened to partake of the everlasting banquet of the saints in glory![43]

Loss in this passage is, like growth, conceptualised as necessary and organic. Death and the religious afterlife are imagined as inevitable parts of a continuous process. Balwhidder implicitly suggests that the 'changes' witnessed by the residents of Dalmailing and the 'changes' their bodies undergo are fundamentally similar. Thus, gradual changes in society are understood in the same way in which the eyes 'become dim' and heads turn grey. Both are inevitable, if not always welcome.

Having given this speech, the minister leaves the pulpit and faces the spectacle of the real community and graveyard:

> in the churchyard all the congregation was assembled, young and old, and they made a lane for me to the back-yett that opened into the manse-garden- Some of them put out their hands and touched me as I passed, followed by the elders, and some of them wept. It was as if I was passing away, and to be no more-verily, it was the reward of ministry-a faithful account of which, year by year, I now sit down in the evening days, to make up.[44]

It is apparent from these early images that the graveyard has a specific symbolic function within this text. Having made an explicit connection between the living congregation in front of him and the graves that surround the church, Balwhidder steps outside to find the kirkyard thronged with those very living generations waiting to mark his retirement. The actions of the parishioners are reminiscent of those of mourners and counter the minister's assertion that death is the end of life on Earth. Although Balwhidder's sermon has suggested a traditional ideation of death followed only by the religious afterlife and remote posthumous example, this passage implies a dynamic relationship between the living community and the graveyard at the centre of their village. Rather than a space whose only function is to provide 'the cold blanket of kirkyard grass' and 'clay pillow', the graveyard becomes a space of living memory as the villagers gather among the gravestones of their ancestors to mark change and remember the past. This is a space that seems to hold a similar temporal status to that of Wilson's 'burial ground, on a green hill'.[45] It is at once an unchanging memorial to the past and a space fully integrated into the life of the community. This simultaneous status is achieved through the invocation of the idea of an enduring community constituted of changing parts, an ongoing cycle of birth, life and death. If read as a mission statement for the *Annals*, Balwhidder's description of the final sermon presents his account of the parish to be one that perches delicately between belief in progress and mourning for the past. He articulates the sort of sub-Burkean vision of gradual historical progress already evoked in works like *Peter's Letters* and *Lights and Shadows*.

Annals contains three possible suicides, and their frequency increases in tandem with local development. In early entries the rural village is apparently a site largely free of suicide, with only one possible example, and the act's creeping presence is only truly felt within the community as it morphs into a working mill town. However, Galt's engagement with suicide and the graveyard space is far more nuanced than this summary would suggest. The novel calls into question the possibility that rural spaces can offer a 'cure' for the nation's malady by emphasising suicide's presence within pre-modern rural space. The invasive presence of Galt's often limited narrator, Balwhidder, also forces the reader to confront history's status as subjective narrative. Balwhidder is far from impartial, and his attempts to integrate the disruptive suicides of his parishioners into his kirkyard vision reveal its fictionality.

In the entry for 1766 an elderly healer, Nanse Birrel, is found dead in a well, leading to speculation that she jumped. This is the first apparent mention of suicide within the text, although its status as a suicide is never confirmed. Balwhidder suggests that the rumour that Nanse jumped into the well may be occasioned by the fact that 'Nanse was a curious discontented blear-eyed woman, and it was only with great ado that I could get the people keepit from calling her a witch wife.'[46] The reference to witchcraft in the brief description of Nanse's death highlights marked differences between the belief systems of minister and congregation. Peter Maxwell-Stuart remarks that by the eighteenth century magic and witchcraft were 'now firmly associated in the educated middle-class mind with popery and the middle ages' in lowland Scotland.[47] Although folk beliefs survived in many communities, records suggest that church investigations into supernatural practices were dwindling. The 1735 Witchcraft Act had made it impossible to be convicted of witchcraft in an English or Scottish court, instead penalising those who pretended to have supernatural powers, a differentiation designed to highlight that belief in witchcraft was no longer part of British legal institutions. The age of witchcraft trials had passed, and belief in witchcraft was increasingly attributed to the 'ignorant' and 'savage'.[48]

In an age of Enlightenment, the educated minister Balwhidder appears to reject the reactions of the villagers to Nanse the 'witch-wife' as leavings from a savage, superstitious time. In life Nanse is called a witch and in death a suicide; the allegation of suicide is treated as an extension of a pre-existing witch hunt designed to exclude Nanse from the community. By linking Nanse's death to her uncertain status within the community, Galt highlights that the origin of the custom of banishing suicide's bodies from the kirkyard is in traditional folk beliefs and systems of justice. Her death highlights the possible ways in which the identification of certain deaths as suicides can operate to police the borders of moral community within the traditional village – borders that Balwhidder, an educated, mid-eighteenth-century minister (imagined by an early nineteenth-century author), is unwilling to continue to enforce. Balwhidder refuses to characterise the healer's death as a suicide and thus allows her to be buried without sanction. Punishing suicides was rapidly going the way of burning witches, and Balwhidder's response to the gossiping villagers can be identified as part of this movement.

The other two suicides in the novel are both associated with the cotton mill erected in Dalmailing in 1788. The first victim Meg Guffaw, the 'haverel lassie', features throughout the novel as a sort of 'idiot-savant' character.[49] Like Madge Wildfire in Scott's *Heart of Midlothian* (1818) or Watty Walkinshaw in Galt's *The Entail* (1823), Meg is presented as a 'daft' character whose eccentricities might be interpreted as leavings from a previous age. Ann Roberts Divine describes Meg as 'a representative of an older age and a symbol of the old ways that are vanishing from the village'.[50] Her suicide in the dam of the modernising cotton mill is thus tied in this reading to the death of an older order. However, although Meg's actions are often reminiscent of the folk customs that are dying out in Dalmailing, the Reverend Balwhidder's descriptions of Meg's behaviours often cast them as an uncanny form of playacting. Even her attempts to prepare her mother's body for burial are described as 'a wonderful and truthful semblance' of a traditional laying out.[51] Meg enacts the different rites traditionally practised by lowland Scots to mark death and yet simultaneously burlesques them: 'making the solemnity of death, by her strange mockery, a kind of merriment, that was more painful than sorrow'.[52] Meg's actions are at once artificial and yet strangely more articulate than the actions of those around her. She seems to exist within the narrative almost entirely to complicate temporal distinctions and Balwhidder's cherished ideas of organic 'progress'. She is a childlike adult who confounds notions of past and present, authenticity and romance.

Meg's own death is attributed to the arrival, and subsequent marriage, of the mill owner's nephew, Mr Melcomb. Meg develops an attraction to the young man when he humours her fancies by allowing her to walk on his arm. Melcomb joins in Meg's playful fantasies, responding to her flirtations and increasingly gaudy costume by handing her 'over the kirkstile, like a lady of high degree' and 'allemanding' her out after church 'in a manner that should not have been seen in any street out of a king's court'.[53] However, when Melcomb's betrothal is revealed in church it becomes apparent that Meg has not been playing. Following Melcomb's marriage, despite the attempts of Balwhidder and the villagers to console her, Meg commits suicide:

> At last she gave a deep sigh, and the water coming into her eye, she said, 'The worm – the worm is my bonny bridegroom, and Jenny with the many feet

my bridal maid. The mill-dam water's the wine o' the wedding, and the clay and the clod shall be my bedding. A lang night is meet for a bridal, but none shall be longer than mine.' In saying which words she fled from among us, with heels like the wind. The servants pursued, but long before they could stop her, she was past redemption in the deepest plumb of the cotton-mill dam.[54]

Meg's poetic rendering of her own fate is the only time when Balwhidder does not cast her words or actions as unsettling instances of mimicry or whimsy. Meg is allowed to speak for herself without being cast as imitative.

Meg's speech and suicide draw upon representational tropes that were common in popular literature and oral culture of the time: the deserted seduced woman and the martyred virgin bride.[55] However, Galt's decision to use the archetype of the local 'idiot woman' to enact these tropes disrupts their message. Meg's suicide is an at once ridiculous and tragic reproduction of a ballad heroine; she kills herself for a love that was ultimately only a playful imitation of its forms. Meg's death is grotesque because it implies a dangerous, ugly vitality to oral tradition; the idealised ballad heroine emerges from verse to take the form of a deranged young peasant woman. Rather than reinforcing an image of country life where the old ways fall victim to industrialisation, Meg's suicide engages with this narrative only to confuse and complicate it. By taking as her model the enduring tropes of the betrayed and suicidal lover Meg invokes a traditional precedent for her actions even as she throws herself into the workings of emerging industrialism. Meg's death complicates notions of suicide as civilisation's shadow by emphasising her mimicry of existing traditional cultural forms.

The double suicide/murder-suicide of Mr Dwining, the failed mill overseer, and his wife in the final chapters of the novel might suggest that Galt's perspective on capitalist development is ultimately pessimistic. However, the cases of Meg and Nanse seem to delineate the limit of local sympathies earlier in the text. They are outsiders, and their cases illustrate the borders of the community even before mills and mines encroach on the village. The rural community has always excluded some and always contained a culture that has, at least imaginatively, incorporated certain forms of suicide.

The Dwinings' deaths take place after the collapse of the Cayenneville cotton business. Having retreated to the village following the failure of his own cotton business in industrial northern England, Mr Dwining finds himself again ruined. Following the mill's financial collapse, Dwining is not seen around the village, but it is noted that his door is open and his sons playing outside:

I happened to pass when they were there, and I asked how their mother and father were. They said they were still in bed, and would not waken, and the innocent lambs took me by the hand, to waken their parents. I know not what was in it, but I trembled from head to foot, and I was led by the babies, as if I had not power to resist. Never shall I forget what I saw in that bed * * * * * * * * * * * * * * * * *.[56]

This is the only instance within the novel where Balwhidder's confidence in his own ability to narrate what he witnesses breaks down and symbols replace words. Balwhidder also chooses not to reproduce the letter he finds on the Dwining's table, stating only that it told him to send the children to an uncle and that 'it is a terrible tale, but the winding-sheet and the earth is over it'.[57] The funeral itself is not a ritual designed to highlight the Dwinings' statuses as suicides. Instead, Balwhidder seems keen to disguise their cause of death from the wider community:

> Two coffins were got, and the bodies laid in them; and the next day, with one of the fatherless bairns in each hand, I followed them to the grave, which was dug in that part of the kirk-yard where unchristened babies are laid. We durst not take it upon us to do more, but few knew the reason, and some thought it was because the deceased were strangers, and had no regular lair.[58]

In the same way that Balwhidder was unwilling to label Nanse's death as suicide, he is here equally unwilling to publicly identify the Dwinings' deaths as such. Instead, he buries the story, keeping the details of the Dwinings' deaths within the private spaces of their home and grave.

The deaths of Mr and Mrs Dwining emphasise the inevitable penetration of market forces and modern ills into rural Scottish space. However, reviewing the three suicide narratives as a group complicates any attempt to cast this moment as one that defines the outlook of the novel as whole. Meg and Nanse occupy uncertain social positions within the community while Mr and Mrs Dwining are economic migrants whose positions are entirely tied to the mill. The Dwinings represent a new type of social outsider in a community that has always excluded some. Dalmailing is thus not an Eden corrupted by the Cayenne mill but a dynamic social space that can both include and exclude. When viewed together, Galt's suicides suggest the complexity of rural development and the impossibility of imposing a progressive or degenerative narrative on these spaces.

This interpretation reads counter to Balwhidder's early need to create a unified and idealised image of the traditional community in his final sermon. Balwhidder's modern discretion is incapable of preventing deaths; it is only capable of bringing the outcast into the graveyard. The living community are often impervious to Balwhidder's edicts and advice; his congregation ignores his attempts to limit the scale of local smuggling, resists his efforts to punish extramarital sexual relationships, and, in some cases, even turns away from his church in the later part of the narrative.[59] However, the graveyard is, like the annals themselves, a representation of Dalmailing that the minister can constitute for himself. His introductory sermon is by the end of the novel laid open to greater scrutiny. The communion between ancestors, living community and future generations that he describes is drawn into question, as he is revealed to act as an author of both local history and graveyard space. The incorporation of the bodies of Nanse Birrell and the Dwinings into the parish graveyard indicates Balwhidder's desire to manufacture a rural space denuded of both the superstitious traditions of the past and the modern negative influences of external capitalist forces. Meg's corpse, lost in the mill dam after a balladic act of martyrdom, symbolises the disruption of this project.

Annals reveals the fictiveness of the *Blackwood's* kirkyard, by exposing the minister and narrator's authorial role in the creation of an idealised kirkyard space. Galt's theoretical history, published alongside the serialisation of his other two 'Tales of the West' in *Blackwood's*, and written with the editorial assistance of the publisher, participates in a dialogue with previous iterations of Blackwoodian rural writing, just as the articles and stories within the magazine speak to one another month to month. Read within this context, his narrator's attempts to rehabilitate the suicides' corpses by returning them to the community of the dead is a symbolic gesture that seeks to manufacture a countryside space denuded of both 'superstition' and deadly market forces; the moralised countryside elucidated in Balwhidder's own final sermon. That this sermon reproduces the image of rural life evinced in Wilson's rural writing is not accidental but central to understanding the ambivalent attitude to national history that drives Galt's novel. Just as the resistance of the narrative to the imposition of a progress plot complicates the central assumptions of Whig historiography, the revelation of Balwhidder's authorial agency in the production of local history casts the eternal, organic kirkyard as a fabrication. Through *Annals'* three suicide scenes, Galt highlights that the nostalgia for true community evinced in the kirkyard is actually a very modern, externally imposed fiction.

A 'Disgusting Oral Tale': Unpacking the Suicide's Grave in *The Private Memoirs and Confessions of a Justified Sinner*

The August 1823 issue of *Blackwood's* features a curious letter from James Hogg, the Ettrick Shepherd, to his *Noctes Ambrosianae* foil

'Christopher North'.⁶⁰ Titled 'A Scots Mummy', the letter opens by recounting a dialogue between Hogg and 'Sir Christy'. The exchange is typical of the *Noctes*: shepherd and editor meet in Ambrose's tavern and discuss their correspondence, revealing their opposing perspectives on writing about rural life. The Ettrick Shepherd was a character who made regular appearances in the *Noctes Ambrosianae*, although Hogg only ever contributed poetry and songs to the series, meaning his speeches were generally authored by one of the other contributors.⁶¹ However, in this instance, the conversation is recounted from the point of view of the shepherd and written by his real counterpart, James Hogg. Given James Hogg's increasing unhappiness with the fictionalised representations of himself as the Shepherd in the *Noctes*, and Wilson's brutal review of Hogg's *Memoir* in 1821, the letter is an instance in which Hogg has the opportunity to reply. In 'A Scots Mummy' the Shepherd writes back.

The exchange begins when North demands to know why the Shepherd rarely writes to him. When the Shepherd declares he has 'naething to write about', North enumerates the 'boundless phenomena of nature' that might furnish appropriate material for a letter: 'you should look less at lambs and rams, and he-goats, Hogg, and more at the grand phenomena of nature. You should drink less out of the toddy-jug, shepherd, and more at the perennial spring.'⁶² This limiting of potential subjects echoes Wilson's 1819 article 'Some Observations on the Poetry of the Agricultural and that of the Pastoral Districts of Scotland, Illustrated by a Comparative View of the Genius of Burns and Ettrick Shepherd', where he had cast the shepherd poet as incapable of commentary on 'the theatre of the world'.⁶³

This fictionalised exchange acts as the stimulus for the main content of the letter, an account that 'is the very thing for old Christy'.⁶⁴ Teasingly, Hogg describes the sublime sights that come under the gaze of the Shepherd, the 'many bright and beautiful appearances on the face of the sky,' and 'the ever-varying hues of the mountains', the obvious subjects that 'old Christy' has had in mind, before having his protagonist reject them because 'they were, in fact, no phenomenons, if I understand that French word properly, nor ever were viewed as such by any of the country people'.⁶⁵ The Shepherd's deliberate misunderstanding serves to deflate North's bombast; it is designed to puncture the rhetoric of North's pastoral sublime.

What follows instead is the first account of the exhumation of 'A Scots Mummy' mentioned in the opening of this chapter. Hogg recounts the 'traditionary history' of a suicide buried on a hilltop in Ettrick.⁶⁶ The story features none of the sublime 'phenomenons' North has demanded. It describes a poor outcast shepherd's suicide, after possibly stealing some cutlery; local rumours that the devil aided in his death, largely fuelled by the fact that 'if you try all the ropes that are thrown over all the outfield hay rigs in Scotland, there is not one among a thousand of them will hang a colley dog'; and the subsequent burial of the malefactor on the wild summit of Cowancroft.[67] This is not the story North or Wilson would have desired, and Hogg is slyly aware of this:

> Well, you will be saying, that, excepting the small ornamental part of the devil and the hay-rope, there is nothing at all of what you wanted in this ugly traditional tale. Stop a wee bit, my dear Sir Christy. Dinna just cut afore the point. Ye ken auld fools an' young bairns shouldna see things that are half done. Stop just a wee bit, ye auld crusty, crippled, crabbit editor body, an' I'll let ye see that the grand *phenomena of Nature's* a' to come to yet.[68]

The grand phenomenon turns out to be the exhumation of the suicide's corpse by two local youths bored of cutting peat near Cowanscroft summit. Just beneath the surface of this grave they find the miraculously preserved body of the suicide wrapped in a blanket and with the rope still around his neck. The young men proceed to partially raise, then handle and loot the corpse, actions that are described with close attention to their materiality:

> One of the lads gripped the face of the corpse with his finger and thumb, and the cheeks felt quite soft and fleshy, but the dimples remained, and did not spring out again. He had fine yellow hair about nine inches long, but not a hair of it could they pull out, till they cut part of it off with a knife. They also cut off some portions of his clothes, which were all quite fresh, and distributed them among their acquaintances.'[69]

Throughout this account, the Shepherd undercuts the physicality of the description with repeated reiterations of his own distaste and disgust, emphasising that he himself has not visited the corpse: 'I never heard of a preservation so wonderful, if it be true as was related to me, for still I have not had the curiosity to go and view the body myself.'[70] Like the 'disgusting oral tale' that preceded it, the account of the preserved corpse is the product of local oral culture.[71] It is not the first-hand account of 'the day dawn, and the sunshine; the dazzling splendours of noon, and the sombre hues that pervade the mountains' that North demanded, but a collection of second-hand rumours about the reopening of a grave.[72] The Shepherd ignores the depopulated sublime landscape his editor requested. Instead, where North imagines an Edenic rural world, the Shepherd reinscribes the human traditions that exist on its surface. Where North would see a wild, majestic summit, the Shepherd identifies a grave and the jumble of 'ugly traditional tales' that cluster around it.[73]

This resistant letter concludes with a note of defiance:

> These are all the particulars that I remember relating to this curious discovery; and I am sure you will confess that a very valuable receipt may be drawn from it for the preservation of dead bodies. If you should think of trying the experiment yourself, you have nothing more to do than hang yourself in a hay rope, which, by the by, is to be made of risp, and leave orders that you are to be buried in a wild height, and I will venture to predict, that though you repose there for ages an inmate of your mossy cell, of the cloud, and the storm, you shall set up your head at the last day as fresh as a moor cock. I remain, my worthy friend, yours very truly,
>
> James Hogg.[74]

The real Ettrick Shepherd addresses North, and perhaps Wilson[75], with an elegant go-hang-yourself. This sort of complex semi-fictionalised literary game-playing between contributors was not unusual within the pages of *Blackwood's*, and, read alone, perhaps all we could take from this letter might be confirmation of the rising animosity between Hogg and senior figures at *Blackwood's* during the 1820s. However, June 1824 saw the publication of an anonymously published novel, *The Private Memoirs and Confessions of a Justified Sinner*, whose closing pages contain an extended excerpt from this text, along with a second conflicting report of the exhumation of an Ettrick suicide. Read in relation to this text, the letter takes on new life.

The novel, and in particular its closing exhumation scene, have been interpreted in numerous ways by different critics but have a habit of eluding any complete explanation; as Susan Manning commented, 'in Hogg's multiple retellings of the suicide's post-mortem existence, the reopening of the grave is a prominent and insistent, though unexplained, aspect of the narrative.'[76] The following analysis proposes reading the 'Scots mummy' as an interpretative key to *Confessions*. I argue that Hogg's rejection of the pastoral sublime in his letter to 'Old Christy' and his adoption of the comic grotesque of oral tradition signpost key ways of looking at the novel and in particular its engagement with the dead. Hogg's decision to use the exhumed body of a suicide as a symbol within this exchange is particularly subversive when considered alongside the fetishisation of the idealised rural Scottish graveyard in the work of many of his *Blackwood's* contemporaries. In repeatedly disinterring the corpse of a suicide, Hogg subverts a fundamental convention of their work: the enduring parish kirkyard.

Interpreting *Confessions*, and in particular Hogg's representation of the novel's 'Editor' figure, as explorations of the growing tensions between Hogg and the editorial team at *Blackwood's* is a common approach in Hogg scholarship.[77] In his reading, Mark Schoenfield interprets *Confessions* and 'A Scots Mummy' as responses to the cruel manhandling of Hogg's *Memoir* in an 1821 review by John Wilson: '*Blackwood's* published a devastating review of Hogg's 1821 *Memoir*. Hogg covertly replied to that review with the short letter, "A Scots Mummy", and, more substantially the anonymous *Private Memoirs and Confessions of a Justified Sinner* (1824).'[78] I extend this interpretation by arguing for a critique on Hogg's part that extends beyond authorial rivalries. 'A Scots Mummy' is not simply a supplementary text to *Confessions*, but a key to the author's intent throughout the text. Tracing the concerns played out in the 1823 letter through the novel reveals not just a personal antagonism between key figures in the *Blackwood's* group but Hogg's radical critique of the kirkyard approach to rural subjects, and of the worldview that this perspective articulates. This critique is embodied in the reoccurring figure of the shifting, degenerating 'Scots mummy'.

Confessions has a tripartite structure. It opens with 'the editor's narrative', an editor's compilation of the 'traditional' account of the fall of the Lairds of Dalcastle following the mysterious murder of the Dalcastle heir, George Colwan, and the disappearance of his illegitimate brother, Robert Wringhim. This is followed by the 'Confessions of a Sinner', a first-hand, conflicting account of these events, apparently authored by Wringhim. Finally, the book concludes with the editor's account of the discovery of the 'Confessions' during the exhumation of a border suicide (the scene described in the introduction to this chapter). These three accounts are close enough in content to convince the reader that they relate to the same events but feature disparities that make it impossible to furnish a cohesive narrative from the materials provided.

The identity of the 'Scots mummy' is one of the many plot features that remains uncertain at the conclusion of the novel. The corpse that is exhumed in the final pages is found with the partially handwritten pamphlet containing the *Confessions* and is therefore generally assumed to be the body of the text's protagonist, Robert Wringhim. However, this identification remains tenuous at best. As Michael York Mason points out, in a text that is full of contradictory accounts, 'the strongest contradictions ... seem to centre on the suicide's grave at Thirlestane Green.'[79] Just as the novel is split into three inconsistent parts, the corpse also has three contradictory narratives assigned to it.'[80] The contradictory nature of the different accounts of the suicide's grave makes definitively identifying the 'remains' that the editor describes impossible. As Mason has illustrated, the features of the three accounts are incompatible.[81] There are several possible explanations for the inconsistencies between the narratives; first, we might argue that the three stories illustrate the inconsistency of human testimony as different storytellers deliberately or accidentally alter key features of the narrative. Alternatively, there may be more than one suicide's grave in the vicinity of Thirlestane and their narratives have been conflated and confused over time. Finally, as Megan Coyer has suggested, the body itself may have changed between accounts: 'the implication may be that Gil-Martin's power over Wringhim's body continues beyond the grave – the flesh remains demonically shiftable.'[82]

What all these possible explanations have in common is that they completely disrupt the conventions of immutability and accurate memorialisation that characterise the idealised kirkyard. Whether the identity of the suicide has been forgotten or confused or has changed within the grave, what is certain is that the grave space that Hogg repeatedly explores in *Confessions* and its associated letter is a complete counter-image of the country graves that Wilson celebrates in *Lights and Shadows*, and that Balwhidder valorises in his final sermon. Orality and superstition re-enter the cleanly symbolic historic kirkyard through the figure of the suicide's grave, suggesting that the past and the rural cannot be divorced from their more unpalatable and 'uncivilised' aspects.

Where the graveyard of *Blackwood's* prose pastoral stories is a place of memorialisation for a stable and unchanging local community, those who visit the grave of Hogg's suicide are not there to remember and have no attachment to the dead man's 'face'.[83] Instead, the young men who exhume the body in 'A Scots Mummy' manipulate its face with their hands so roughly that they leave an impression in the flesh that 'did not spring out again'.[84] The group who return to disinter the suicide in *Justified Sinner* are equally unattached to the body's identity; their search is for a dehumanised scientific specimen, and the editor notes that he was 'very anxious to possess the skull'.[85] The scenes at the grave imagine the resurrection of Scotland's past in two equally damning ways; as mindless defacement or ghoulish trophy hunt. If the first men to resurrect the corpse are bored youths interested in the body only as a distraction from their labours, the second exhumation party are urban voyeurs, come to exhume the body of an unknown suicide and take away souvenirs. These scenes represent a complete inversion of the ancestral relationships between the dead, the living rural community and the urban literary class that Wilson had imagined. Locals bring up their traditions, their stories and their dead with an iconoclastic zeal, and allow the gentlemanly visitors to loot the grave.

This rejection of the kirkyard is set within a wider reimaging of rural Scottish landscapes and culture. In *Confessions* the rural community is not the repository of a pure vein of poetry, and stories of the past do not serve to cement a moral community with national application. The rural characters described in *Confessions* never inhabit a community with an obvious heart or centre; instead, we encounter isolated castles and cottages in a menacingly depopulated borderland. Rumours and gossip swirl in this space, but their sources are shrouded. The Dalcastle estate appears to be at the heart of a host of rumours and traditions, but the relationship between its inhabitants and those who live around it is one of surveillance rather than community. The final isolated and misremembered grave of the suicide refutes any attempt to cast rural Scottish spaces as repositories of true social connection or continuity through time.

Further, there is no modernising, moderate middle-class character there to right the wrongs of rural tradition and gossip as Balwhidder tries to in Dalmailing. The benevolent minister figure, Mr Blanchard, is unceremoniously shot at close range early in the sinner's account and no equivalent character subsequently emerges.[86] Instead, religion is presented as a dangerous force that allows characters to ignore and defile social bonds. In the figure of the Reverend Wringhim, Hogg describes a minister whose function within society is not to create ties but dissolve them. Where ministers like Balwhidder and those depicted in *Lights and Shadows* are moderate Evangelicals who attempt to unite their communities, the Reverend Wringhim's main aim is the creation of controversy and the destruction of family and community connections that fall outside of his own branch of Calvinist belief. Responding to Lady Dalcastle's complaints against her husband, the Reverend asserts not only the absolute relativity of moral codes, 'to the wicked all things are wicked; but to the just, all things are just and right', but the complete lack of interconnectivity between the 'just' and those around them: 'we have no more to do with the sins of the wicked and unconverted here, than with those of an infidel Turk; for all earthly bonds and fellowships are swallowed up in the holy community of the Reformed Church.'[87] Robert Wringhim's own faith is about the differentiation of the individual from those around him: 'I deemed myself as an eagle among the children of men, soaring on high, and looking down with pity and contempt on the creatures below', and allows him, according to his own account, to commit fratricide, matricide and, eventually, suicide.[88] Hogg reminds the reader of the divisiveness of religion within Scotland's recent past and its potential to ferment social fragmentation. Where Galt's Balwhidder tries to use an account of the undisturbed graves of Covenanters to neutralise the problematic and violent history of Scottish rural spaces, Hogg does the opposite, exhuming a suicidal fanatic's corpse to reveal the fractures in Scotland's recent past.

Schoenfield has argued that representations of Hogg within *Blackwood's* consistently imagined him as an artefact from the past, a static leaving from a previous time:

> Where Hogg recognised himself as a historiographic agent, constructing, through his works and public persona, interpretations of history, the editors of *Blackwood's* relegated him to historical object, subject to their interpretations. Like so many of the found items that permeate *Blackwood's*, the recurrences of Hogg, rooted to his Scottish ancestry and shepherding origins, enforced a nascent Tory historiography counterpoised to the *Edinburgh's* construction of historical progress.[89]

In Schoenfield's reading, Hogg's role within the magazine's imaginative scheme was as a symbol of a lost past but this symbolic role denuded him of agency. The 'Ettrick Shepherd' was central to the *Blackwood's* brand, 'Hogg's significance to *Blackwood's* ... is as a precursor, a legitimating figure, and a mode of exploring the uniqueness of Scottish culture.'[90] However, the importance of Hogg as a symbolic figure also limited his possible roles as a writer within the magazine. The shepherd could not, and should not, become an urbane literary wit but must remain in his role as rustic autodidact. The objectification that Schoenfield identifies is tied to Hogg's status as rural labourer.

This is the background that informs 'A Scots Mummy' and the exhumation scenes of *Confessions*. Although the exchanges between Hogg and his editors are personal controversies, the conflict between an imagined static peasant poet and the living author behind this mask is symptomatic of a wider problem with the temporality of kirkyard Romanticism. The exhumation scenes function to expose and question *Blackwood's* presentation of Hogg and the tradition he comes from as the modern Blackwoodian's buried ancestor. The personal and the abstract are inherently linked in Hogg's critique; in criticising his own treatment as rural Scottish writer, Hogg exposes a broader problem with the *Blackwood's* view of Scotland. Scottish rural space, like Hogg, cannot change in any radical way because its primary function is symbolic. The kirkyard is at the heart of this project, a tangible image of *Blackwood's* ideological agenda. The shapeshifting, isolated corpse that Hogg describes in the closing chapter of his novel problematises these attempts to cure and preserve the countryside and those who inhabit it.

Hogg's approach to the suicide's body is one that foregrounds the incongruities of early nineteenth-century literary approaches to Scottish history. A similar preoccupation with temporal contradiction is apparent in Galt's use of the suicide's grave. Whether adopting the theoretical history's form or rejecting it through the re-inscription of orality, Hogg's and Galt's texts play havoc both with the progress plot and the kirkyard's attempt to ringfence a static 'spot of time' from that flow. The images of suicide they employ play upon, not just the historic outsider status of suicide's outcast corpses, but on the historiographical uncertainty of the suicide in the years around 1823. The suicide's position is emblematic of that of the literary rural parish in this moment, marooned between the disgusting past and the maddening future.

Suicide, Modernity and Foreshadowing in *The House with the Green Shutters* (1901)

If the figure of the suicide's body operates in these texts as a temporal disruptor, then this offers an interesting lens through which to examine the three suicides that litter the final pages of George Douglas Brown's early twentieth-century intervention into the Scottish provincial novel tradition. Douglas Brown's bleak novel of small-town life and death *The House with the Green Shutters* (1901) was published in the wake of, and in response to, the 'kailyard school' of Scottish fiction.[91] Characterised by its vivid imagery and pessimism, the novel charts the downfall of George Gourlay, a small-town big man, and his hubristic folly, the eponymous house with the green shutters. The text has been described as an 'antikailyard' novel and Douglas Brown defined his own work against 'the sentimental slop of Barrie, and Crockett, and Maclaren'.[92] As previous scholars have explored extensively, the novel invokes a series of classic kailyard tropes (for example the lad o' pairts, the benevolent minister and schoolmaster, the mediating learned-but-local narrator) only to darken and disrupt them.[93] However, not all responses to the novel have characterised the relationship with the kailyard as an oppositional binary. Ian Campbell argues that *The House with the Green Shutters* should be understood, not just as a response to the kailyard group, but as part of an expanded kailyard tradition alongside Romantic predecessors like Wilson and Galt.[94] My own argument also sees Douglas Brown's novel within a continuous line of Scottish rural fiction but seeks to step beyond the kailyard conversation. Instead, I propose that Douglas Brown's text is best understood within a longer tradition of Scottish provincial writing, extending back to the early decades of the nineteenth century, and that one of the characteristic motifs of this literary conversation is the kirkyard.

Reading *The House with the Green Shutters* alongside Hogg's *Justified Sinner* and Galt's *Annals* highlights the centrality of modernity and temporality to all three texts. One of Douglas Brown's core projects is to counter the reification of an idealised and moralised vision of lowland Scotland; the formation of an idealised 'spot of time'. The conversion of rural Scotland from living space to memory is depicted through the figure of Jock Allan in the Edinburgh portion of the novel. Allan's desire to reconnect with his past through the young men who come to Edinburgh to study at the university is attributed to physical and temporal distance:

> Allan, like most great-hearted Scots far from their native place, saw it through a veil of sentiment; harsher features that would have been ever-present to his mind if he had never left it, disappeared from view, and left only the finer qualities bright within his memory. And idealizing the place he idealized its sons. To him they had a value not their own, just because they knew the brig and the burn and the brae, and had sat upon the school benches … A Scot revisiting his native place ought to walk very quietly. For the parish is sizing him up.[95]

These scenes take place halfway through the novel when the reader has already spent time in a small town that stands in contrast to the sentimentalised Barbie of brig, burn, brae and school bench of Allan's imagination. It is clear that Allan has constructed his own kailyard. He stands in for a wider readership whose relationship with the Scottish countryside is one underwritten by an impossible desire for return to an imagined better past.

In contrast, the real Barbie is shown to be a space heavily affected by external forces. John Gourlay is a character whose inability to adjust to incursions by the railway and modern commerce is an important factor in his downfall. Following the collapse of his business ventures, and his son's failure at the university, the deaths of the Gourlay family happen in rapid, melodramatic succession over the final chapters of the novel. These scenes are reminiscent of the suicides of the Dwinings in *Annals of the Parish*. Both families are, in one reading, victims of the forward momentum of progress and the incursion of these forces into rural space.

However, where Balwhidder is there to bury the dead and draw a veil over the Dwinings' last moments in Galt's novel, there is no such euphemising narrator in Douglas Brown's parish. The texts' expurgations are flipped as Douglas Brown includes details of the suicides' deaths but not their burials. The narrator vividly describes as the patriarch is murdered by his drunkard son with a poker and John Jnr ends his own life with poison. His body is discovered by his mother and sister in the darkened pantry in a scene of detailed Gothic horror: 'his legs had slipped to the floor when he died, but his body was lying back across the couch, his mouth open, his eyes staring horridly as if his father's eyes had watched him from aloft while he died.'[96] Left alone the women of the house are slowly driven to suicide by the collapse of the Gourlay empire. Their final scene is a strange parody of 'The Cotter's Saturday Night' as the matriarch reads the Bible 'in the high exaltation of madness', nerving herself and daughter to also swallow poison.[97]

This summary might suggest a narrative where the village of Barbie is the idyllic 'spot of time' Allan imagines destroyed by the forces of modernity. However, Barbie prior to the arrival of the railway and James Wilson is not a prelapsarian Eden but a space of corruption and stagnation. As Cairns Craig notes, in Douglas Brown's account: 'Scottish life is grim and vindictive, a place governed by the repression of personal feeling and policed by public malice and gossip.'[98] The forward motion of history is cruel but so too is the culture and society it obliterates. The Gourlay family are also far from simple victims. John Gourlay is a brutal patriarch, his wife and children damaged and selfish. Gourlay's greed and attempts to monopolise control of trade in the village combine with his inability to adjust to economic development in his downfall.

Imagining the deaths of the Gourlays as a simple critique of historical progress negates, not just Barbie's corruption, but also the way that the text complicates ideas of linear history through its use of foreshadowing. *The House with the Green Shutters* has been discussed in relation to both Greek and Shakespearean tragedy and likened to Thomas Hardy's realist tragedy *The Mayor of Casterbridge* (1886).[99] The novel shares with these texts a sense of inevitability that seems to negate any idea of progress or improvement. Douglas Brown himself commented of the Gourlays:

> I saw no end for them but the one I brought them to – their doom was implicit in themselves – they suffered the results of their own characters. We all do that, of course which is an inevitable law on earth as it is the old Greek law which means that we must all bear the consequences of our own action or want of action. That may not be a comfortable doctrine, but it is bracing and true.[100]

The future of the Gourlays is predestined from the early pages of the novel, and notably, the reader's access to the talk of the village bodies means they already have the keys to the novel's final tragedy by the midway point of the text.[101] This sense of foreboding reaches its zenith in the final death scenes. Gourlay's slow ascent of the ladder, and the repeated mentions of hammer and poker, build a horror-film-like tension predicated on the inescapability of disaster. The deaths of Janet and Mrs Gourlay also have a strange inevitability; Mrs Gourlay's repeated incantation 'there's two thirds of the poison left' seems to obviate any possibility of escape just as do the revelations of the women's terminal diagnoses.[102] Free will and the capacity to change or grow are absent from the novel. As Craig has argued:

> by superimposing a story of modern merchantile greed on the framework of Greek tragedy, Brown challenges the ideology of progress on which commercial society is based, forcing his readers to acknowledge human experience as cyclic rather than progressive[103]

Like Wilson's cotters whose deaths are the objects of their lives, the Gourlays' existence is entirely presented within the text in terms of its end. The rise of commercial success is understood, not as progress, but as the precursor to an inevitable fall. Suicide in Douglas Brown's novel maintains the power to disrupt the temporal assumptions of Enlightenment-derived progress. However, in leaving the bodies of the Gourlays unburied and on ignominious display to the reader and the gossips of Barbie, Douglas Brown also sidesteps the fiction of the enduring rural kirkyard. Like their kirkyard predecessors, Douglas Brown's suicides reveal the limits of historical narrative.

Notes

1. Hogg, *The Private Memoirs and Confessions of a Justified Sinner*.
2. Ibid., p. 185.
3. Ibid., p. 186.
4. Some notable examples include: Mason, 'The Three Burials in Hogg's *Justified Sinner*'; Mack, 'The Body in the Opened Grave'; Coyer, 'The Embodied Damnation of James Hogg's Justified Sinner'. Manning's article title 'That Exhumation Scene Again: Transatlantic Hogg' perhaps best encapsulates how widely the scene has been discussed.
5. Chandler, *England in 1819*, p. 128.
6. Hopfl, 'From Savage to Scotsman', p. 19.
7. Makdisi, *Romantic Imperialism*, p. 2.
8. Löwy and Sayre, *Romanticism against the Tide of Modernity*.
9. Makdisi, *Romantic Imperialism*, pp. 12, 13.
10. Jeffrey includes Galt's writing in his 'Secondary Scots Novels' review. As explored in Chapter 1, Wilson explicitly engages with Hogg's writing as a precursor to his own work alongside the poetry of Burns.
11. Duncan, *Scott's Shadow*.
12. Duncan has argued that Galt and Hogg approach the problem of history in their fiction with two contrasting strategies: 'Galt's affirmation of theoretical history by way of a refusal and then critique of romance, identified with the conventions of an extensive artificial plot, makes for a striking contrast with Hogg whom we found subverting the Enlightenment scheme of theoretical history in order to reclaim the critical force of "traditionary" narrative modes.' While Duncan explores these two methodologies in relation to Walter Scott's 'dialectic between romance and history', this

chapter places them alongside the static and virtual historical time of the kirkyard focusing particularly on the historiographically inflected motif of the suicide's grave. Duncan, *Scott's Shadow*, p. 220.
13. Alvarez, *The Savage God*, p. 231.
14. Houston, *Punishing the Dead?*, pp. 189–90.
15. Gates, *Victorian Suicide*, p. 7.
16. Qtd in MacDonald and Murphy, *Sleepless Souls*, pp. 348–9.
17. Ibid., p. 23.
18. Ibid., p. xiii.
19. McGuire, *Dying to be English*, p. 9.
20. Ibid., p. 9.
21. Cheyne, *The English Malady*, p. i.
22. Wood, 'Goldsmith's English Malady', p. 65.
23. Halliday, *A General View of the Present State of Lunatics and Lunatic Asylums in Great Britain and Ireland*, p. 24.
24. Brown, *What asylums were, are and ought to be*, p. 84.
25. Kushner, 'Suicide, Gender and the Fear of Modernity', p. 25.
26. In his literary autobiography *The Literary Life and Miscellanies of John Galt*, Galt claims that he started work on *Annals* in 1813, but laid it aside 'as I was informed that Scottish novels would not succeed (Waverley was not then published)' (p. 153). The *Literary Life* describes the manuscript's rediscovery 'years after' and subsequent submission to Blackwood. Galt, *The Literary Life and Miscellanies of John Galt*, p. 154.
27. Henderson Scott, 'Galt, John', *Oxford Dictionary of National Biography*.
28. Irvine, 'Introduction' to Galt, *Annals of the Parish*, p. xviii.
29. Jeffreys, 'Secondary Scottish Novels'.
30. Irvine, 'Introduction', p. xvii.
31. Morrison, 'John Galt's Angular Magizinity', p. 204.
32. See Chapter 1.
33. Hewitt, 'Introduction: Observations and Conjectures', p. 1.
34. Qtd in Costain, 'Theoretical History and the Novel', p. 343.
35. See Costain, 'Theoretical History and the Novel'; Jarrells, 'Reading for Something Other Than Plot'; McKeever, '"With Wealth Comes Wants"', pp. 69–93.
36. Jarrells, 'Reading for Something Other Than Plot', p. 123.
37. Duncan, *Scott's Shadow*, p. 227.
38. Ibid., p. 229.
39. Galt, 'Annals of the Parish', p. 3.
40. A scene which heavily parallels the kirkyard sermon in Lockhart's *Peter's Letters to His Kinfolk*.
41. Galt, 'Annals of the Parish', p. 4.
42. Ibid., p. 4.
43. Ibid., p. 5.
44. Ibid., p. 5.
45. Wilson, *Lights and Shadows*, p. 147.
46. Galt, 'Annals of the Parish', p. 33.
47. Maxwell-Stuart, 'Witchcraft and Magic in Eighteenth-Century Scotland', p. 91.

48. Ibid., p. 82.
49. Galt, 'Annals of the Parish', p. 308.
50. Divine, 'The Changing Village', p. 124.
51. Galt, 'Annals of the Parish', p. 87.
52. Ibid., p. 87.
53. Ibid., p. 122.
54. Ibid., p. 123.
55. Ballads which describe suicide and madness in the face of disappointed love or desertion were popular during the late eighteenth and early nineteenth century, with titles like 'Bess of Bedlam' and 'The Plymouth Tragedy' reoccurring in different chapbooks published in Scotland during the period. The image of the bride transformed into a corpse is also a recurring one in chapbooks and other street publications like 'The Bride's Burial', 'Andrew Lammie; or, The Mill of Tiftie's Annie'. In these texts the martyred virgin, dying for love but simultaneously untarnished by the act of love, is morally exalted for her constancy and purity, which is guaranteed by death. See Evans, 'Courtship, Sex and Marriage in Eighteenth-Century Popular Literature'.
56. Galt, 'Annals of the Parish', p. 152.
57. Ibid., p. 152.
58. Ibid., p. 152.
59. See Galt, 'Annals of the Parish', pp. 11, 52, 147.
60. Hogg, 'A Scots Mummy', in *Contributions to Blackwood's Edinburgh Magazine*.
61. See 'Introduction' for descriptions of *Noctes Ambrosianae*.
62. Hogg, 'A Scots Mummy', p. 132.
63. Wilson, 'Some Observations on the Poetry of the Agricultural and that of the Pastoral Districts of Scotland', p. 521.
64. Hogg, 'A Scots Mummy', p. 140.
65. Ibid., p. 140.
66. Ibid., p. 140.
67. Ibid., p. 141.
68. Ibid., p. 142.
69. Ibid., p. 143.
70. Ibid., p. 142.
71. Ibid., p. 141.
72. Ibid., p. 140.
73. Ibid., p. 142.
74. Ibid., p. 143.
75. The character Christopher North is often associated with Wilson in *Blackwood's*.
76. Manning, 'That Exhumation Scene Again', p. 103.
77. In his 'Introduction' to the 1969 Oxford University Press edition of *Confessions*, John Carey traces the relationship between Wilson and Hogg during the early years of the 1820s, suggesting that 'Wringhim's divided attitude to his "elevated and dreaded friend" can, without much imagination, be paralleled in Hogg's relationship with Professor Wilson. Kelly E. Battles has argued that Confessions constitutes a response to the boorish, licentious images of Hogg which had become common currency

within the magazine, where the writer was increasingly cast as 'a naturally talented but unschooled and undisciplined writer who, because of his coarse background, has no sense of propriety.' She argues that, in *Confessions*, Hogg casts 'the editor', whom Battles identifies as a 'stand-in for John Wilson', as the one struggling with improper appetites. When the body of the suicide is uncovered, Battles contends that the Editor's necrophiliac and homoerotic desires are revealed: 'the true nature of the Editor's appreciation rather than being the pure and disinterested aesthetic pleasure of the connoisseur or the similarly disinterested critical gaze of the scientist, is a sexualised, erotic pleasure directed at a doubly taboo object: a male corpse.' Similarly, Ian Duncan suggest that, when the James Hogg depicted at Thirlestane Market refuses to guide the party of antiquarians to the suicide's grave in the last pages of the novel, 'he takes back his folk identity from the Blackwood's wits to utter a gruff rejection of the unseemly business of exhuming the countryside for public amusement', although Duncan also notes that this is what 'as anonymous author of *The Private Memoirs and Confessions of a Justified Sinner*, he has been doing all along.' Carey, 'Introduction', in *The Private Memoirs and Confessions of a Justified Sinner*, p. xx; Battles, 'Bad Taste, Gothic Bodies and Subversive Aesthetics', pp. 54, 57, 62; Duncan, *Scott's Shadow*, p. 173.

78. Schoenfield, *British Periodicals and Romantic Identity*, p. 203.
79. Mason, 'The Three Burials in Hogg's *Justified Sinner*', p. 17.
80. Ibid., p. 18.
81. Ibid., p. 21.
82. Coyer, 'The Embodied Damnation of James Hogg's *Justified Sinner*', p. 13.
83. Hogg. 'A Scots Mummy', p. 149.
84. Ibid., p. 143.
85. Hogg, *Justified Sinner*, p. 185.
86. Ibid., p. 107.
87. Ibid., p. 13.
88. Ibid., p. 88.
89. Schoenfield, *British Periodicals and Romantic Identity*, p. 203.
90. Ibid., p. 205.
91. See Chapter 1.
92. Hart, *The Scottish Novel*, p. 131. Barrie qtd in Veitch, *George Douglas Brown*, p. 153.
93. Campbell, 'George Douglas Brown's Kailyard Novel' and Craig, 'Introduction', in *The House with the Green Shutters*.
94. In his article 'George Douglas Brown's Kailyard Novel', Campbell suggests that 'the kailyard can be traced in the weaker fiction of John Galt and John Wilson', p. 62.
95. Brown, *House with the Green Shutters*, p. 137.
96. Ibid., p. 245.
97. Ibid., p. 248.
98. Craig, 'Introduction', p. vi.
99. See Campbell, 'George Douglas Brown's Kailyard Novel'; Royle, 'The Ghost of Hamlet in *The House with the Green Shutters*'; Egan, 'The

Indebtedness of George Douglas Brown to *The Mayor of Casterbridge*', respectively.
100. Qtd in Veitch, *George Douglas Brown*, p. 158.
101. Douglas Brown, *House with the Green Shutters*, p. 126.
102. Ibid., p. 245.
103. Craig, 'The Modern Scottish Novel', p. 413.

Chapter 4

The Doctor and the Dead: Anatomy, Feeling and Genre

In October 1824 a new serial debuted in *Blackwood's Edinburgh Magazine*. Featured some nine pages before an episode of Caroline Bowles's already familiar Chapters on Churchyards series, 'Wonderful Passage in the Life of Mansie Wauch, Tailor' describes the incursion of body snatchers into the rural kirkyard of Dalkeith. It opens *in medias res* as the population of Dalkeith become aware of rumours that their dead have been exhumed:

> About this time there arose a great sough and surmise, that some loons were playing false with the kirkyard, howking up the bodies from their damp graves, and harling them away to the College. Words canna describe the fear, and the dool, and the misery it caused. All flocked to the kirk yet.[1]

Mansie's first-person narrating voice is immediately distinctive and identifiable as one drawn from regional Scotland. His use of broad Scots and his description of bodies taken '*away* to the College' indicates to the reader the story's status as a regional tale, set beyond the boundaries of the cities with their growing medical schools. As Bowles and Wilson so often do, Moir begins his rural story in the churchyard, but rather than a place of tranquil contemplation and memorialisation this kirkyard is the focus of a disturbance as locals 'flock' to protect their dead.

The early passages of the tale foreground the effect of the grave robbing on the local community. The citizens of Dalkeith rush to the kirkyard as a dismayed group to inspect a crime that has been committed against them. Moir focuses on the case of one bereaved family whose recently interred mother's corpse has been taken from the grave.[2] The choice of the elderly matriarch as the victim of the grave robbers creates a particularly emotive scenario. The grey-haired mother is symbolic of the safety and comfort of home and hearth; the theft of her body from the graveyard is therefore an action that attacks the family-centred community values of idealised small-town Scotland. In the same issue of the magazine where Caroline Bowles describes the sentimental death and burial of a wronged peasant maiden in a peaceful 'secluded burial-ground', Moir opens his long-running series of rural tales by presenting a possible threat to this vision of recuperative rural graveyard space.

Mansie's emotive encounter with the resurrection men is one of a number of fictionalised responses to their crimes published by kirk-yard writers. This chapter examines a cluster of body-snatching tales published in *Blackwood's* between 1821 and 1831. I argue that, in these tales, the twin spectres of the exhumed cadaver and the ambitious anatomist become useful symbols for the evils of a society that prioritises economic and scientific progress over feeling. These symbols are underwritten by the existing idea of the kirkyard as a national sanctuary and repository foregrounded in conservative Scottish rural fiction. If the undisturbed ancestral burial ground contains the building blocks of the nation, then this can be endangered by the theft of bodies from their graves. The connections of kinship and community are overridden by the demands of a system where the pursuit of economic and scientific improvement is prioritised. The tale writers engage with the crimes of the body snatchers and Burke and Hare to critique this model of society and offer an alternative vision.

What is at stake in these conversations is the role of emotion in the formation of the national community. William Christie has noted that '*Blackwood's* argument with the *Edinburgh* reviewers ... was that they employed "only the national intellect, and not the national modes of feeling"' – in essence, that the *Blackwood's* mode of Romantic nationalism prioritised feeling over theory when it came to thinking about national community.[3] In the previous chapter, I explored how the image of the suicide's grave was used by Scottish authors to engage with ideas of time, problematising post-Enlightenment progress but also the kirkyard's Romantic 'spot of time'. In this chapter, I instead foreground another aspect of the kirkyard writers' Romantic critique of modernity by looking at their representation of emotional engagement and detachment. Authors like Wilson play into a well-established conservative understanding of the nation as a quasi-familial set of relations built on strong feelings of loyalty and identification. The vision of the Romantic nation that Wilson and Lockhart assembled, from the materials provided by thinkers like Burke and Schlegel, was grounded in the prioritisation of the emotional over the rational or theoretical. Lockhart's complaint that 'a single generation of abstract reasoners is enough to vitiate the pedigree of national sentiment and association' is addressed in these texts through the invocation of strong emotion in the reader, countering what Andrew Lincoln terms the 'detachment and moderation fostered by enlightened rationality'.[4] The pre-eminence of tales of terror and sentimental regional fiction in early *Blackwood's* is therefore, arguably, not coincidental. Authors use sentiment and terror to co-opt readers into intense emotional identification, even as they argue for the importance of emotion in forming the bonds that constitute the imagined community. Genre and message are tied together in a mutually beneficial embrace.

In this chapter, I examine a group of stories about grave robbing that were published in *Blackwood's*. I explore their use of generic conventions to evoke strong emotions in the reader and to criticise a lack of emotion in modern society.[5] I then trace the legacies of these emotive body-snatching tales into the later nineteenth century. When Robert Louis Stevenson recreates the archetypal 'tale of terror' in his magazine fiction he returns to the kirkyard and the crimes of the resurrectionists. This is a deliberate strategy that draws upon the legacies of kirkyard Romanticism to assemble a resistant and Romantic critique of contemporary anglophone letters.

The Resurrectionist in the Village: 'Mansie Wauch', the Doctor, and the Dead

D. M. Moir's *The Life of Mansie Wauch Tailor in Dalkeith* series ran in *Blackwood's* from 1824 and 1827, before being collected and published as a book in 1828. Moir was a highly prolific *Blackwood's* contributor and a professional physician based in Musselburgh. His works included poetry, commentary and fiction, but he is perhaps remembered for his *Mansie* stories. The series employed couthy Scots humour and a small-town setting, following good-natured but naive hero Mansie from an apprenticeship in Edinburgh to life as a successful tailor in Dalkeith. The stories fit in among the *Blackwood's* tales of Scottish life; George Douglas notes that 'the autobiographical tailor, with his unconscious self-revelation, is obviously suggested by the Provosts and Micah Balwhidders' of Galt's writings, and Moir dedicated the single-volume edition of the series to the Ayrshire author.[6]

The stories are gentle and slow-paced; they seem designed for a mixed, perhaps family, audience. Reading *Mansie Wauch* is often presented as a communal experience by subsequent commentators. Douglas comments that 'this book was never meant for closets and the midnight oil, but to be read aloud over the fire on winter's eves in the family circle', while T. F. Henderson's introduction to *The Life of Mansie Wauch* asserts that 'in Scotland, there were districts where country clubs awaited impatiently for the Magazine, met monthly, as soon as it was issued, and had

Mansie read aloud by one of their number among expressions of congregated laughter.'[7] These images of the imagined consumption of the text indicate the social and often domestic reading experience associated with the *Mansie* series. Moir's farce is gently comedic, allowing a wide range of readers to join in the laughter. The stories are not designed to address an individual reader but a collection of listeners. Moir doesn't just describe a provincial community; the reading of his stories, written in broad lowland Scots, seems designed to create one, to precipitate scenes of familial conviviality like those Burns and Wilson had described around 'the big ha' bible'.

As Megan Coyer has explored, Moir was committed to both literature and medicine throughout his life but displayed anxiety about the compatibility of these two roles.[8] In her account of Moir's writing, Coyer ties this anxiety into a wider politicised conversation about the role of feeling and art in medical training and practice. She argues that reacting to an increasing perception of the doctor as removed from the religious and moral social body, Moir participated in 'the formulation of a redemptive counter-discourse in Scottish letters' that paved the way for the figure of the 'doctor hero' in Victorian literature.[9] Moir's *Blackwood's* writing is concerned then with the reintegration of the professional medic into the moral community. The kirkyard offers an effective symbol of this ideal. In *Mansie Wauch*, doctors reoccur on several occasions. Their entanglements in the acquisition of cadavers and the practice of anatomy give Moir opportunities to explore the relationship between the medical profession and a moral national community.

Resurrection Men and Monstrous Doctors: The Two Transformations

The historical background to Mansie Wauch's first encounter with the resurrection men was the decade leading up to the passing of the Warburton Anatomy Act of 1832, a piece of legislation that fundamentally changed how human subjects for anatomical dissection were acquired. These legislative changes were precipitated by an increasing black-market trade in bodies. As the medical schools and research hospitals of eighteenth- and early nineteenth-century Britain expanded and became ever more committed to hands-on dissection as a tool for training and investigation they required an ever-growing number of cadavers. However, the number of bodies they could officially access remained static. Before 1832 the only cadavers officially available for dissection in Britain were the bodies of recently executed felons as laid down by the provisions of the 1752 Murder Act.[10] Supply rarely met demand, and ambitious anatomists were therefore increasingly likely to accept and pay for bodies that had been acquired from other unregulated sources. This problem was particularly marked in Edinburgh as the city's strong reputation for medical education attracted a huge number of medical students. The demand for bodies was driven by the ambitions of the many surgeons competing for students and professional acclaim. Official sources simply could not keep up with the requirements of the booming medical sciences.

The gap between supply and demand was filled through the theft and importation of corpses.[11] Body snatching, the practice of exhuming or otherwise co-opting the bodies of the recently deceased to sell, was widespread in early nineteenth-century Britain. The grave robbers were often groups of professional resurrectionists, although students and anatomists also sometimes took matters into their own hands and collected the bodies themselves. They operated at night, exhuming recently interred bodies secretly and delivering them to the schools under cover of darkness. Bodies were also covertly imported into Britain on board ships from Ireland and France.

Public opinion was frequently hostile towards body snatching. Even those who argued for the need to further medical science through anatomical investigation often took steps to secure their bodies and those of their loved ones from the body snatcher's grasp.[12] There were riots in some Scottish cities when rumours of body snatching and anatomical malpractice came to public attention. Caroline McCracken-Flesher cites 'clashes' between 'citizens' and 'students and surgeons' in Glasgow throughout 1813 and 1814 following the discovery of a cargo of corpses hidden within 'rag bales at the city docks'.[13] Anatomical science remained a contentious issue throughout the early decades of the nineteenth century, as the public maintained what Ruth Richardson terms 'a very brittle tolerance' of the anatomical schools that could easily be damaged by the perceived overstepping of boundaries.[14]

One of the issues that provoked this response was dissection's association with the posthumous punishment of criminals. However, this punishment was based on an even deeper sense that the dissection of the body was an act that annihilated and dehumanised. Michael Sappol describes how many would have viewed dissection as 'the final and definitive annulment of their [the dead's] social being'.[15] The body of a person was (ideally) placed in a graveyard at the centre of their community with the story of their life over them in the form of their epitaph, whereas a cadaver was an object that was bought and dissected with little regard for its humanity. The corpse that had gone into the grave as a person and ancestor was transformed on the dissecting table into a commodity.

This uneasy status quo of the body-snatching era was brought to an abrupt close in part due to the West Port murders of 1828. The murderers, William Burke and William Hare, were Irish immigrants who had migrated to Edinburgh to work as labourers during the construction of the Union Canal. The men stumbled upon a new income source when a tenant of Hare's wife's lodging house died without settling debts. Burke and Hare sold his body to the assistant at an extramural anatomy school. Now aware of the profits to be made from flesh, the men proceeded to prey on the most vulnerable citizens of Edinburgh, murdering them and selling their bodies. In response to the public outcry that these murders, and the subsequent London 'Italian Boy' murders of 1831, generated, along with the conviction of two doctors for grave robbing in 1828, an act made its way through the British Parliament that radically altered the way anatomical subjects were sourced.[16]

The murders shocked and fascinated the public far beyond Scotland's capital, generating responses in the press, periodicals and popular fiction. In the street literature that addressed the West Port murders, anger and blame were often directed at the figure of the professional surgeon. Many texts focused on the guilt of, not just the murderers, but their employer, Dr Robert Knox. A contemporary broadsheet exemplifies this argument: 'What induced that Monster, Burke, to Murder so many human beings? Nothing but the price offered to him by the Surgeons. And what can induce those infernal fiends to pillage churchyards? Nothing but the price paid them by the Lecturers on Anatomy!'[17] *Blackwood's* also joined the throng of voices berating the Edinburgh anatomist. In the *Noctes Ambrosianae* for March 1829 conversation turns to the recent execution of William Burke. After sketching unflattering portraits of the two murderers and their wives based on the principles of physiognomy, Christopher North, Timothy Tickler and the Ettrick Shepherd turn their attention to Dr Knox and his anatomy school:

Shepherd-But what o' Dr. Knox?
  North-The system established and acted on in the dissecting-rooms of that anatomist is manifestly of the most savage, brutal and dreadful character. It is allowed by all parties, that not a single question was ever put – or if ever, mere mockery – to the wretches who came week after week with uninterred bodies crammed into tea-chests – but that each corpse was eagerly received and fresh orders issued for more. Nor is there any reason to believe, but every reason to believe the contrary, that had the murderers brought sixty instead of sixteen murdered corpses, they would not have met an instant market.
  Shepherd-Fearsome-Fearsome![18]

The exchange follows this pattern throughout, with either Tickler or North making long passionate speeches about the Doctor, prompted and concurred with by a servile and at times naive Shepherd. The Shepherd makes a lengthier exposition at the end of the discussion, vividly describing the haunting of the Burkers and doctors:

> Shepherd – Naebody believes in ghosts in touns, but every body believes in ghosts in the kintra. Let either Hare or Knox sleep in a lanely wood, wi' the wund roarin' in the tap branches o' the pines, and the cheepin' in the side anes, and by skreich o' day he will be seen flyin' wi' his hair on end, and his een jumpin' out o' their sockets, doon into the nearest toon, pursued, as he thinks, by saxteen ghaists a' in a row, wi' Daft Jamie at their head, caperin' like a paralytic as he was, and lauching like to split, we' a mouth drawn a' to the ae side, at the doctor or the doctor's man, distracted at the sicht o' sae mony spirits demandin' back their ain atomies.[19]

By 1829 the *Noctes* were under the authorial control of John Wilson, and the way in which he chooses to represent the dialogue between the Scots-speaking Shepherd and English-speaking North and Tickler is indicative of the relationship between science and tradition that he wishes to present. The culpability of Dr Knox is something that *Blackwood's* urban and rural characters can agree on. These murders combine professional ambition, unchecked modernisation and free-market greed in a single potent image. Knox represents the march of progress and personal ambition that *Blackwood's* so often identifies and condemns in contemporary society. However, in the *Noctes* conversation, the ability to critique the workings of the laboratory and the law is given to the educated North and Tickler, while the Shepherd's area of expertise is in the province of the supernatural. *Blackwood's* urban and rural voices unite from their different perspectives to indict Knox. Together, their voices form a damning Tory chorus that attacks the ambitious and unethical doctor.

The scandals of West Port have often been identified as the point of the origin for the monstrous or inhuman doctor who played an increasing role in Gothic writing from the nineteenth century onwards. A. W. Bates comments that 'the sinister anatomist of early Victorian fiction was a stock character' and traces the popularity of this figure back to the West Port and Italian Boy murders.[20] Tim Marshall supports this view, but dates the emergence of these ideas in literature prior to the detection of Burke and Hare's crimes, arguing that 'in the anatomy literature there is much slippage between the surgeon, the dissector, the murderer'.[21] The monstrous doctors of the nineteenth century tend to be characterised by two interrelated features that remove them from the wider social world: ambition and clinical detachment. Marie-Luise Kohlke explains:

[A]s representatives of a 'masculine' empiricist rationality, they [doctors] acted as purveyors of scientific knowledge, social reform and progress; yet their expertise and practice often rendered them objects of fear as much as veneration, suspected of narcissistically abusing their powers over life and death for profit and other immoral even unhallowed pursuits.[22]

In 1759, in *The Theory of Moral Sentiments*, Adam Smith had already posited the idea that the practices of the surgeon might blunt or annihilate that most important tool of human connection, sympathy: 'some people faint and grow sick at the sight of a chirurgical operation … One who has been witness to a dozen dissections, and as many amputations sees, ever after, all operations of this kind with great indifference, and often with perfect insensibility.'[23] In a theory that postulates sensibility as the premier mode of social connection, 'insensibility' and 'indifference' place the surgeon outside of the webs of sympathetic connection that make human society possible.

Concern about the relationship between the medical professional and society continued throughout the early nineteenth century. During these years medical practitioners attempted to elevate their status within contemporary society through professionalisation and increasingly differentiated the modern science that they practised from the 'quackery' of untrained practitioners. Catherine Crawford has argued that in the medical periodicals of the period 'a common feature of the various perspectives on medical improvement was concern about the social status of the profession'.[24] One of the ways in which the elevation of medical science was to be affected was through the banishment of emotion and 'the curious' from medical discourse. The physician of the early nineteenth century was, Meegan Kennedy has argued, 'more objective and more skeptical' than his predecessors and attempted to adopt a 'homogenous, professional medical discourse' in his case histories and other medical writings.[25]

However, alongside the increasing drive towards professionalisation and social elevation, a parallel anxiety persisted about the possible ways in which professional detachment and ambition might sever the professional from wider society. Caroline McCracken-Flesher quotes the response of that most famous of Edinburgh Tory professionals, Walter Scott, to the Burke and Hare trial:[26]

Scott declared his suspicion of a science divorced from human values, saying: 'I am no great believer in the extreme degree of improvement to be derived from the advancement of science; for every pursuit of that nature tends, when pushed to a certain extent, to harden the heart, and render the philosopher reckless of everything save the objects of his own pursuit' (*Letters.* 11:127). He questions his similar dedication to the courts, for 'I have myself often wondered how I became so indifferent to the horrors of the criminal trial, if it involved a point of law.'[27]

In Scott's account, the ambition and detachment required to practise law or medicine successfully also serve to threaten the sympathetic responses of the professional. Sympathy and professionalism mutually endanger one another. The professional is always at risk of losing his ties to the broader social world.

This concern about the blunting of feeling in medical professionals was one that Moir playfully engaged with in his fiction prior to the West Port murders. Doctors again feature in the episode of *Mansie Wauch* titled 'Benjie on the Curtain', published in *Blackwood's* in 1827. In this episode, Mansie's wife Nanse suggests that their teenage son, having shown academic promise in school, might become a doctor:

> 'Doctor!' answered I – 'Keh, keh, let that flee stick to the wa'; it's a' ye ken about it. If ye was only aware of what doctors had to do and see, between dwining wains and crying wives, ye would have thought twice before ye let that out. How do ye think our callant has a heart within him to look at folk bluiding like sheep, or to sew up cutted throats with a silver needle and silk thread, as I would stitch a pair of trousers; or to trepan out pieces of cloured skulls, filling up the hole with an iron plate; and pull teeth, maybe the only ones left, out of aud women's heads, and so on, to say nothing of rampaging with dark lanterns and double-tweel dreadnoughts, about gousty kirkyards, among humlock and long nettles, the hail night over, like spunkie-shoving the dead corpses, winding-sheets and all, into corn-sacks, and boiling their bones, after they have dissected all the red flesh off them, into a big cauldron, to get the marrow to make drogs of?'
>
> 'Eh, stop, stop, Mansie!' cried Nanse, holding up her hands.
>
> 'Na,' continued I, 'but it's a true bill – it's as true as ye are sitting there. And do ye think that ay earthly compensation, either gowpins of gowd by way of fees, or yellow chariots to ride in, with a black servant sticking up behind, like a sign over a tobacconists door, can ever make up for the loss of a man's having all his feelings seared to iron, and his soul made into whinstone, yea into nether-mill-stone, by being art and part in sic dark and devilish abominations?'[28]

Mansie's knee-jerk reaction to the suggestion his son become a doctor forms the climax of a comedic set piece in which Nance suggests a variety of socially respectable professions that Mansie uses his rather idiosyncratic logic to reject. Moir is having a little fun with the Gothic reputation of his own profession here, and perhaps giving a playful wink to those readers who were in on the secret of the anonymous author's identity.[29] However, Mansie's comments also reflect a caricatured version of the image of the monstrous, detached doctor who was to loom large in response to the West Port murders. Although Mansie's rant is supposed to appear overblown and preposterous, it is built on a series of attitudes that already existed within public discourse. Just as the body became an object in the anatomy theatre, the anatomist appeared to transform himself, through the cultivation of detachment, into a monstrous machine – 'his feelings seared to iron, and his soul made into whinstone'. If the dissected body was transformed from social being into object, a comparable transformation could be affected on the dissector.

While Moir's Mansie is highly critical of the anatomist, Moir himself was a small-town doctor who had received his training in the anatomy theatres of Edinburgh. He had direct experience of the necessity of anatomical training to contemporary medical education but would also have been aware of the difficulties that body snatching could create for medical practitioners in the affected communities. His presentation of the 'horrors of grave-robbing' through his provincial hero can be read, not as an indictment of this aspect of medical training, but as an argument for anatomical provision to be regulated through new legislation in the form of the 1832 Act.[30] We can see this most clearly in Mansie's first encounter with the grave robbers. Mansie's reflections on the stolen bodies in Dalkeith focus on the impact of body snatching on local social relations:

> Tell me that doctors and graduates maun hae the dead; but tell it not to Mansie Wauch, that our hearts maun be trampled in the mire of scorn, and our best feelings laughed at, in order that a bruise may be properly plaistered up, or a sair head cured. Verily, the remedy is waur than the disease.[31]

In Mansie's encounter with the resurrectionists, he argues primarily against the social effect of body snatching. Body snatching seems completely unrelated to the daily realities of bruises and sore heads to people like Mansie. It is a practice that, in its effects on the local community, causes far more damage than any disease. However, Moir avoids stating that anatomy itself is entirely unnecessary. If we follow Mansie's argument to its logical conclusion, if corpses were not part of a social matrix then their dissection would not be abhorrent. The issue is not the inherent morality of investigating the body through dissection, but the possible ill effects that appropriating bodies might have on the social harmony of the conservative rural idyll.

The Tale of Terror and the Professional Observer

While the Scottish regional tale was rapidly becoming a hallmark of William Blackwood's output, another distinctive tradition, with a seemingly very different approach to the dead, was also emerging as a recurring feature in the publisher's flagship magazine. The tales of terror were a prominent genre within *Blackwood's* early fiction.[32] Morrison and Baldick describe how these tales foreground 'the recorded "sensations" of a first-person narrator witnessing his own responses to extreme physical and psychological pressure'.[33] The reader's perspective is limited and entirely identified with the narrator's subjectivity. This narrator is often isolated or trapped in a very restricted and extreme environment. They make limited reference to events prior to the experience they describe or beyond the environment they inhabit. These strategies create an intense and highly emotive reading experience where the reader seems to experience the narrator's terror.

Like the kirkyard novels and tales, the tales of terror are littered with bodies but, unlike the rural dead described in Wilson's, Lockhart's and Bowles's regional writing, the dead in these Gothic stories are rarely left to lie peacefully in their graves. Protagonists find themselves trapped amid the piled bones of the deceased, as in 'A Night in the Catacombs' by Daniel Keyte Sandford (1818), witness to the deaths and dissections of murderers, like the narrator of Robert McNish's 'An Execution in Paris' (1828), and themselves rising from the dead, as in Henry Thomson's 'Le Revenant' (1827) and Galt's 'The Buried Alive' (1821). As Yael Shapira notes, the *Blackwood's* tale of terror presents the Gothic corpse directly to the viewer and lingers on its horrors.[34] Just as these tales are often identifiable by the minute description of the physical experience of terror, they are also characterised by the minute and visceral observation of the dead body.

Tim Killick's account of the development of the Blackwoodian tale of terror notes the importance of the medical case study as a source for their innovative content and formal strategies.[35] The reproduction of 'curious' medical case studies was an existing feature of many contemporary periodicals but in drawing their stylistic features and content into the realms of fiction the authors of the *Blackwood's* tales of terror sought 'to develop new ways of telling stories that drew on the language of medicine and psychology, and their associated discourse of cause and effect'.[36] *Blackwood's* tales regularly adopt a register that David Macbeth Moir termed the 'medico-popular', in reference to Blackwood's tales and essays with a medical component.[37]

Just as a knowledgeable middle-class mediator often accompanied the reader into the cottages of the rural poor in the kirkyard tales, in the tales of terror a similar intermediatory narrator is used. This intermediatory narrator differentiated these tales from more demotic crime writing of the period. To bring sensational stories of crime and violence into the polite reader's parlour, writers often employ the professional expert as a mediating agent.[38] The use of professional narrators means that these stories offer access to spaces and experiences that would otherwise remain private. The reader is invited into the sickroom and the dissecting chamber and shown their secrets by an expert from their own world.

The employment of the 'professional' gaze also means that the text can model its own distanced reading. The reader is invited into the profession for the time they read the text. Their concern is accurately describing physical sensations rather than ascribing moral meaning. These reports are not for the public at large but for educated insiders. The terror stories draw upon the emerging professions for their Gothic potential, their implications of exclusivity, and, perhaps most importantly, their perspective.

However, as the *Noctes* response to the Burke and Hare murders indicates, *Blackwood's* is never truly comfortable with the fully detached professional. Coyer observes that, in contrast to the impersonal medical case study, the tale of terror is often narrated by a developed first-person narrator, whose thoughts and feelings intrude on their account of events. This focalisation creates 'a dialectic between the empirical narrator's sensational relation of the events and the putatively authoritative medico-scientific narrative'.[39] The objective professional gaze is undercut by the interjection of the feeling man.

'I still could hear, and feel, and suffer': Anatomy as Gothic Transformation

John Galt's short story 'The Buried Alive' is an oft-cited example of the *Blackwood's* tale of terror that explores the twin transformations of the doctor and the dead man in the dissection room.[40] Published in *Blackwood's* in 1821, the story describes a man's experience of his own death, exhumation and attempted dissection.[41] In the course of the tale the protagonist finds himself upon his deathbed but realises that, although his body cannot move, he has retained full mental consciousness. Locked in and unable to communicate with those around him, he is mourned, prepared for the grave, and buried before being exhumed by a party of grave robbers and transported to the dissecting table where a series of experiments are performed on his body for an audience of medical students. Only with the application of a scalpel to his chest does the protagonist revive. The story, like many tales of terror, maintains a limited and almost claustrophobic focus on the sensations and interiority of the first-person narrator. As his eyes are closed by a friend, he comments that 'the world was then darkened, but I still could hear, and feel, and suffer', and this perhaps sums up the content of the story that never expands beyond the perspective of the 'hearing', 'feeling' and 'suffering' man trapped within his own body.[42]

This transfiguration of a living man into a cadaver is presented as a form of Gothic metamorphosis. Galt's use of a first-person narrator, who witnesses his own transformation, foregrounds the corpse's transition from person to commercial object. The transformation of the middle-class male narrator into a saleable commodity also effects a complete reversal of power relations; he is taken from his privileged position in society and transformed into an object. Andrew Mangham has argued that, during the nineteenth century, 'the idea of being buried alive emerged as a ghastly emblem of knowing – *truly* knowing – what it was to be beleaguered, victimised and terrified.'[43] Galt's narrator temporarily experiences the nightmare of absolute reification and social deletion. The story is a horrifying version of Adam Smith's individualised sympathy which places 'our own living souls in their inanimated bodies'.[44] It is the living dead man's body that imprisons him and causes his interment and attempted dissection. The site of terror is not the anatomy theatre or the graveside but the body itself.

However, there is a second transformation that takes place over the tale as the revelation that the cadaver is alive provokes an emotional response in the previously detached medical students. In the anatomy theatre an 'accent of awe and compassion' replaces the 'hustle' and cries of 'admiration' as the students recognise the 'good subject' as a person they have known.[45] The dehumanised cadaver is revealed to be a living man, horrifying those who have come to watch the spectacle of its dissection. The narrator/cadaver teaches the room of gawping students to recognise their own kinship with the dead.

Galt's tale of terror is thus both sensationally entertaining and slyly didactic. A complicated system of identifications informs the narrative. The reader is placed within the living dead man's body through the employment of a first-person narrative but is also to some extent an observer, like the medical students, who is to be educated. What disturbs the students in the auditorium, even before the narrator has been revealed to be alive, is that they know the subject; they have socialised with him and he is of their social class. When they recognise him they wish that 'it had been some other'.[46] Similarly, what is frightening to the educated reader of *Blackwood's* magazine is that the first-person narrator is just like them. Relatively wealthy and socially respectable but otherwise unidentifiable, the man at the centre of Galt's text could be any one of *Blackwood's* intended readers. He is a middle-class man who knows doctors and students, can afford to employ undertakers to carry out his funeral, and has a working understanding of galvanism. 'The Buried Alive' uses Galt's unnamed narrator to produce a chilling sense of personal identification in the reader. Galt reattributes personhood to the body: literalising the fears of contemporary readers and relying on the retained humanity of the corpse to produce horror. This Gothic description of anatomy forces the reader, like the students, to confront the humanity of the anatomical subject.

Across Moir's and Galt's regional tales and tales of terror there are a shared series of concerns and attitudes to death and anatomy. Although the stories belong to very different genres, they ponder the same problem and critique the same perceived social ills. Both the tale of terror and the sentimental regional tale are concerned with provoking strong emotion in the reader. They also participate in an intergeneric conversation, using the cadaver and the doctor as twin symbols of the dangers of emotional detachment.

Samuel Warren's popular series *Passages from the Diary of a Late Physician* ran from August 1830 to August 1837 in *Blackwood's* and mingled the discourses of sentimental and terror fiction. Warren, whom we first encountered in the introduction to this book, was a lawyer and an author who was to have an ongoing relationship with Blackwood into the 1850s.[47] The *Passages* are presented as a series of professional anecdotes from the diary of a physician, detailing incidents from his training and practice. While episodes from the series are anthologised and classified as tales of terror, as Coyer has noted, the late physicians' encounters 'range from the macabre to the sentimental'.[48] The physician is not just a proxy through whom the reader has the voyeuristic opportunity to view sequestered professional spaces and experience; he is also a man of feeling.

Written after the West Port murders, amid growing calls for burial reform, Samuel Warren's *Blackwood's* tale 'Gravedoings' is an early story in the series and was published in June 1831 as the debates around anatomical reform gained in volume and intensity. The story describes a 'grotesque if not ... ludicrous' attempt to exhume a body from a rural graveyard.[49] The protagonist, two fellow medical students, and an Irish porter named Trip travel to a graveyard in a village outside London in pursuit of the body of 'a young and rather interesting female' patient whose family have refused to allow the doctors to carry out a post-mortem.[50] Their inexperience and zeal are exposed as they find themselves the victims of a thunderstorm, a wayward ass and a farcical incident in which they mistake their own coachman for the deceased girl's enraged brothers.

The story is less a tale of terror than a parody of these tales. It repeatedly describes the protagonist's terrified responses to supposed horrors only to reveal each time that they have been founded on misapprehension. The tale can productively be approached in the way that Yael Shapira approaches a fellow tale of terror, 'A Night in the Catacombs' by Daniel Keyte Sandford, a story that she argues 'gestures towards the historical function of the corpse as a means of instruction ... only to render it subtly ironic'.[51] Like Sandford's hysterical reader of Gothic fiction, whose time in the Parisian catacombs offers a cure for morbid sensibility, the youthful Physician's experiences in the graveyard demystify the terrors of grave robbing through farce and humour.

This 'de-terroring' has a double function: it educates not only the medical student in the story but also the reader. Warren's wider argument across the story is that superstition and prejudice have caused the scandals of the anatomy era. Early in the tale the narrator chides his readers for their concerns about medical dissection: 'it is your own groundless fears, my fair trembler! – your own superstitious prejudices – that have driven me, and will drive others of my brethren, to such dreadful doings as those hereafter detailed.'[52] It seems that just as the horrors that terrify the would-be grave robbers are revealed to be imagined, so too are we as an audience being shown the misapprehension behind our fear of the anatomy theatres of modern medicine.

However, this reading is complicated by the conclusion of the text, as the protagonist becomes increasingly disenchanted with the work he must undertake. By the closing lines of the episode the protagonist's outlook on events seems to have undergone a radical shift and, although he does not retract his avowal of the need for body snatching, his opinions on undertaking the task coalesce with those of the previously comedic Irish porter: 'I heartily resolved with him, on leaving the coach, that it should be "the divil's own dear self only that would timp me out agin *bodysnatching*!"'[53] In both Moir's *Mansie* stories and Warren's body-snatching tale the voices of provincial dialect-speaking characters are naive and used to humorous effect but also contain a grain of truth or morality. Mansie is ridiculous but also the emotional and moral heart of Moir's series, and in Warren's story Tip's responses to the exhumation of the body are hyperbolic but contain a sentiment that the English-speaking Physician is eventually driven to echo. This is also true of the way that the Ettrick Shepherd is sometimes employed in the *Noctes* to reinforce the points made by other more urbane characters, as in the March 1829 *Noctes* discussed earlier in this chapter. In effect, this technique allows the *Blackwood's* author to bring together the urbane and traditional parts of the magazine's character. Like the dialect-speaking characters, the traditionary elements of the magazine operate as a moral heart or conscience for the modern, educated narrator and reader. They are the voice of an old father, out of touch with modern life, somewhat humorously so, but still capable of giving sound moral guidance to his sophisticated urban progeny.

In Warren's tale the two perspectives of the narrator and the unwilling Irish porter are not exclusive. It is quite possible that Warren, who had spent some time at Edinburgh's medical college before training as a lawyer, could have both championed the necessity of anatomical education and simultaneously rejected body snatching as an effective strategy to feed the dissection table. The story instead seems designed to imply the need for a more systematic, and perhaps less 'ludicrous', mode of supplying the medical schools. Warren does not demonise the practices that have underpinned the development of modern medicine; rather, he attempts to soften the reader's attitude to them through the deployment of humour. The comedic element of the farce in the graveyard negates the sinister aspect of the medical man's role in the exhumation.

The physician narrator's opening plea for clemency on the part of the reader implies a broader approach that the reader might apply to medical anatomy's controversial history:

> My gentle reader-start not at learning that I have been, in my time, a RESURRECTIONIST. Let not this appalling word, this humiliating confession, conjure up in your fancy a throng of vampire-like images and associations or earn your 'Physicians's' dismissal from your hearts and hearths.[54]

In presenting the trip to the graveyard as an act of youthful folly, Warren personifies the progress of medicine, attributing the life cycle of the doctor to his profession. Just as the young medical students will progress from excitable boys to respectable professionals, the story implies that body snatching is part of an anatomical science still in its adolescence that will mature into a more respectable profession. Body snatching is not a sinister systematic operation rather the resurrection men represent the boisterous early steps of a profession in progress. This presentation of body snatching humanises the development of anatomical science. If Burking terror is underwritten by a fear of the faceless, unyielding process of scientific progress, then this comparison naturalises anatomical science and returns it to the world of gradual, humane change that underwrites kirkyard Romanticism.[55]

Warren's tale is then designed to both dismiss the Gothic associations of anatomy and to reassert the respectability of the anatomically trained physician as a trustworthy professional and, more importantly, as a feeling man. The 'Late Physician' stories were an extremely popular feature of the magazine between 1830 and 1837, and they were often characterised by the sentimental or emotive tone of the physician's observations. Based on this tendency towards emotion Meegan Kennedy has argued that the narrator 'endangers the professional standing of the physician by insisting on his subjective embodiment rather than his rational, distanced perspective'.[56] However, it seems to me that, in a context where the doctor is characterised as a monster with a soul of 'iron' and 'whinstone', Warren's insistence on the subjectivity of his protagonist does quite the opposite. By June 1831 the fictional 'Physician' had been addressing the *Blackwood's* readership with passages from his diary every month for almost a year. They had witnessed his struggles as a fledging doctor, they had shared his terror in scenes of madness and violence, and they had watched him tend to the needy in sentimental scenes worthy of Wilson's *Lights and Shadows*.[57] In short, just as readers of the magazine grew to feel that they knew the bickering contributors depicted in the *Noctes Ambrosianae*, by the time that 'Gravedoings' was published they would have felt a certain intimacy with this 'Physician' who visited them each month. Warren's body-snatching story domesticates the anatomically trained doctor, and occasional grave robber, by making him a man with whom readers already held a great deal of fellow feeling. The story aims to return the monstrous doctor to the readers' 'hearts and hearths', using both humour and sympathy to remind them, in the wake of West Port, that doctors were not inhuman, Gothic creatures but members of their social world.

Terror Haunted: Robert Louis Stevenson in the Kirkyard

Some sixty years after the heyday of the kirkyard, Robert Louis Stevenson authored a quintessentially Blackwoodian body-snatching tale. Drawing upon genre-forming terror tales and kirkyard writing, in 'The Body Snatcher' (1884) Stevenson once again brings professional Edinburgh and rural Scotland into collision over the grave.[58] Examining Stevenson's 'The Body Snatcher' in relation to previous body-snatching stories reveals a pervasive relationship between Stevenson's tale and the tale of terror. It also gestures towards Stevenson's participation in a particularly Scottish tradition of resistant Romanticism.

Stevenson's tale opens with a confrontation between 'an old drunken Scotsman' named Fettes, and a respected surgeon, Dr Wolf MacFarlane, in an almost contemporary English pub.[59] This incident provides the frame for Fettes's account of the gruesome events that took place during the men's time as medical students in Edinburgh in the late 1820s. Working for the sinister Dr K, a clear reference to the infamous Dr Knox, the students accept deliveries of bodies for dissection from an Irish duo on his behalf, despite increasing evidence that the victims did not die of natural causes. Events take a further dark turn when MacFarlane murders an acquaintance and disguises his crime by selling the body to the school as a specimen with Fettes's assistance. However, the climactic horror of the tale is not, as we have perhaps come to expect, directly related to the crimes of Burke and Hare. Stevenson disappoints reader expectation by making no further reference to the West Port crimes and instead situates the narrative's crisis in a body-snatching venture the two students make to a rural parish, Glencorse, near Penicuik. Here the body of the old woman whom they have exhumed appears to supernaturally transform into that of MacFarlane's long-dissected victim.

At the tale's opening, the ageing Fettes is described as a Cleishbotham-type figure: a benign feature of the cosy pub fireside that he habitually occupies: 'his blue camlet cloak was a local antiquity, like the church spire. His place in the parlour at the George, his absence from church, his old crapulous, disreputable vices, were all things of course in Debenham.'[60] However, this entombment within the stasis of rural life is broken by the arrival of Dr MacFarlane. The mention of his name jolts the drunk into sobriety: 'we were all startled by the transformation, as if a man had risen from the dead.'[61]

This frame, and metaphorical resurrection, rehearses the larger collision described in the body of the story, that can perhaps be best illustrated by engaging with the author's extended description of the graveyard that Fettes and MacFarlane plunder:

> there came the news of a burial in the rustic graveyard of Glencorse. Time had little changed the place in question. It stood then, as now, upon a crossroad, out of call of human habitations, and buried fathoms deep in the foliage of six cedar-trees. ... once in seven days the voice of the bell and the old tunes of the precentor, were the only sounds that disturbed the silence around the rural church. The Resurrection Man – to use a by-name of the period – was not to be deterred by any of the sanctions of customary piety. It was part of his trade to despise and desecrate the scrolls and trumpets of old tombs, the paths worn by the feet of worshippers and mourners, and the offerings and the inscriptions of bereaved affection. To rustic neighbourhoods where love is more than commonly tenacious, and where some bonds of blood or fellowship unite the entire society of a parish, the body snatcher, far from being repelled by natural respect, was attracted by the ease and safety of the task. To bodies that had been laid in earth, in joyful expectation of the resurrection of a far different awakening, there came that hasty, lamp-lit, terror-haunted resurrection of the spade and mattock. The coffin was forced, the cerements

torn, and the melancholy relics, clad in sackcloth, after being rattled for hours on moonless by-ways, were at length exposed to uttermost indignities before a class of gaping boys.[62]

The image of a rural space in which one steps out of the narrative of linear time is again repeated in this description, with even the image of the reputable old church reprising its symbolic function. These rural spaces become allied with the grave.[63] Glencorse kirkyard is a space reminiscent of the Romantic kirkyards of the earlier century; a space that represents the pre-Enlightenment social values attributed to rural spaces 'where love is more than commonly tenacious, and where some bonds of blood or fellowship unite the entire society of a parish'. The pervasive Blackwoodian image of the sentient body's journey to the dissection table is also indicated in the passage's final sentence which recaps a plot used in 'The Buried Alive', Henry Thomson's 'Le Revenant' and James Hogg's 'Terrible Letters from Scotland'.[64]

Stevenson was highly aware of the *Blackwood's* tradition. He reviewed the new edition of the *Noctes* in 1876 for *The Academy*. His review is favourable; he recognises Wilson's resistant, adversarial agenda, and suggests that the wild, shocking prose of the *Noctes* could stir up his own literary milieu:

> this book is not only welcome because it takes us on a visit to Wilson when he is in his best vein, but because Wilson in all his veins is the antidote or at least the antithesis of much contemporary cant. Here is a book full of the salt of youth; a red-hot shell of animal spirits calculated, if anybody reads it, to set up a fine conflagration among the dry heather of present-day Phariseeism. Touch it as you will, it gives out shrewd galvanic shocks, which may perhaps brighten and shake up this smoke-dried and punctilious generation.[65]

For Stevenson, the resistant Romanticism of the *Noctes* provides a vital riposte to his own literary age. Liam McIlvanney also indicates that Stevenson considered serialising his novel *Weir of Hermiston* in *Blackwood's* because of its history of publishing 'queer' 'scotch' writing: 'he reflected, there was one magazine worth trying: "It has occurred to me that there is one quarter in which the very Scotchness of the thing would be found a recommendation and where the queerness might possibly be stomached. I mean *Blackwood*."'[66] This perception of the character of the magazine illustrates familiarity with the history of the periodical, and the reputation for scandal, Scottishness and the strange that had sealed its success during the early century. Stevenson's invocation of Blackwoodian tropes in 'The Body Snatcher' is traceable to a familiarity and identification with this tradition, and an awareness of the magazine's antagonistic ethos.

Stevenson's self-avowed project was, like the kirkyard writers before him, aesthetically oppositional. In his 1882 essay 'A Gossip on Romance' he critiques the British public's appetite for novels of modern life, stating that 'English people of the present day are apt, I know not why, to look somewhat down on incident, and reserve their admiration for the clink of teaspoons and the accents of the curate.'[67] He portrays his own artistic aesthetic as a 'romantic' antidote to this trend. Stevenson defines his own style of writing by differentiating between writing that focuses on the moral dilemmas of everyday life and Romantic writing where characters must weather and adapt to events that happen to them. For him the superiority of Romantic writing lies in its ability to tap into the desires and fantasies of the reader. He argues:

> The great creative writer shows us the realisation and the apotheosis of the day-dreams of common men. His stories may be nourished with the realities of life, but their true mark is to satisfy the nameless longings of the reader, and to obey the ideal laws of the day-dream.[68]

Romance, then, is an aesthetic that resists the prosaicness of contemporary realism just as Wilson offers the 'antidote' to 'contemporary cant' in Stevenson's review. Emotional engagement is central to Stevenson's vision of the Romantic. Tapping into 'nameless longings', the Romantic text is not the 'clever'[69] plotless novel of manners but the text where 'situation is animated with passion, and passion clothed upon with situation'.[70] Just as identification with the protagonist animates the tale of terror, for Stevenson romance is 'when the reader consciously plays at being the hero'.[71]

'The Body Snatcher' uses terror to inspire intense identification in the reader. While the early use of framing might seem to distance the reader from Fettes, the protagonist, the presence of the mediating narrator is increasingly submerged as the tale develops until the reader feels an immediate connection with Fettes' emotions and sensations. Any sense of distance slowly disintegrates until the reader and the frightened student are one. In the tense moments before the body is transformed, individualised physical sensation places the reader within his body: 'A nameless dread was swathed, like a wet sheet, about the body, and tightened the white skin upon the face of Fettes; a fear that was meaningless, a horror of what could not be, kept mounting to his brain.'[72] There is a doubled sense of identification in this passage. Even as the reader is trapped within the consciousness of Fettes, Fettes's sensations are tied to those of the body. He feels a dread that swathes his body 'like a wet sheet' – a metaphor that mirrors the real 'flapping' 'dripping' sack that covers the stolen cadaver and that has repeatedly touched and troubled the body snatchers.[73]

Although, like Warren's physician, Fettes is revisiting experiences from his youth with the distance of age, the latter part of the story is not mediated by this mature perspective. The story does not offer the sense of comforting resolution of the earlier body-snatching tales, closing amid the action as:

> a wild yell rang up into the night; each leaped from his own side into the roadway: the lamp fell, broke, and was extinguished; and the horse, terrified by this unusual commotion, bounded and went off toward Edinburgh at a gallop, bearing along with it, sole occupant of the gig, the body of the dead and long-dissected Gray.[74]

Over the course of the story the reader has been brought ever closer to Fettes, but at this point their perspectives diverge. Rather than following Fettes along the path that will bring him to safe entombment in a Debenham inn, these final scenes focalise the now unburied and careening corpse. Stevenson's tale journeys across genres, transporting the reader from the safety of the kirkyard to the intense emotional extremity of the terror tale without offering a route back.

Stevenson's use of kirkyard figures and themes in 'The Body Snatcher' and his employment of the intense emotional immediacy of the tale of terror suggests the possibility of a continuous tradition of resistant Romanticism in Scottish writing. As Shaw has noted Stevenson was part of a 'loose, vibrant group' of authors who participated in the Scottish 'Romance Revival' of the turn of the century but he has rarely been considered in this context.[75] The recognition of the influence of the kirkyard in his work might open new ways to place Stevenson within this wider Scottish Romantic tradition.

Notes

1. Moir 'Wonderful Passage in the Life of Mansie Wauch, Tailor', p. 456.
2. Ibid., p. 456.
3. Christie, '"Where Personation Ends and Imposture Begins"', p. 177.
4. Lockhart, 'Remarks on Schlegel's History of Literature', p. 500; Lincoln, *Walter Scott and Modernity*, p. 25.
5. A group of texts which Marshall defines as 'essentially the literature that concerns the social ideologies which triumphed in 1832, the year of the Great Reform Bill' and traces back from this date to the latter half of the eighteenth century. Marshall, *Murdering to Dissect*, p. 14.
6. Douglas, *The 'Blackwood' Group*, p. 106.
7. Douglas, *The 'Blackwood' Group*, p. 107. Henderson, 'Introduction', in Moir, *The Life of Mansie Wauch, Tailor*, p. x.
8. Coyer, *Literature and Medicine in the Nineteenth-Century Periodical*, pp. 94–5.

9. Ibid., p. 115.
10. The 1752 Murder Act states that 'in no Case whatsoever the Body of any Murderer shall be suffered to be buried'. See Richardson, *Death, Dissection and the Destitute*, p. 37.
11. It is important to note here that, although terms like 'grave robbing' were commonly employed, corpses were not classed as property as so could not legally be stolen. See Sappol, *A Traffic in Dead Bodies*, p. 20.
12. MacDonald quotes the surgeon George Guthrie expressing his horror at the idea of dissecting a body which had been 'a beloved mother, wife or sister', while Richardson highlights that the renowned anatomist and surgeon Astley Cooper was buried in a stone sarcophagus and multiple inner coffins to avoid being exhumed. MacDonald, *Possessing the Dead*, p. 9; Richardson, '"Trading Assassins" and the Licensing of Anatomy', p. 82.
13. McCracken-Flesher, *The Doctor Dissected*, p. 11.
14. Richardson, '"Trading Assassins" and the Licensing of Anatomy', p. 92.
15. Sappol, *A Traffic in Dead Bodies*, p. 17.
16. Richardson, *Death, Dissection and the Destitute*, p. 7.
17. *Resurrection*.
18. 'Noctes Ambrosianae', *Blackwood's Edinburgh Magazine*, 25 (March 1829), p. 387.
19. Ibid., p. 389.
20. Bates, *The Anatomy of Robert Knox*, p. 163.
21. Marshall, *Murdering to Dissect*, p. 13.
22. Kolhke, 'The Neo-Victorian Doctor and Resurrected Gothic Masculinities', p. 123.
23. Smith, *The Theory of Moral Sentiments*, p. 30.
24. Crawford, 'A Scientific Profession', p. 219.
25. Kennedy, 'The Ghost in the Clinic', pp. 333, 342.
26. Walter Scott studied law at the University of Edinburgh and qualified as a lawyer in 1792. During his career he practised as an advocate for a period and served as Sheriff-Depute of Selkirkshire and Principal Clerk of the Court Session. His treatise for admission into the Faculty of Advocates in 1792 focused on the legal status of the bodies of criminals showing a marked interest in the issues that animated the anatomy debates. See McCracken-Flesher, *The Doctor Dissected*, p. 54.
27. Ibid., p. 43.
28. Moir, 'From the Autobiography of Mansie Wauch, Tailor', p. 41.
29. Moir is generally referred to in the magazine by his pseudonym 'Delta' and marked his submissions to *Blackwood's* with the Greek letter in place of his name.
30. Coyer, *Literature and Medicine*, p. 103.
31. Moir, 'Wonderful Passage in the Life of Mansie Wauch, Tailor', p. 456.
32. See Morrison and Baldick, 'Introduction', in *Tales of Terror from Blackwood's Edinburgh Magazine*, pp. vii–xviii; Sucksmith, 'The Secret of Immediacy', pp. 145–57.
33. Morrison and Baldick, 'Introduction', p. xiv.
34. Shapira, *Inventing the Gothic Corpse*, p. 222.
35. Killick, *British Short Fiction in the Early Nineteenth Century*, p. 170.

36. For curious case studies, see Coyer, *Literature and Medicine*, p. 42; Killick, *British Short Fiction in the Early Nineteenth Century*, p. 168.
37. Coyer, *Literature and Medicine*, p. 173.
38. I discuss this strategy in greater depth in Sharp, 'A Club of "murder-fanciers"'.
39. Coyer, *Literature and Medicine*, p. 48.
40. Galt, 'The Buried Alive', pp. 262–4.
41. In 1821 the story is included in the magazine as a standalone tale but it would be later republished as part of *The Steamboat* when that series was collected as a book in 1822.
42. Galt, 'The Buried Alive', p. 262.
43. Mangham, 'Buried Alive', p. 10.
44. Smith, *The Theory of Moral Sentiments*, p. 13.
45. Galt, 'The Buried Alive', p. 263.
46. Ibid., p. 263.
47. Dunlop, 'Warren, Samuel'.
48. Morrison and Baldick, 'Introduction', in *Tales of Terror from Blackwood's Edinburgh Magazine*, pp. vii–xviii; Coyer, *Literature and Medicine*, p. 124.
49. Warren, 'Passages from the Diary of a Late Physician – Chap X – A Slight Cold, Rich and Poor and Gravedoings', p. 960.
50. Ibid., p. 960.
51. Shapira, *Inventing the Gothic Corpse*, pp. 223–4.
52. Warren, 'Passages from the Diary of a Late Physician – Chap X – A Slight Cold, Rich and Poor and Gravedoings', p. 960.
53. Ibid., p. 967.
54. Ibid., p. 960.
55. 'Burking' was a contemporary term used to describe the act of murdering for dissection.
56. Kennedy, 'The Ghost in the Clinic', p. 330.
57. In his entry on Warren for the *Oxford Dictionary of National Biography*, C. R. B. Dunlop quotes Warren's characterisation of the 'Passages' as moral tales: 'He later described his views and feelings in writing the book as "those not of a Novelist, but of a Moralist" whose "steady purpose … was to exhibit deathbeds".' As I discuss in Chapter 1 and in my previous work, this is also one of the models on which Wilson's short fiction is based. See Sharp, 'A Death in the Cottage'.
58. Stevenson, 'The Body Snatcher'.
59. This frame is set probably sometime between 1870 and 1880 based on the ages of the two men.
60. Stevenson, 'The Body Snatcher', p. 67.
61. Ibid., p. 68.
62. Ibid., p. 80.
63. Glencorse's name itself contains an archaic form of the word for a dead body making it literally 'valley of the corpse'.
64. The 'Terrible Letters' are discussed in Chapter 4 of this book.
65. Stevenson, 'Review: The Noctes Ambrosianae: The Comedy of the Noctes Ambrosianae', p. 231.
66. McIlvanney, 'Mohowks: Review – The House of Blackwood: Author–Publisher Relations in the Victorian Era by David Finkelstein', p. 7.
67. Stevenson, 'A Gossip on Romance', p. 57.

68. Ibid., p. 56.
69. Ibid., p. 57.
70. Ibid., p. 58.
71. Ibid., p. 61.
72. Stevenson, 'The Body Snatcher', p. 84.
73. Ibid., p. 83.
74. Ibid., p. 84.
75. Shaw, *The Fin-de-Siècle Scottish Revival*, p. 34.

Chapter 5

'Burking, Bill and Cholera': Death, Mobility and National Epidemic

James Hogg's poem 'One Thousand, Eight Hundred and Thirty One', published in the issue of *Fraser's Magazine* for February 1832, playfully responds to the previous year's events:[1]

> O Eighteen Hundred Thirty-one
> Thou hast been an intolera-
> Ble year for fume, for fudge, and flame,
> For Burking and for Cholera![2]

The poem's use of sing-song metre, enjambement and forced rhyme might seem to make light of the year's travails and this is a reading that Hogg satirically acknowledges, '"Hold, Shepherd! Hold thy impious breath! / It would be most intolera- / Ble thus to laugh at flames and death, / At Burking and at Cholera!"'[3] However, it ties together a series of concerns that would reoccur in public discourse throughout the 1832 cholera epidemic. Hogg characterises 1831 as a year defined by 'Burking, Bill and Cholera!' and presents all three as harbingers of social unrest.[4] The three current issues cross-pollinate in the poem to create the impression of a society struggling with change and internal discord.

The tying of these three issues together in Hogg's poem reflects the connections that were made between grave robbing, reform and epidemic disease in print media during the first British outbreak of cholera. The disease struck Britain during the autumn of 1831 and continued to spread rapidly throughout 1832, killing an estimated 23,000, almost 10,000 of whom were Scottish.[5] It hit the country at a time when Burking hysteria and social tension related to the Great Reform Bill were both raised to the point of fever pitch. The three issues were debated and discussed in newspapers and magazines as 'the apparent volatility of society and its institutions was linked in the press to the mysterious threat of the new illness'.[6]

One of the areas of contemporary life most severely disrupted by the cholera outbreak was the burial of the dead. To stem the disease's progress, public health regulations were put in place that prohibited many traditional mourning practices such as wakes, corpse viewings and funeral processions, and called for the placement of cholera bodies in mass graves away from traditional burial sites and family lairs.[7] Cholera was a new and terrifying disease that encroached on traditional burial practices and sites. Its arrival in the UK, and sudden disruption of interment, in the direct aftermath of the Burke and Hare anatomy murders led to fear and social unrest among the population, at its most extreme precipitating violent anatomy riots.

In the politically charged months leading to the Great Reform Act approaches to cholera were informed not just by contemporary scientific knowledge but also by social ideology. With no universally accepted explanation for its spread, contagious and non-contagious explanations of the disease became tied to different political perspectives. At the heart of this conflict over the nature of a national epidemic, then, was a wider conflict over the nature of society and the nation. British responses to cholera in 1832 are informed by the same questions as the kirkyard texts of the previous decades.

Due to this context, when literary texts intervene in these conversations the dead function as a potent political metaphor. This chapter looks at two responses to the cholera dead published in the periodical press by writers with ties to *Blackwood's*. In James Montgomery's 'Cholera Mount' and James Hogg's 'Terrible Letters from Scotland' we encounter two contrasting responses to cholera and its victims. Both authors use the cholera dead to comment on the state of the nation, articulating contrasting perspectives on social and geographical connection. Where Montgomery promotes a cohesive national relationship between the dead and the living, Hogg situates rural space within conflicting webs of national and international connection and contagion.

The chapter argues that this difference in response expresses contrasting ideas of national community. Montgomery adopts a teleological approach, casting the cholera dead as casualties of, or even sacrifices to, the wider progress of the British nation. Cholera is portrayed as an external aggressor that the British have collectively fought and repelled. The dead are the casualties of this struggle around whose memory the national community can rally. Hogg's tales, written in the early months of the outbreak, are less willing to read the disease in this way. Their invocation of the kirkyard archetype resists any totalising narrative of national progress by mapping the impact of the epidemic onto regional space.

At the same time, Hogg's tales complicate the 'local associations and traditional ties' that Anthony Jarrells has identified as central to *Blackwood's* regional fiction.[8] The good peasants of John Wilson's villages are socially and geographically static; their lack of physical mobility is tied implicitly to a lack of social mobility. Buried in the kirkyard with their ancestors, they ensure the continued stability of British society. Cholera, a disease whose transmission could be traced across the British world in real time, has the potential to disrupt this allegiance and reveal the manifold connections that characterise an increasingly mobile and globalised society. Through the unquiet graves of cholera victims Hogg articulates a disquiet about the complexity and instability of modern social relations.

The chapter's coda then turns to a later account of epidemic disease and Scottish rural life. John Buchan's novel *Witch Wood* (1927) describes the coming of plague to the already conflict-riven Borders community of Woodilee in 1644. The novel speaks to and subverts the *Blackwood's* tradition of writing about Scottish parochial life. Like Hogg a hundred years earlier, Buchan uses plague to articulate the relationship between insider and outsider, stasis and change; but where Hogg's stories identify mobility as a source of dangerous infection, Buchan casts the stagnant kirkyard parish as the site where sickness festers.

Contagion, Conservativism and the Colonies

One of the defining features of the kirkyard archetype in Wilson's work was its rejection of the increasing mobility of the British population in favour of an image of geographical stasis. Despite the increasing importance of urbanisation and colonisation in early nineteenth-century Scottish life, the village kirkyard in the texts is often one whose inhabitants have lived within the surrounding parish all their lives. In Wilson's *Lights and Shadows* tale 'The Elder's Funeral' local ties are privileged over those that extended across global space:

> To those who mix in the strife and dangers of the world, the place is felt to be uncertain wherein they may finally rest. The soldier – the sailor – the traveller, can only see some dim grave dug for him, when he dies in some place obscure-nameless-and unfixed to the imagination. All he feels is that burial will be – on earth – or in the sea. But the peaceful dwellers who cultivate their paternal acres, or tilling at least the same small spot of soil, shift only from a cottage on the hillside to one on the plain, still within the bounds of one quiet parish, – they look to lay their bones at last in the burial-place of the kirk in which they were baptised, and with them it almost literally is a step from the cradle to the grave.[9]

In this passage the kirkyard is immutable; a form of immortality is guaranteed by the unchanging nature of local life. This characterisation of the rural graveyard as a repository of memory and tradition is typical of the graveyards we encounter in Wilson's writing. The wandering soldier, sailor or traveller cannot be incorporated into the kirkyard; their mobility banishes them from the static community of the dead, while the local cottager moving between cottages on the 'hillside' and 'plain' becomes part of the kirkyard and of local history. Wilson's commitment to continuity means that his idealised kirkyard cannot contain Britain's increasing army of colonial servants, military personnel and traders.

In his work on the representation of the British colonies in *Blackwood's*, Anthony Jarrells has argued that Blackwoodian engagements with colonial space in the early issues of the magazine are designed to counter 'the liberal line on empire' that was 'reformist, universalist, and grounded in the stadial theory of Scottish Enlightenment political economy'.[10] He argues that *Blackwood's* writers employed similar representative techniques to those used in its regional fiction when engaging with colonial locations, often focusing on the specific regional features of 'so-called settler colonies (such as Upper Canada) and ... India'.[11] Just as in the magazine's Scottish fiction, this approach counteracts narratives of 'reform' and improvement by re-emphasising the importance of tradition, heritage and kinship: 'the provincial strain that finds its way into many of the magazine's foreign policy pieces can be understood as part of a more general distrust of liberal politics.'[12]

Wilson's colonial servant-free kirkyard and *Blackwood's* counter-Whig approach to empire are both important contexts for Hogg's and Montgomery's texts because of cholera's strong associations with Britain's colonial territories in the East. The outbreak that reached Britain in 1831 was thought to have started in Jessore in the Ganges Delta and travelled to Britain across Asia and Europe.[13] The disease quickly acquired the moniker 'Indian' or 'Asiatic' cholera to differentiate the epidemic from a milder native infection referred to as 'English cholera' or 'cholera morbus', although these names are sometimes confused in articles not written by medical men. Cholera was thus widely recognised as a disease that had issued from Britain's colonies in India and that had been conveyed back to Britain from these territories. As Alan Bewell describes it, 'an imperial age produced an imperial disease'.[14] Cholera was often imagined as a dangerous, foreign agent that had invaded Britain; Thomas Siek refers to a contemporary British caricature that depicts John Bull grappling with the figure of King Cholera wearing a turban.[15] This concept of a colonial attack on the centre of empire was profoundly disturbing; it suggested that, just as wealth could pass back into Britain from her colonies, so too could foreign disease. This conclusion could have far-reaching implications for the commerce and conquest that Britain increasingly depended on, and consequently the Whig commitment to international trade.

The route that the disease had taken to the British Isles was well documented in contemporary coverage of the disease. Prior to the first confirmed reports of cholera in the United Kingdom, its movement across Europe from India had been charted in the British press, and once the disease arrived in Britain many medical practitioners sought to retrospectively sketch the route the disease had taken. These reports often charted the role that traders and the military had in propagating the infection.[16] Cholera was a disease that could be clearly mapped onto Britain's global mercantile and military projects. Bewell describes the symbolic impact of this connectivity:

> spread along the main transportation and commercial arteries of the nineteenth century – by river, sea, road, and later by railway – cholera mapped the many lines of communication between Britain and its colonial possessions. Its spread thus demarcated the reach of empire, demonstrating that there were no longer any boundaries.[17]

Cholera could be understood as a global epidemic propagated by Britain's global aspirations; the hypermobility of goods and troops between regions allowed the disease to easily travel from location to location.

Cholera swept towards Britain with plague-like unpredictability: it 'killed swiftly and randomly', apparently unaffected by the wealth or status of its victims.[18] The disease therefore gained more attention in the press and periodicals than other diseases that would prove to be far more deadly in terms of annual death toll. Reports on the approach of cholera often focused on the disease's potential to spread throughout the social body. In May 1831 *The Englishman's Magazine* reports: 'cholera is capricious in the selection of its victims. The infirm and debilitated are its favourite subjects. Yet the best health will not ensure exemption.'[19] Unlike diseases of the poor such as typhus, cholera appeared to have the potential to transcend barriers of rank and class; in those first tense months it was felt that no one was safe from this plague. Once it had infiltrated the national body it had the potential to circulate and infect all of its parts. Cholera could be understood as a crisis that revealed the porous, undifferentiated nature of the modern nation. Just as the disease could reveal the dangers of unrestrained movement between different colonial locations, it could also be used to indicate a lack of social boundaries at home.

Official and public dread were heightened by the fact that doctors were unable to come to a consensus on how the disease spread. Medics were divided between those who believed the disease was contagious, and anticontagionists who argued that it originated in miasmas caused by rotting waste. A report from *The Eclectic Review* of March 1831 laments, 'we are too much in the dark ourselves, to undertake the business of enlightening others', and urges that 'no time ought to be lost in ascertaining the precise nature of the disease, and in settling the proper mode of treatment'.[20] The possibility of a catastrophic plague-like epidemic seemed a terrifying prospect for the British medical men and government officials who watched cholera's unpredictable advance towards Britain's shores but they also feared raising levels of alarm in a country whose economy relied heavily on imports and exports. The contest between contagionist and anticontagionist views of the disease was tied to political interests.[21] A contagious epidemic would mean the need for limits on the movement of people and goods. These measures were highly unpopular with anyone with ties to trade. As Edwin H. Ackerknecht has argued: 'quarantines meant to the rapidly growing class of merchants and industrialists a source of losses, a limitation of expansion.'[22] A contagionist approach was tied to what Ackerknecht terms 'old bureaucratic power' while more liberal commentators favoured explanations that would allow trade and movement between locations within and beyond Britain to continue.[23] Laura Otis summarises the political motivations behind the two perspectives on disease:

> Anticontagionist reformers, largely liberals and radicals, fought for scientific, commercial, and individual freedom simultaneously, regarding the three as inseparable. While the middle class stood to benefit from free trade, the landed gentry and other traditionalists had nothing to fear from embargoes that favoured national interests. Contagionism consequently attracted conservatives, officers and bureaucrats who thought that centralised power structures, not individual citizens or local authorities, should control policies affecting public health.[24]

Conceptions of the infection were therefore tied into the political tensions that dogged British society in the early 1830s. The decision to quarantine or impose sanitary regulations was tied not just to scientific research but to perceptions of society.

An article entitled 'To the Future Electors of Great Britain', published in *Blackwood's Edinburgh Magazine* in August 1832 and attributed to the staunchly Tory advocate and historian Archibald Alison, illustrates how politics and attitudes to the disease could interact within the magazine's pages.[25] In this article Alison links the new cholera legislation's restrictions on burial to a Radical desire to challenge established religion:

the whole Radical party in Parliament voted against any recognition of the Supreme Being, in the act relating to the cholera. If, therefore, the electors of Great Britain wish to destroy the faith and religion of their fathers – if they would see Sunday abolished, churches closed, the dead buried without a blessing ... they have nothing to do but support the Revolutionary candidates at the next election. [26]

The limits placed on traditional burial by legislators are portrayed as challenges to key bastions of the Tory nation: established religion and patriarchal inheritance ('the faith and religion of their fathers'). Alison overtly connects burial rites with *Blackwood's* vision of the godly nation and casts the passing of legislation that disrupts them as an attack on this archetype.

However, it is important to note that Alison perspective on burial regulation is not indicative of an overarching anticontagionist position within the magazine. Megan Coyer has highlighted the very vocal contagionism of key medical contributors D. M. Moir and Robert Macnish.[27] Jessica Roberts notes that in its employment of political metaphor *Blackwood's* uses images of both contagion and poison.[28] What Alison's comment on cholera does indicate, though, is how tightly intertwined the medical and the political were in 1832 and the way that burial could become a lightning rod for these issues.

James Montgomery and Monumentalising 'The Cholera Mount'

In the early verses of his elegy for the cholera dead in the November 1832 issue of *Blackwood's*, the Ayrshire-born poet and hymn writer James Montgomery characterises the movement of the disease from India across Europe in the preceding year as the march of a marauding army:

> Far east its race begun,
> Thence around the world pursued by the westering sun;
> The ghosts of millions following at its back
> Whose desecrated graves betray'd their track;
> On Albion shore, unseen, the invader stept;
> Secret, and swift, and terrible it crept.[29]

For Montgomery, cholera desecrates the grave by banishing cholera victims from established religious graveyards and consigning them to burial sites that Tim Marshall has described as 'isolated mass graves'.[30] Cholera is represented as a foreign invader disrupting community customs and traditions. The cholera victims are removed from the society they inhabited in life and forced to become part of a new form of 'sad community' characterised by fragmentation and the breaking of social ties:

> In death divided from their dearest kin,
> This is 'a field to bury strangers in;'
> Fragments lie here of families bereft,
> Like limbs in battle-grounds by warriors left;
> A sad community![31]

In these early lines, the cholera victim is removed from their previous position within their community and made a 'stranger' through their body's invasion by the disease. This sense of the breaking down of social relations continues throughout the main body of the poem as Montgomery focuses on the traumatic fracturing of domestic relations – 'many a home of them left desolate; / Once warm with love, and radiant with the smiles / Of woman, watching infants at their wiles' – and of ancestral lineage – 'when they knock'd for entrance at the tomb, / Their fathers' bones refused to make them room'.[32]

However, Montgomery's earlier references to battle-fragmented bodies and invasion create a precedent for the themes that are introduced in the final verses of the elegy. The poet reconstructs the cholera pit as a form of national war memorial, reappropriating the banished bodies of the dead by placing them within a culture of national remembrance. The mothering body of Britain in the form of Nature claims the dead as part of a national family unit:

> 'Live!' to the slain she cried: 'My children, live!
> This for an heritage to you I give;
> Had Death consumed you by common lot,
> Ye, with the multitude, had been forgot;
> Now through an age of ages ye shall *not*.'[33]

The last stanza presents the resting place of the dead as a memento mori within the eternal pastoral landscape of rural Britain. Rather than being lost, the memory of the cholera sufferers becomes a shared heritage for future communities, functioning as a message to 'generations long to come'.[34] Their influence extends beyond the familial and local ties they enjoyed in life and becomes one that creates national and human ties of fellowship.

This call for unity is particularly interesting when viewed alongside the account of the poet's political affiliations in his biography. Although politically radical in his early life (he was imprisoned twice for publishing inflammatory political material in the later decades of the eighteenth century), by the time Montgomery wrote 'The Cholera Mount' it appears that he had adopted a more conservative worldview.[35] Although he remained concerned with the fate of the poor in Sheffield and was heavily involved in the foundation of a wide range of charitable schemes, particularly those related to religious and literary education, Montgomery was increasingly disassociated from calls for large-scale political reform. As his biographer J. W. King commented: 'he had seen the passing of the Reform Bill without any radical emotions in favour of the one step in advance towards that freedom for which he wrought so hard in his youth.'[36] Montgomery's approach to the world around him and the inequality endemic within Sheffield at this time appears to have had more in common with the liberal perspectives of contemporary Evangelical sanitarians such as Edwin Chadwick, with their focus on personal morality and charity, than the radicals and Chartists who advocated large-scale social change.[37]

The *Noctes Ambrosianae* in the December 1825 issue of *Blackwood's* includes a brief discussion of Montgomery's retirement from *The Isis*, the Sheffield newspaper he had edited since 1794. The Ettrick Shepherd and Christopher North, two recurring characters in the series, debate whether Montgomery's retirement speech was overly long-winded for the editor of a provincial newspaper before raising a toast to him. They then turn their attention to Montgomery's politics. The Shepherd proposes a toast to Montgomery's politics but is challenged by North:

> North – James, do you know what you're saying? The man is a Whig. If we do drink his politics, let it be in empty glasses.
> Shepherd – Na, na. I'll drink no man's health, nor yet ony ither thing, out o' an empty glass … James Montgomery is, I verily believe, a true patriot. Gin he thinks himself a Whig, he has nae understanding whatever o' his ain character. I'll undertake to bring out the Toryism that's in him in the course o' a single *Noctes*. Toryism is an innate principle o' human nature – Whiggism but an evil habit.[38]

This exchange highlights Montgomery's public reputation as a Whig in the early nineteenth century but also *Blackwood's* continued efforts to champion the poet despite his political allegiances. This slightly paradoxical situation could be attributed to the controversy that had surrounded the publication of Montgomery's early poem *The Wanderer of Switzerland* in 1806. The *Edinburgh Review* had published such a brutal review of Montgomery's poem that it is mentioned in Byron's attack on the *Review* in 'English Bards and Scotch Reviewers' (1809). Thus, in taking Montgomery under its wing, *Blackwood's* differentiated itself from arch-rival Constable's *Edinburgh Review*. The position of

Montgomery in the Edinburgh periodical wars of the early century is evinced in an 1831 *Blackwood's* article, 'An Hour's Talk about Poetry', where Wilson makes the difference between the two magazines' positions on the poet explicit: 'It was said by *the Edinburgh Review* that none but maudlin milliners and sentimental ensigns supposed that James Montgomery was a poet. Then is *Maga* a maudlin milliner – and Christopher North a sentimental ensign.'[39] Montgomery was by 1832 an avowedly Whig poet with a strong association with the still-militantly Tory *Blackwood's Edinburgh Magazine*.

'The Cholera Mount' functions as a call for social cohesion as an alternative to social change. As in a war, Montgomery envisions the 'invasion' of cholera as an opportunity for national unity across regions and class divides. Although it engages with domestic paradigms, 'The Cholera Mount' rejects Blackwoodian localism in favour of a more obviously national and universalised role for the dead, and this allows Montgomery to side-step contagionism and colonialism. In Montgomery's poem cholera is not carried to Britain by irresponsible traders; it is an anthropomorphised invader approaching British shores through its own volition. Nor is the cholera pit representative of the crumbling of established religion. Instead, Montgomery presents the cholera pit as everyone's monument. The mass grave does not express the individual identities of the deceased to their community; rather, it functions as a marker of identity for the civic or national community. Cholera is cast as an external aggressor and the cholera victim as the community's own martyr. In Montgomery's elegy the identity of the individual cholera victim is subsumed by the larger cohesive function that their deaths are seen to serve within society. The poet avoids issues of local and colonial space, or British economic inequality, by characterising cholera as a battle between nation and disease that the nation has resoundingly won.

Cholera Humbug

However, issues of social inequality were central to many popular responses to the disease. The mass graves of cholera victims could also function not as nationally unifying monuments, or radical attacks on established faith, but as symbols of a deep-rooted social antagonism. When the Privy Council introduced the quarantine and burial regulations, these regulations were perceived by the sections of the population most directly affected, the poor and emerging working classes, to be attacks on their freedoms and civil liberties, invasions of their domestic lives by burking doctors. Cholera was perceived by many not as a foreign invader but as an attack on the poor that issued from within the nation's boundaries.

This antagonism was expressed in a conspiracy theory propagated in radical newspapers and pamphlets. A series of beliefs that R. J. Morris refers to as 'cholera humbug' had strong currency among radical factions during the early months of the outbreak, and this set of beliefs became widespread among the poor and the working classes in many areas of Britain.[40] Within the context of an already heightened political climate, and with anxieties regarding the medical profession at a particularly high level following the West Port murders, a theory emerged that cholera was an 'anti-reform measure' designed to distract the poor and working classes from political agitation, co-opt their bodies for dissection and medical science, and thus reduce population excess.[41]

This belief had its roots in a variety of additional cultural factors. Although Malthus's *Essay on the Principles of Population* had been published in 1798,[42] discussion of its content was particularly widespread in the years leading up to the revision of the English Poor Law Act in 1834, and during the debates about the efficacy of the Scottish system of Poor Relief of the 1830s and 1840s.[43] Proponents of the new, stricter Poor Law in England and supporters of the old Church-based system of assessed aid in Scotland cited the essay as evidence that supporting the destitute led to the unchecked growth of population and used this to support their policies. The raised profile of Malthusian logic alongside suspicion of the 1831 census proved a potent combination.[44] Radical publications proposed that there was no cholera; it was just an elaborate tool of social coercion, an artificially created Malthusian 'positive check'. Gilbert describes how widespread these suspicions were:

> the readings that we can recapture from personal histories, broadsheets, radical newspapers, and so forth, suggest that many among the working-classes saw the cholera in terms of negative social control, providing an opportunity for the upper-classes to seize working-class rights, voices and even bodies.[45]

These fears led to sometimes violent resistance against the removal of cholera victims to hospitals and burial places, and a series of riots across the country in the early months of the epidemic, including an infamous day of unrest in Paisley in March 1832 that was widely reported in the British press.[46] Montgomery's retrospective identification of cholera as an event that unified the nation followed a year in which the disease had highlighted and widened social divisions in Britain.

'When Fire Is Set to the Mountain': James Hogg's 'Terrible Letters' and Treating the Social Body

When James Hogg published his own cholera stories, at the height of the outbreak in April 1832, his approach to the social legacy of the cholera victims was considerably more ambivalent than Montgomery's would be a few months later. In the immediate aftermath of the riots in Paisley, James Hogg published a collection of three short fictional accounts of cholera 'Some Terrible Letters from Scotland' in the April 1832 issue of *The Metropolitan Magazine*.[47] Written and submitted to the London journal during Hogg's time in the city, the stories are unusual and mischievous in their Gothic representation of a disease that was only beginning to be reported in London. Joan McCausland has suggested that Hogg's stories are likely to be based on the sensational reports of the epidemic in Scotland that were appearing in the London papers at the time, sparked by events like the riots at Paisley and the high death tolls in the small towns of East Lothian.[48] The stories draw on the conflicting accounts of the disease current in the press at the time to create a text that ambiguously combines competing registers of Gothic horror and dark humour. Each letter appears to be the first-person account of a witness who wishes to publish the 'truth' about the epidemic. However, the increasingly obvious presence of vested interest, misunderstanding and supernatural explanation in their accounts challenges the reader's assumption of objective truth, complicating the experience of reading a first-hand account.

Although published in the libertarian and reform-minded *Metropolitan*, Hogg's cholera tales remain committed to exploring the relationship between the contemporary world and rural Scotland that characterised kirkyard writing.[49] Hogg's letters each describe contact between cholera and a Scottish provincial space. In two of the tales the dead rise. In the first, a man sits up in his coffin and flails grotesquely, his shroud obscuring his face, and a mother and daughter are possibly buried alive. In another, two ghostly women rise from their grave to take their mother to the tomb with them in vengeance. These rising corpses reference the horrifying upright corpse figure that both John Barrell[50] and Ian Duncan[51] have identified as a central feature within Hogg's writing. However, in this text the uncertain status and position of the dead is tied to the uncertainty of social borders. Hogg's rural spaces are rendered permeable in the 'Terrible Letters' as goods and diseases move between locations, challenging the immutable, inward-looking pastoral of the kirkyard. Tracing how corpses move in and out of graves in Hogg's stories, and exploring how these displaced bodies are tied into wider webs of exchange and commercial connection, reveals a British nation where trade and mobility tie populations together with potentially deadly consequences.

The stories never overtly discuss the fears that had sparked the riots in Paisley, yet, particularly in the first and third letters, Hogg constantly brings together the ideas of cholera and resurrection. The stories play with these themes from so many perspectives that body snatching appears conspicuously absent. The first narrator, Andrew Ker, introduces himself to the letter's recipient through reference to the West Port murders: 'I have wrought on your farm for some months with William Collins that summer that Burke was hanged.'[52] Having introduced the narrator through the events of the West Port murders, the author disappoints reader expectation by presenting us with a story where, instead of the dead being exhumed, murdered or dissected, the living are prepared for burial. Reminiscent of John Galt's classic tale of terror 'The Buried Alive', the letter describes the Gothic experience of Ker, a carter who appears to die from cholera only to sit up in his coffin wrapped in his winding sheet. The protagonist, Ker, believes himself to have died from cholera but retains consciousness even though he cannot move or speak: 'all the while I had a sort of half-consciousness of what was going on, yet had not the power to move a muscle of my whole frame.'[53] McCausland suggests that the story may be a fictional response to published reports that during the January of 1832 a man suffering from cholera had been buried alive in Haddington.[54]

Lines between life and death are also blurred in the third story. The protagonist James McL—awakes from a dream in which his mother is spirited away by his reanimated sisters. He sets out to visit the graves of his apparently risen sisters in a scene that also echoes the language used to describe the resurrection of Christ in Mark 16:

> I said nothing of what I had seen; but went straight to the churchyard, persuaded that I would find my sisters' graves open, and they out of them; but, behold! they were the same as I left them, and I have never seen mother and sisters more. I could almost have persuaded myself that I had been in a dream, had it not been for the loss of my mother; but as she has not been seen or heard of since that night, I must believe all that I saw to have been real. I know it is suspected both here and in Edinburgh that she has been burked, as she was always running about by night; but I know what I saw, and must believe in it though I cannot comprehend it.[55]

The ghostly presence of the anatomy murderer is once again invoked, in a way which means that the letters are bookended by apparently casual references to him. These strange stories, full of opened graves and rising bodies, seem designed to gesture to the fears of the choleraphobic masses. Although no bodies are overtly resurrected or murdered, the resurrection men and the Burkers lurk at the edges of the accounts, casting long unexplained shadows.

The uncertain borders between life and death are mirrored in the porous borders between different places and groups of people in the stories. In each letter the connections between people and geographical locations function as channels for the spread of disease: in the first letter, Ker, a cart driver, fatally brings cholera into the home of his sweetheart; in the second, a dog escapes a trading ship docked in an isolated Highland village; and in the third it is the mother's self-interested visits to the deathbeds of her neighbours that bring the infection of her own family. Hogg's fascination with movement and connectivity within the 'Letters' is part of the contemporary conversation about contagion, capital and nation that saw contagionist and anticontagionist perspectives clash along scientific and economic lines. In his 'Letters' Hogg seems committed to mapping a contagious outbreak onto rural Scotland. The spread of cholera allows Hogg to trace the social and economic connections that tie the different parts of society in a mutually fatal embrace.

At the opening of the first letter Ker fears for his own safety should he become infected with the disease: 'I often thought to myself, if I should take that terrible Cholera Morbus, what was to become of me, as I had no home to go to, and nobody would let me within their door.'[56] A travelling cart driver, without family or friends, Ker's profession both displaces him and allows him to circulate without regulation. He has no place within society. Instead, he is constantly in motion communicating and making connections between different people and locations. Later in the tale, following his miraculous resurrection, Ker comments upon the dangers of complacency in the face of the disease:

> it is amazing that the people of London should mock at the fears of their brethren for this terrible and anomalous plague; for though it begins with the hues and horrors of death, it is far more frightful than death itself; and it is impossible for any family or community to be too much on their guard against its baleful influence.[57]

These words function as both warning and threat. If Ker the cart man represents the possibility of circulation and communication, then his escape from East Lothian to the Borders in the guise of a shepherd suggests the possibility that the disease could also travel invisibly from one site to another. An invisible enemy can circulate within the nation. The Londoners who dismiss the disease from afar have forgotten the ties of national kinship and trade that bond them to the afflicted Scots.

The interdependency of different groups within the British population is perhaps most suggestively articulated in Hogg's second letter, which contains a darkly farcical account of a captain's dog's escape from a cholera-afflicted ship into a Highland village. The story is largely about miscommunication and misunderstanding; the Gaelic-speaking villagers have heard of the 'Collara Mor' but have not understood what it is.[58] They therefore interpret the dog as a physical embodiment of the cholera and flee the village when they see the black dog approaching. The Highlanders are as foreign to the story's narrator, a ship's mate, as any colonial people. He takes a jarringly light-hearted approach to the narrative, depicting the villagers as simple-minded and credulous peasants whose speech is almost unintelligible: he quotes the local explanation that the deadly illness was a result of having 'peen raiter, and te raiter too heafy on te herring and pot-hato'.[59]

The sailors may not be able to communicate effectively with the Highlanders but they are capable of communicating infection. The trading ship expressly disregards quarantine regulations by docking in the Highland village when the sailor 'cannot aver that ... [the] ship was perfectly clean'.[60] The sailor takes an ambiguous position in relation to his own personal responsibility for the outbreak suggesting that the transference of the disease might not be the result of contagion: 'whether the disease was communicated to them by the dog, by myself, by the fright or the heat they got in running I cannot determine; but it is certain the place suffered severely.'[61] However, given the pattern of cholera transmission across the three letters these alternative explanations have little power. Cholera, this text suggests, reaches the Highlands through the irresponsibility of British profiteering and free trade and from there is carried into the rest of the population. Although the Highlanders seem isolated and unrelated to the population of Britain, they are vulnerable to infection and capable of infecting others. Like the Irish widow in Thomas Carlyle's *Past and Present* (1843), the Highlanders are an indictment of the individualism of laissez-faire economics.

This representation of the Highlands is typical of Hogg's later writings, which are increasingly interested in the place of the Highlands within the British nation. If lowland country dwellers were cast as direct ancestors in *Blackwood's* kirkyard fiction, Highlanders existed as an Ossianic legend of their ancient origins. David Manderson has characterised the representations of the Highlands within the *Noctes Ambrosianae* as ones that dismiss the contemporary Highlands in favour of fantasy: 'in the world created in the *Noctes* by the new owners of empire ... there was no place for the real Highlands, still less for the people who lived there.'[62] Hogg's first engagement with the Highlands was in his accounts of his *Highland Journeys* of 1802, 1803 and 1804.[63] In the *Journeys* Hogg's lauds the efforts of Highland landlords to effect agricultural improvement through the introduction of large-scale sheep farming, events that are now commonly referred to as the Highland Clearances. However, by the 1820s and 1830s Hogg offered a more critical perspective on the recent history of the region. H. B. de Groot, in his introduction to the *Highland Journeys*, describes the journeys as the first steps towards Hogg's 'powerful account of the destruction of Highland society after the battle of Culloden in *The Three Perils of Woman* in 1823'.[64] By 1832 Hogg was an author with an obvious investment in, not just challenging, limiting notions of lowland Scotland as a repository for national tradition, but also similarly restrictive perspectives on the Highlands. Hogg's second cholera 'Letter', in its critique of the ignorance and irresponsibility of the sailor narrator, and its insistence on the place of Highland villages in the webs of connection that characterise modern Britain, challenges overwhelming contemporary rhetoric that presented the region as one trapped in a previous stage of 'civilisation'. Like much of his lowland writing, it insists on the contemporaneity of rural Scottish life and its problems, refusing both narratives of improvement and the uncritical idealisation of Scottish rural life.

Reinforcing this reading, the relationship between economic exchanges and the circulation of disease is sketched again, this time in miniature, in the third story of the trio. In James McL-'s strange dream, his sisters lead their mother away to the graveyard, and she is never seen again. The revenant sisters claim that she has brought cholera into their home through her morbid delight in visiting and assisting families afflicted with the disease in return for 'drams and little presents'.[65] The narrator also conceives of the mother's exchanges as the carriers of disease: 'ye winna leave aff rinning to infectit houses … Do ye no consider that ye are exposing the whole o' your family to the most terrible of deaths; an' if ye should bring infection among us, an lose us a', how will ye answer to God for it?'[66] The mother's greed makes her willing to visit the sick, and these visits eventually lead her to communicate disease to her own children.

The exploration of social connection across the three letters suggests a wider critique of the impact that international trade and modernisation have on the traditions of rural life. At the close of the first letter Ker struggles to draw a moral conclusion from his experiences, alternating between belief in human autonomy and in fate. His conclusion, while partially based on the idea of an all-powerful Old Testament God, also draws on the ideas of sub-Malthusian social selection that inspired contemporary choleraphobia. Even though it has culled his sweetheart and her mother, he comments of the disease:

> it is as infectious as fire. But when fire is set to the mountain, it is only such parts of its surface as are covered with decaying garbage that is combustible, while over the green and healthy parts of the mountain the flame has no power; and any other reasoning than this is worse than insanity.[67]

Similarly, the narrator of the second letter also conceptualises the disease as an agent of social selection, commenting of the Highlanders killed in the outbreak his ship causes that, 'the glen being greatly overstocked, they were not much missed'.[68] In both instances Hogg's narrators use dehumanising metaphors, reducing the cholera victims to so much 'decaying garbage' or, even more suggestively, to livestock. The 'overstocked' glen within a context of contemporary clearance and enforced emigration in the north and west of Scotland is a highly charged metaphor.[69] Its use alludes to the improvement of the Highland estates where the human population were compared in terms of profitability to sheep. The glen's stock problems and the clearing of areas of brush on the burning mountain both seem apt metaphors for the type of large-scale social engineering that was taking place in late eighteenth- and early nineteenth-century rural Scotland. These images present the largely poor victims of cholera as socially undesirable citizens who will be 'not much missed' and link the disease to processes of improvement. Hogg's 'Terrible Letters' operate as a rebuttal of the concept of a self-regulating capitalist society. They imply that improvers, in their attempts to use free-market forces to engineer an ideal society, create diseases that will eventually infect the entire national body. Motivated by profit they fail to protect their own lower classes, weakening the social body as a whole. The fire does not run out of garbage and die off, but proceeds to consume the green.

Hogg's disturbed cholera graves represent the disturbed social relationships around them. The webs of local, national and international connection that Hogg weaves into the fabric of his three stories create dynamic, complicated and fragmented narratives and rural spaces. The economic and imperial decisions that have brought cholera to Scotland's shores have created a context in which even the dead will not lie still. Cholera operates as a Frankenstein's monster of colonialism and free-market economics. Where Montgomery represents the 'story' of cholera as one shared by a civic and national community, Hogg uses the restless regional graves of the cholera dead to depict an increasingly restless Scotland.

'Air and light': Plague in John Buchan's *Witch Wood* (1927)

The potent symbolism of the plague grave is carried into John Buchan's 1927 historical novel *Witch Wood*. While analysis of the more popular Richard Hannay novels has tended to dominate Buchan's posthumous literary reputation, casting him as the 'father of the twentieth-century spy thriller'[70], he has also increasingly been acknowledged as an inheritor of older Scottish literary traditions. *Witch Wood*, in particular, has been understood as an intervention into a pre-existing 'tradition of Scottish historical and social fiction'.[71] Buchan's contemporaries were alert to the connection. 'For *Witch Wood* specially I am always grateful,' wrote C. S. Lewis: 'all that devilment sprouting up out of a beginning like Galt's *Annals of the Parish*. That's the way to do it.'[72] With its rural setting, focus on kirk, minister and parish, Covenanting historical context, and evocations of the sinister and the supernatural, *Witch Wood* deliberately recalls the Romantic Scottish fictions of Scott, Hogg, Galt and Wilson.

Although the forest and hills play significant roles in the symbolic geography of Buchan's imagined parish, the kirkyard recurs as both location and metaphor. In the early parts of the novel, references to the grave draw upon a vision of death familiar from kirkyard fiction like Wilson's *Lights and Shadows of Scottish Life*. David Sempill's visit to the deathbed of a shepherd's wife, Marion of Greenshiel, invokes the motifs of the good cottar death. The elderly couple at Greenshiel console one another through their poverty. When the husband questions his own survival after Marion's death, Sempill's invocation of God's plan provides ready comfort. The new minister interprets the scene as a parable:

> The young man's heart was full with the scene which he had left. Death was very near to men, jostling them at every corner, whispering in their ear at Kirk and market, creeping between them and their firesides. Soon the shepherd of the Greenshiel would lie beside his wife; in a little, too, his own stout limbs would be a heap of dust.[73]

Similarly, the rites of Marion's burial cement this idealised vision of Scottish rural life and confirm the minister's role in his new community: 'he had an assurance of his vocation. The crowd at the kirkyard, those toil-worn folk whose immortal souls had been given into his charge, moved him to a strong exultation. He saw his duty cleared from all doubts.'[74] Just like the parishioners who throng the kirkyard in *Annals of the Parish*, *Peter's Letters* and *Adam Blair*, the Woodilee mourners function as exemplars of the moral rural community.

However, the atmosphere of Woodilee, and Buchan's employment of the kirkyard trope, changes as Sempill becomes increasingly disillusioned with his new parish. Images that previously confirmed the community's moral righteousness transform into others that indicate its disfunction. Following the revelation of diabolical pagan rituals in the wood, Sempill imagines the village as a revenant: 'Man, there's times when Woodilee seems as quiet and dead as a kirkyard. But there's a mad life in its members, and at certain seasons it finds vent.'[75] Uncanny and unsettled, the seemingly quaint, placid village becomes a site where the past, in the form of pre-Christian folk belief, survives and threatens to resurface. The earlier godly kirkyard vision of the funeral is a mask.[76]

Unlike Hogg's villages, subject to Gothic encroachments of a diseased modernity, Woodilee is made terrible by its very isolation, retrogression and resistance to outward interference. David Daniell's description of the text as a 'tight black vortex' accurately describes a novel in which thick woodland, religious orthodoxy and communal insularity enclose the action.[77] The coming of plague further develops this motif. Following the imposition of quarantine, the already isolated village becomes a 'noisome cage': the dead litter 'byre and stable', they are left entombed in their quarantined houses, and 'staring unshrouded' corpses lie 'in the nettles of the manse loan'.[78] Sempill seeks to break free from this suffocating isolation. Adopting a hygienist approach to the outbreak, he seeks to bring 'air and light' into the homes of the sick, burn infected buildings and bury the dead.[79] Disease here is imagined not as a traveller or invader but as a corruption that brews in the community's own darkness. Like the pagan rituals that have corrupted the residents of Woodilee, the plague germinates in the snug 'shuttered cottages' of the traditional village.

However, as Alan Massie has noted, the novel does not limit its account of events to the third-person narration.[80] Although Buchan's text gives less credence to alternative viewpoints than Hogg's tales, it too invokes the multivocality of tradition and history. *Witch Wood* opens and closes with a fictionalised prologue and epilogue that detail the efforts of the narrator to gather Sempill's story from conflicting sources, and the novel itself is interspersed with reported rumour and gossip. Consequently, festering local malignancy is not the only available source for interpreting the plague's spread; it is not, we learn, the narrative adopted by the people of Woodilee. While the narrator's account links the approach of the disease to the onset of strange weather, in its wake contending contagionist and religious explanations among the villagers blame the already unpopular minister:

> Practical folk said that he had been in Edinburgh in the time of plague, and had brought maybe brought back the seeds of it. The devoted averred that the uncanny weather had followed upon his public sins, and that the east had come close on the heels of the Presbytery's condemnation. Was there not the hand of God in this, a manifest judgement?[81]

Some chapters before these events, Sempill travels to Edinburgh to witness his father's death due to 'the plague in a new form'.[82] The alignment of the villagers' suspicions with the reader's knowledge of this earlier excursion works to undermine the authority of the apparently omniscient third-person narrator. Although we view events largely through his eyes, we are made aware of the possibility that Sempill's schema for understanding both disease and parish may not be reliable.

The final parts of *Witch Wood* narrate the minister's excommunication from the kirk and escape from the village. They also see his story absorbed into the cluster of conflicting local myths and traditions that open and close the novel. Buchan situates these conversations in the kirkyard, as the congregation wait to enter Sempill's former kirk. Seated 'on the flat gravestones' and leaning on the gate, the local people's mingled stories of his downfall begin to form the Romantic, religious and supernatural tales that will eventually constitute the minister's legacy. This brief scene once again evokes scenes in Lockhart's *Adam Blair*, in which the congregation gather in the kirkyard to reminisce and gossip. In both novels, the graveyard is a site that generates enduring, and not always benign, stories.

In contrast, the burial of Sempill's otherworldly beloved, Katrine Yester, in the greenwood represents an escape from the scenarios of toxic enclosure. The Reverend Fordyce notes how Katrine's burial will place her beyond the bounds of community memory:

> 'It is not the way of our Kirk,' he said, 'to consecrated ground for the dead. All earth is hallowed which receives Christian dust. But lest the graves of the departed be forgotten, it has been the custom to gather them together in some spot under the kirk's shadow. In a wild wood among bracken and stones it will be ill to keep mind of a place of sepulchre.'[83]

Katrine's memory is thus reserved only for those who know where she has been laid.

Although its representation of contagion's relation to social connection differs from Hogg's, Buchan's narrative builds on the same system of kirkyard tropes. Hogg and Buchan, almost a hundred years apart, challenge the more comforting conservative mythology of Wilson's cotters and kirkyard in the same symbolic language. As I mentioned in the introduction to this book, Douglas Gifford has described a Scottish Romantic tradition 'with its indigenous themes, patterns and symbolism, and its own deconstructive agenda'.[84] In the article where he makes this point, Gifford argues that Buchan is one of a group of turn-of-the-century Scottish authors who participate in 'the sustained subversion of Scottish historical romanticism'.[85] Reading *Witch Wood* alongside the 'Terrible Letters' and the wider kirkyard group, we can trace a continuous tradition of Romantic intertextuality, subversion and deconstruction. Drawing upon the imagery of previous Scottish writers, Buchan is able to unsettle the kirkyard into the twentieth century.

Notes

1. A periodical edited by long-term *Blackwood's* contributor William Maginn, who had left *Blackwood's* and founded rival monthly *Fraser's* in 1830.
2. Hogg, 'One Thousand, Eight Hundred and Thirty-one', p. 84.
3. Ibid., p. 84.
4. Ibid., p. 84.
5. Marshall, *Murdering to Dissect*, p. 242. Morrison and Baldick, 'Notes', *The Vampyre and Other Tales of the Macabre*, p. 266.
6. Gilbert, *Cholera and Nation*, p.17.
7. The legislation demanded that 'those who die of this disease should be buried as soon as possible, wrapped in cotton or linen cloth saturated with pitch, or coal tar, and be carried to the grave by the fewest possible number of persons. The funeral service to be performed in the open air.' Qtd in Richardson, *Death, Dissection and the Destitute*, p. 105.
8. Jarrells, 'Tales of the Colonies', p. 267.
9. Wilson, *Lights and Shadows of Scottish Life*, p. 144.
10. Jarrells, 'Tales of the Colonies', p. 269.
11. Ibid., p. 269.
12. Ibid., p. 269.
13. Bewell, *Romanticism and Colonial Disease*, p. 244.
14. Ibid., p. 243.
15. Siek, '"A Rose by Any Other Name"', p. 27.
16. Bewell quotes a report in the *Lancet* medical journal from November 1831 which emphasises the role of military and trading connections in spreading the disease: 'the rise of British naval commerce with Bombay after 1815 is credited for the city's emergence as "a centre and point of departure for the itinerary lines, by which the cholera advanced to the Persian Gulf, to the Mediterranean, the Caspian and the Baltic; and we may now, unfortunately, add, to the German ocean and the river Wear".' Bewell, *Romanticism and Colonial Disease*, p. 246.
17. Ibid., p. 244.
18. Devine, *The Scottish Nation*, p. 334.

19. 'The Nature and the Cure of the Indian Cholera', p. 158.
20. 'Review: Observation on the Nature and Treatment of Cholera and on the Pathology of Mucous Membranes', pp. 244, 246.
21. See Morris's examination of the debate surrounding imports of flax from cholera-infected Eastern Europe, in *Cholera 1832*, p. 30.
22. Ackerknecht, 'Anticontagionism between 1821 and 1837', p. 8.
23. Ibid.
24. Otis, *Membranes*, p. 11.
25. Archibald Alison contributed political content to *Blackwood's* and published his *History of Europe* with the publisher in 1833. His High Tory perspective on this subject was satirised by Disraeli in his portrait of the Tory historian Mr Wordy in his 1844 novel *Coningsby*. Alison was a key voice in the formation of *Blackwood's* political point of view: Milne has argued that '*Blackwood's* took its political character from him more than from any other single contributor'. See Milne, 'Archibald Alison', p. 420.
26. Alison, 'To the Future Electors of Great Britain', p. 278.
27. Coyer, *Literature and Medicine in the Nineteenth-Century Periodical Press*, p. 112.
28. Roberts 'Medicine and the Body in Romantic Periodical Press', p. 248.
29. Montgomery, 'The Cholera Mount', p. 802.
30. Marshall, *Murdering to Dissect*, p. 261.
31. Montgomery, 'The Cholera Mount', p. 802.
32. Ibid., p. 803.
33. Ibid., p. 803.
34. Ibid., p. 803.
35. Hatfield, *The Poets of the Church*, p. 439.
36. King, *James Montgomery*, p. 358.
37. Ibid., p. 356.
38. 'Noctes Ambrosianae', 18 (December 1825), p. 759.
39. Wilson, 'An Hour's Talk about Poetry', p. 476.
40. Morris, *Cholera 1832*, p. 96.
41. Ibid., p. 98.
42. The essay stated that population growth would always outstrip the possibilities of food production, describing what Malthus terms 'the constant tendency in all animated life to increase beyond the nourishment prepared for it'. This growth could be controlled by either preventative or positive checks. Preventative checks reduced birth rate and were generally voluntary (for example abstinence) whereas positive checks increased death rate and might include famine, disease and war. Malthus, *An Essay on the Principle of Population*, p. 14.
43. Hamline and Gallagher-Kamper, 'Malthus and the Doctors', p. 128.
44. Hamline and Gallagher-Kamper describe the early decades of the nineteenth century as characterised by a 'pervasive Malthusianism'. Ibid., p. 122.
45. Gilbert, *Cholera and Nation*, p. 51.
46. These events are described by both Gilbert and Morris in their respective accounts of the epidemic: Gilbert, *Cholera and Nation*; Morris, *Cholera 1832*.
47. *The Metropolitan Magazine* was founded in 1831 by the publisher James Cochrane and edited by Thomas Campbell. The magazine was

intended to replace *The Naval Chronicle* which had ceased publishing in 1819. However, the periodical was targeted at a wider readership than its predecessor and, according to Duncan Ingraham Hasell, it aimed to 'compete with more general-interest magazines like *Fraser's*'. See Hasell, *Material Fictions*, p. 147. Hogg was at the time, like many of the original Blackwoodians, increasingly offering his work to multiple periodicals rather than publishing exclusively with *Blackwood's*. The publisher of *The Metropolitan Magazine*, James Cochrane, was Hogg's London publisher. See Garside, 'Hogg and the Book Trade', p. 29.

48. McCausland, 'James Hogg and the 1831–32 Cholera Epidemic', p. 44.
49. Camlot describes the journal as 'libertarian' in outlook. Camlot, *Style and the Nineteenth-Century British Critic*, p. 60. Sullivan highlights that in its note 'To Our Readers' the first issue of the magazine described itself an 'unflinching advocate of a Reform in State and Church'. Sullivan, *British Literary Magazines: The Romantic Age, 1786–1836*, p. 305.
50. Barrell, 'Putting down the Rising', *Scotland and the Borders of Romanticism*, pp. 130–8.
51. Duncan, *Scott's Shadow*, p. 207.
52. Hogg, 'Terrible Letters', p. 99.
53. Ibid., p. 101.
54. McCausland, 'James Hogg and the 1831–32 Cholera Epidemic', p. 44.
55. Hogg, p. 112.
56. Ibid., p. 99.
57. Ibid., p. 103.
58. Ibid., p. 107.
59. Ibid., p. 108.
60. Ibid., p. 106.
61. Ibid., p. 108.
62. Manderson, 'The Hidden Highlander', p. 102.
63. Hogg, *Highland Journeys*.
64. De Groot, 'Introduction', in Hogg, *Highland Journeys*, p. xxix.
65. Hogg, 'Terrible Letters', p. 108.
66. Ibid., p. 109.
67. Ibid., p. 105.
68. Ibid., p. 107.
69. The representation of the Highland Clearances by kirkyard writers is further examined in Chapter 6.
70. Waddell, *Modern John Buchan*, p. 4.
71. Gifford, 'The Roots That Clutch', p. 18.
72. Daniell, *The Interpreter's House*, pp. 181–2.
73. Buchan, *Witch Wood*, p. 29.
74. Ibid., p. 51.
75. Ibid., p. 118.
76. This masking is also apparent in the burial of Bessie Todd, the elderly woman tortured by the witch pricker: 'the dead woman was buried decently in the kirkyard, and her male kin attended the funeral as if there had never been a word against her fair fame', ibid., p. 225.
77. Daniell, *The Interpreter's House*, pp. 182–3.
78. Buchan, *Witch Wood*, p. 243.

79. Ibid., p. 249.
80. Massie, 'Introduction', in Buchan, *Witch Wood*, p. xiii.
81. Buchan, *Witch Wood*, p. 251.
82. Ibid., p. 152.
83. Ibid., p. 266.
84. Gifford, 'The Roots that Clutch', p. 18
85. Ibid., p. 18.

Chapter 6

'To lay our bones within the bosom of our native soil': The Kirkyard in the Age of Migrants

Midway through John Galt's North American emigration novel *Lawrie Todd* (1830), a careful reader, one familiar with his previous works, might be surprised to encounter a feeling of déjà vu. Following the collapse of his farming ventures in the New World, the protagonist, Todd, is seized by illness and falls into a strangely familiar trance: 'although my body was immovable, and all the powers of corporeal life stood still, my mind was vividly awake; I heard everything that passed in the chamber.'[1] The scenes that follow echo those of Galt's 1821 short story 'The Buried Alive', at times invoking their exact language, but relocate the hearing and feeling narrator from the professional urban world of Galt's original tale to the colonial homestead. Galt's decision to revisit the cataleptic trance in his novel is a peculiar one, perhaps intended simply to recycle the thrills that his short story elicited in the previous decade. However, as this book has argued so far, the dead had, over the 1810s and 1820s, become important motifs for the group of writers, like Galt, who had built their careers writing Scottish fiction for Blackwood. We can read the author's return to the living dead man as a gesture to an existing body of writing about the dead and perhaps an existing set of ideas about society. Galt, although writing a different type of fiction for a different publisher and locating his story in a quite different region of the world, fleetingly invokes his tale of terror and the cultural concerns that underpin it.

In previous chapters we explored a series of Romantic responses mounted through the dead and the kirkyard. The modern nation, I have argued, is cast in these texts as a space riven by unchecked development, rationalism and globalisation, and the kirkyard, whether peaceful or disrupted, operates as a Romantic site removed from, or endangered by, these processes. This chapter is interested in how authors who subscribed, or at least responded, to an image of nation founded in the local space of the Scottish kirkyard situated that idea in relation to colonial space. Where is the kirkyard in Britain's empire? Can the idea of the kirkyard survive transportation to Britain's far-flung colonial outposts?

To answer these questions, the chapter begins by exploring the phenomenon of the forgotten grave in the poetry of John Wilson and D. M. Moir. I highlight the similar representational strategies employed to describe Highland and colonial locations in these texts, noting how both these locations are presented as sites of historical absence. Unlike the well-trodden kirkyard gravesites, these burial grounds are presented as spaces outside the bounds of memory. However, the lonely grave poem, by describing these scenes to the reader, creates a virtual community of mourners, allowing forgotten sites to be incorporated into the memories of the feeling nation.

I then explore how *Blackwood's* writer John Howison blends elements from the tale of terror and the regional tale in his colonial stories for the magazine. In his tales Howison draws upon the idea of colonial emptiness to engender terror but often employs Indigenous or local characters to counteract that threat.[2] In doing so, I argue, he complicates the progress plot of stadial history and repeoples the seemingly empty colonial landscape. My analysis focuses on the burial scene in the Canadian tale 'Adventure in the North West Territory', which, I argue, assigns Indigenous characters a similar role to the peasant protagonists of Scottish regional writing. I then return to Galt's North American novels. In these works, I argue, narratives of absence and return foreground the relationship between colonial space and Scottish rural space. While *Lawrie Todd* (1830) suggests that homecoming may be possible for Scotland's colonial diaspora, in *Bogle Corbet* (1831), Galt's most pessimistic American novel, colonialism is recognised as part of an inevitable modernising process that will make any return to the kirkyard idyll impossible. Across the chapter I argue that, for the kirkyard Romantics, the grave site, which had already provided a symbol for an alternative mode of imagining Scotland, becomes an obvious emblem through which to explore the contradictions of the country's role in empire.

This application of the representational tools of Scottish Romanticism to the peripheries of the growing British world sets up an influential mode of imagining colonial identity. In the final parts of this chapter I consider how a nationally symbolic dead can effectively articulate a subnational identity in colonial space. When Thomas McCombie cites Scott, Warren and Bowles in his Australian sketch he suggests an international use for the kirkyard, born of its strong unionist nationalism and complex relationship with temporality. For McCombie Scottish Romanticism is not just a talismanic tradition brought from home but a useful precedent for imagining an Australian identity that can exist within a British colonial one. I argue that it is thus particularly productive to consider early settler colonial literary traditions alongside nineteenth-century Scottish literature, not just because Scots were highly represented among migrants, or because Scottish literature was widely read, but because many canonical Scottish Romantic authors were articulating ideas of region and nation that translated effectively across peripheral contexts.

Imagining the Scottish Empire

In the *Noctes Ambrosianae* sketch for the September 1829 issue of *Blackwood's* John's Wilson's recurring alter ego, Christopher North, notes that the Scots have taken 'two-thirds of all the colonies, rump and stump, to ourselves'.[3] These claims are not entirely bluster. Scots were significantly overrepresented in the ranks of colonial servants and migrants that participated in the expansion of the British Empire during the late eighteenth and early nineteenth century. In an 1821 letter Scott acknowledges the centrality of empire to the prospects of Scotland's landholding classes, referring to India as 'the corn chest for Scotland, where we poor gentry must send our youngest sons as we send our black cattle to the South'.[4] The years between 1815 and 1914 have been termed 'Britain's Imperial Century' by Ronald Hyam and saw British interests expanding globally.[5] As Britain's empire grew, so too did the number of Scots participating in that expansion. During the nineteenth century somewhere in the region of two million people left Scotland for Britain's settler colonies and Scots disproportionately participated in the imperial project at all levels.[6]

Britain's imperial growth, like the union with Scotland, created new challenges for existing definitions of the British nation. Ian Baucom notes that, although Britain has historically been imagined in spatial terms, the expansion of its borders means that who and where can be termed British has often become unstable and contingent:

> as England conquered Ireland, crowned a Scottish king, united with Scotland, and established colonies in North America, the Caribbean, the Pacific, the Indian subcontinent, and Africa, the recourse to a territorial definition of collective identity meant that Britishness, at least as a legal concept, was to become as elastic as the nation's imperial boundaries.[7]

However, even when regions and peoples became part of a global British imperial space, this did not mean that they were imagined as equally British. Instead, the colonial location or subject often functioned as an 'other' against which or whom Britishness could be defined.

For both Edward Said and Linda Colley, the colonial other becomes essential to ideas of self within the colonising nation.[8] However, as postcolonial thinkers including Mary Louise Pratt and Homi K. Bhabha have foregrounded, this binary between self and other is constantly undermined by the creation of innumerable colonial 'contact zones'.[9] Just as Scotland's relationship with Britishness reveals the 'tensions and ambiguities that result from trying to articulate any national identity', the British Empire denaturalises any seeming consensus about who and what is British.[10] The peripheries, Celtic and colonial, simultaneously define and complicate ideas of the national.

This is in part due to the way that such peripheries are imagined in temporal terms. The establishment of a grand narrative of human development was one of the projects of the Scottish Enlightenment. The liberal vision of empire, as it emerges in the years following the Enlightenment, seeks to understand the world through what Uday Singh Mehta terms 'liberal universalism' and Saree Makdisi refers to as 'universal world history'. Makdisi describes how in James Mill's *History of British India*, a landmark of early-century liberal engagement with empire, the author attempts to conform India's past to a 'diachronic story within a rational, logical, and above all, historical narrative'.[11] Conceiving of history as a continuous and universal global narrative, liberal thinkers like Mill try to integrate the 'other' into 'a history narrated by Europeans, a history at the end of which stands Europe'.[12] At a basic level these thinkers understand human history as a single system founded on a shared model of advancement from primitivity to civilisation (with urban Europe as the epitome of that civilised state) and seek to understand the peoples that come under British colonial dominion through this lens.

As we have explored in earlier chapters of this book, post-Enlightenment ideas of civilisation and barbarism underwrote the way that Scotland's regions were imagined: allowing historical processes to be written onto geographical space. These interpretations of stadial history also had a significant role in underwriting the logic of empire. Just as different groups who lived in Britain might be classified as more or less developed, so too could peoples beyond Britain's shores be understood as savages or civilised men. These categorisations often depended on the way that people related to the land they inhabited. Stadial modes of classifying human development could justify the dispossession of native peoples in global settler locations by casting them as survivals from a past pre-agricultural age.[13]

Romanticism, as we have explored throughout this book, can be understood as a mode of resistance to this emerging world order but also develops congruently with it and assists in its construction.[14]

The kirkyard writers engage with empire in ways that both engage with and challenge narratives of universality. The critique of liberal approaches to history and nation that had often underwritten provincialism in their works carried into their writing on empire. This may seem surprising given these authors' relationship with *Blackwood's Edinburgh Magazine*, whose later nineteenth-century reputation was as a magazine concerned with and consumed in, what Finkelstein has termed, the 'comfortable drawing rooms of the British Empire'.[15] However, the earlier *Blackwood's* line on empire, although certainly not anti-imperialist or radical, was, as Jarrells has suggested, concerned with countering 'prevailing' liberal perspectives on colonialism.[16] Writing at first within, and then beyond, the pages of *Blackwood's* and the volumes published by William Blackwood, the kirkyard writers use the grave to formulate an alternative Romantic imperialism.

The Forgotten Grave: Dying outside History

Within the world of John Wilson's rural fiction to die abroad is to die in exile. The deaths of soldiers and sailors in colonial and Napoleonic conflicts are tragedies, not just because of the loss of life, but because their graves are removed from those of their ancestors and inaccessible to their surviving kin.[17] This characterisation of the remote gravesite as tragedy is consistent across Wilson's fiction. In the *Lights and Shadows* tale 'Consumption' a dying maiden expresses her relief that she will die at home, before she can travel to Italy to convalesce, in horticultural terms:

> The thought is sweet to lay our bones within the bosom of our native soil. The verdure and the flowers I loved will brighten around my grave – the same trees whose pleasant murmurs cheered my living ear will hang their cool shadows over my dust, and the eyes that met mine in the light of affection will shed tears over the sod that covers me, keeping my memory green within their spirits![18]

Here Wilson makes use of a lexicon of organic imagery that recurs across kirkyard writing to articulate a nativist and fatalistic perspective on national identity. It is better to die and live on in memory within the regional world of the kirkyard than to chance recovery or obliteration through travel beyond these bounds. In an increasingly globalised world Wilson's regional fiction remains deeply ambivalent about the possibility of death abroad. Rather, memory is a plant that will remain green only in its native soil. To go out into the world is to risk not just untimely death but the death of memory.

However, burial within Scottish rural space does not guarantee the survival or preservation of memory. Wilson's 1817 poem 'Lines Written in a Lonely Burial Ground on the Northern Coast of the Highlands' describes a windswept and forgotten burial ground. In this poem the Highlands are presented as a depopulated and remote space where, following a fatal shipwreck, there is no one to remember and mourn the dead. Written in the same year as 'The Desolate Village', 'Lines Written ...' shares a focus on the aestheticisation of degeneration and depopulation. The burial ground is defined by absence, and Wilson does not explain this desolation:

> I see no little kirk – no bell
> On Sabbath tinkleth through this dell.
> How beautiful those graves and fair,
> That lying round the house of prayer,
> Sleep in the shadow of its grace!
> But death has chosen this rueful place
> For his own undivided reign! [19]

The burial ground is described through its contrast to an idealised village kirkyard. The presence of both a religious institution, and a living community to heed its bell, are missing from the 'rueful place'. This absence leaves the onlooker with nothing that assures them of a religious or secular afterlife: 'Hope with Memory seems dead!'[20] The space is instead only animated by nature. The speaker describes the sounds of the roaring ocean, wailing seabirds and humming mountain bees, and the sight of the 'sickly wild-flowers' that adorn the graves.[21]

Wilson's poem evokes an existing Ossianic discourse in its portrayal of Highland space. The 'extinguished kingly race' whose 'name on earth no longer known / Hath moulder'd with the mouldering stone' are not the occupants of the graves Wilson describes but their invocation places this lonely grave poem within the wider context of contemporary literary responses to the Highlands.[22] James Macpherson's Ossian poems of the 1760s inaugurated a mode of looking at the Highlands that would dominate Romantic presentations of the region. Macpherson's Ossian is the last of his race, a bardic figure whose function is to commemorate and lament a lost age. The Ossian poems are presented as fragments, translated from Gaelic, that give lowland and English readers fleeting access to a lost, ancient and unknowable world. These poems are not associated with a living or vital culture instead, as Juliet Shields notes, Highlanders 'were incorporated into Romantic poetry as symbols of the nation's primitive past'.[23] Subsequent writing, like Wilson's, draws upon this bank of images and ideas. If the rural lowlands contain the wisdom and history of modern Britain's forefathers, the Highlands are the home of far more ancient ancestors whose practices are at a much greater remove from those of the reader. They are, as Susan Manning vividly noted, 'properly rotted and consigned to a more primitive, noble past'.[24] Highland history, recorded in fragmented Gaelic verse, is already lost and unknowable, unlike the lowland rural idyll that is always just within living memory. The Highlands are, in cultural terms, already empty.

This mode of imagining the Highlands and Highlanders through a lens of historical obsolescence is underwritten by the changes to the Highland landscape that followed the Jacobite Rebellion of 1745 and the Clearances. In the years after Culloden, the Highlands were subject to what Andrew Mackillop terms a 'legislative assault upon the institutional and legal framework of clanship ... matched by the proscription of what Westminster believed were vital cultural symbols for the Gael; namely bagpipes and tartan'.[25] The subsequent pastoral revolution in Highland agriculture involved the removal of many Highlanders from the land to make way for livestock. This dispossession was often understood by contemporary commentators in terms of development or improvement.[26] The wild Highlands were to be tamed through the removal of wild Highlanders. Only once these belated inhabitants were cleared from the land could modernisation fully take place and the Highlands be incorporated into the modern nation.[27]

Even as these historical events were in progress, literary accounts of the Highlands often pre-empt the region's depopulation, casting it as an inevitable, and already completed, tragedy. Famously, Scott's epilogue to *Waverley* comments of the Jacobite Highlanders that 'this race has now almost entirely vanished from the land'.[28] Wilson's poem participates in this imaginative depopulation. Denuded of any local community and recorded only in the fragmentary poetry of an 'extinguished' race, Scotland's northern coast is presented as outside the limits of memory and nation.

D. M. Moir's colonial graveyard poem 'Lines Written in a British Burial Ground in India' was published in *Blackwood's* in 1821 and describes another lonely grave. A Musselburgh-based medic and writer, Moir had himself never travelled to India. Instead, his poem draws upon the images and ideas of India that were current during a period when the British East India Company continued to control large swathes of the region. In this poem, it is not the emptiness of the landscape that leads to the grave's loneliness. Rather the contingency of colonial sojourn comes into conflict with the grave's function as an enduring national memorial. The emotional weight of the poem stems from India's reputation as a hazardous place for colonial servants and the impermanence of British communities in the country. Following a similar formula to Robert Blair's eighteenth-century graveyard poem 'The Grave', the poem's speaker describes his wanderings in the burial ground and ponders the fates of various stock figures of the Indian empire (the soldier, the young wife, the missionary) who have died far from their homeland.

Although set in India, the poem is less interested in describing the colonial landscape than in contrasting the Indian burial ground with the archetypal ancestral churchyard. Just like Wilson's burial ground, Moir's graves are defined by absence. The early lines of Moir's poem draw an image of the 'home' kirkyard and its relationship to memory:

> no sacred pile
> Here calls the heart from brooding o'er the grave,
> Or spreads its holier influence round the scene.
> No father here, beside the ancient church,
> May shew his sons their honour'd grandsire's tomb.[29]

The British burial ground in India in Moir's poem is characterised by what is not there and these missing features correspond with the key icons of kirkyard Romanticism: the 'sacred pile', the family, descendants and the ancestor's bones. All are absent, leaving only 'the stranger here by stranger's side'.[30]

Just as 'circling palms' shut out 'rays of morn' from the gravesites, so too are the 'British dead' shut out from familial commemoration and national memory.[31] In the final stanzas of the poem, the soldier's widow joins her husband in the grave. The speaker, seemingly a colonial sojourner, reveals his own imminent departure: 'sad scene, farewell! / thus numbering all thy tombs, / How oft have I the mournful evening passed, / Till all thy lonely paths were lost in shade.'[32] The dead and their graves fade into obscurity, as into twilight, and the soldiers, missionaries and administrators of Britain's empire die or return to their home soil. Without a living, local community of British mourners the British dead cannot be fully integrated into history as it is imagined through the kirkyard. Burial in India carries with it the possibility of being forgotten.

Notably, the tribute of 'the passing Indian' is not a substitute for this absence.[33] Moir's India is not depopulated, but its inhabitants, even when they mourn the dead who lie in lonely graves, are not admitted into the community of national memory.[34] The tributes of Indian mourners cannot replace those of white British colonial sojourners and do not ensure that the dead are remembered. A similar erasure of alternative modes of history is apparent here to that exercised on the Highland past. Makdisi has discussed the tension between the perceived 'chaos of India's past' as it was recorded in Hindu mythology, and the colonising impulse to 'absorb contemporary India into the narrative of a universal history' apparent in the writings of thinkers like Mill.[35] In Moir's poem history as it is remembered by the native population is not given the status of true history. Even as the foregrounding of the grave might seem to subvert or interrupt the positivist flow of 'universal history', Moir does not suggest that India might be the source of an alternative narrative. Even when imagining empire through the pathos of the lonely grave, a white British witness is required. The India described by Moir may be a populated landscape but it is still lonely due to its position beyond the limits of European history.

In both poems the conventional home kirkyard is the foil against which the lonely grave's loneliness can be measured. The lonely grave is the counterimage to the kirkyard grave, a grave planted in land without tangible history or memory. If the kirkyard is rich in endangered, degenerating memory and must be preserved on the page, the lonely graves exist in a place without memory or textual record where their extinction seems inevitable.

However, to read either of these lonely grave poems as pure lament is to miss a double register. In both, the graves of the sailors and sojourners take on the attributes of pioneer graves. Moir's mournful register is balanced by its seeming celebration of those who 'valour claimed' and who 'ruled the plains' in Britain's name.[36] Wilson's lost sailors too are considered by the poet in terms of their manhood and fortitude.[37] The lonely grave can, then, be understood as a founding monument and an emblem of sacrifice. By depopulating, or de-historicising, the spaces they describe the poets clear the land for a new heroic myth of origin. The lonely graves become to some extent first graves that begin the integration of the land into the vision of the nation that kirkyard writing articulates.

The poems arguably offer a mode of reintegrating lonely graves into British national memory through something akin to Westover's 'imaginary pilgrimage'.[38] Although geographically removed from the 'little platoon' of memory, the grave need not be forgotten due to its inclusion in a virtual nation inhabited by readers. Just as the kirkyard allows the modern reader to virtually visit a disappearing and idealised rural world, the lonely grave poem also allows a readerly community to gather and mourn an imagined dead. These are literary graves of unknown soldiers that provoke a collective identification and offer a virtual gathering place, even as they wring pathos from the dead's supposed isolation and erasure. The lonely grave poem offers a mode of imagining these 'emptied' spaces and integrating them into history through feeling. The readership is united in its role as sentimental witness to history and the poem's subject is transformed from a lonely grave to a mass monument. Rather than lost in a world beyond history, the graves of these sailors and sojourners operate to bring these sites into the representational domain of the kirkyard and the nation. The presence of the grave makes these spaces legible.

John Howison and the *Blackwood's* Colonial Tale: Homing the Wilderness

Just as the sentimental periodical poetry of Moir and Wilson uses the pathos of the lonely grave to incorporate the peripheral into Romantic national history, the growing range of colonial fiction published within *Blackwood's* also sought ways to imagine colonial space beyond 'liberal universalism'. From its earliest issues it is possible to see *Blackwood's* privileging a Scottish perspective, foregrounding its status as an Edinburgh magazine, and cementing a reputation for Scottish, often antiquarian, content. Colonial content, although present, is at first less prominent, and colonial fiction does not immediately feature in the magazine's pages. The inclusion of multiple short stories by John Howison in the magazine throughout 1821 is an important landmark in the growth of the *Blackwood's* colonial story. Howison was a writer and medic who spent much of his career as a colonial surgeon.[39] This experience appears to have underpinned his writings which span the British colonial world. The first of John Howison's stories for the magazine, 'Vandecken's Message Home', was published in May 1821 and describes a ghostly encounter at sea off the Cape of South Africa. John Howison subsequently became one of *Blackwood's* most prolific contributors of fiction during 1821: publishing 'The Fatal Repast' in July, 'The Florida Pirate' in August, 'Adventure in the North-Western Territory' in September, 'The Floating Beacon' in October and 'Vanderbrummer: or, The Spinosist' in December. His first book, *Sketches of Upper Canada*, is reviewed by John Galt in the December issue. Further books of colonial sketches and stories would follow, including *Foreign Scenes and Travelling Recreations* (1825), *Tales of the Colonies* (1830) and *European Colonies* (1834), although by this time Howison had defected from the publisher.

The majority of Howison's *Blackwood's* stories describe a highly mobile nautical and colonial world, far removed from the idealised stasis of Wilson's archetypal Scottish tale. The settings of these tales are marked by their strangeness and their depopulation, operating as almost empty canvases upon which their protagonists' responses to extreme experiences can be minutely detailed. The colony as a space of individualised terror plays upon wider conceptions of colonial lands as uninhabited wildernesses. Much of the settler colonialism undertaken in the Americas and Australasia was conceptualised as the taming of a wasteland for the use of European settlers.[40] The concepts of *vacuum domicilium* in colonial America and *terra nullius* in Australia categorise land that had not been developed for habitation and cultivation, according to European standards, as unclaimed.[41] These 'new lands' are imagined as empty spaces of almost infinite potential, through the dispossession of their prior inhabitants and the devaluing of existing cultures. As Moreton-Robinson has noted through this 'legal fiction', Indigenous people are transformed from inhabitants to trespassers on their own ancestral lands.[42] Similar representational strategies are employed beyond the settler colonial locations of the Americas and Australasia. Mehta notes that even in colonial contexts where *terra nullius* is not legally relevant, like India, liberal accounts of empire present a similar understanding of colonised lands as empty or without history: 'the image one gets of India is of a vacant field, already weeded, where history has been brought to nullity and where extant social and political practices are narrowly contained, or altogether absent, primed for reform and constructive efforts.'[43] We might think here not just of the absence of memory in Moir's and Wilson's poems but of the encroachment of the natural environment in its place. Locations like Moir's India and Wilson's Scottish Highlands are, like the settler wilderness, ripe for cultivation and re-inscription.

The characterisation of colonial space as a wilderness without history means that Howison can, initially, use these locations in the way that other authors of tales of terror use coffins, bells and catacombs.[44] The conventions of the tale of terror allow Howison to represent the colonial environment through European eyes as an empty and inhospitable landscape where a terrifying death seems inevitable. This idea of emptiness is challenged when Howison introduces the generic conventions of the regional tale to his tale of colonial terror. In doing so, Howison dramatises the transformation of this space into something habitable and comprehensible through the knowledge of the native.

The colonial landscape is imagined as a site of extreme Gothic isolation in the early passages of 'Adventure in the North West Territory'. Set in a remote Canadian fur-trading outpost, it describes a fur trader's near-death experience when he becomes trapped on a thawing ice floe in a frozen lake and then lost in a vast forest. His peril is further heightened when he falls in with a party of 'Indians' only to learn that one of them plans to revenge his father's death by killing the lost trader.

Although the specific geographical, cultural and climatic features of the Canadian environment are important to its plot, the unnamed protagonist's mental and physical sufferings are the primary focus of much of the story. The Indigenous men who find the protagonist are at first placed somewhere between natural dangers and threatening trespassers in the scheme of the text.

Indigenous North Americans had taken on an emblematic role in accounts of Enlightenment stadial history where Tim Fulford suggest they were imagined as 'living examples of an earlier society'.[45] This use of Indigenous people as the antithesis of 'Modern Man' employs a familiar temporal logic of uneven development where a contemporary community is imagined as a survival from another age. Like the Highlanders and cotters, the Indigenous North American is denied coevalness with the contemporary world. McNeil argues that conversations around the dispossession of Indigenous peoples in the Americas were informed by existing attitudes to Highland migration.[46] The removal of Highlanders and Indigenous North Americans would create spaces without history or memory that were ripe for the inculcation of new cultures and memories. The empty land that so terrifies and threatens Howison's protagonist, prior to his encounter with the hunting party, is a desired stage of settler colonial conquest.

However, the death of a member of the Indigenous hunting party shifts the generic profile of the story and arguably challenges the idea of the Indigene as a trespasser. Strikingly, when the vengeful Thakakawerenté is killed by another member of his party, Outalisso, the description of his burial takes on a different register. The pace slackens as the narrator records the preparation of the body and Outalisso's explanation of his actions:

> 'Are you ignorant of our customs?' said he: 'When an Indian dies all his property must be buried with him. He who takes anything that belonged to a dead person will receive a curse from the Great Spirit in addition ...' Outalisso now proceeded to arrange the dress of the dead man, and likewise stuck the tomahawk in his girdle. He next went a little way into the forest for the purpose of collecting some bark to put in the bottom of the grave.[47]

Earlier in the story, we are largely aware of the inhospitableness and strangeness of the landscape to the protagonist, his inability to understand or survive in the Canadian wilderness, and its unhomeliness. Here, when he ejaculates, 'Are you ignorant of our customs?', the reader is made aware that Outalisso is at home in this same landscape.[48] By enacting burial customs, Outalisso demonstrates his relationship to the land in a way which is recognisable to a reader already familiar with the burial scenes of *Blackwood's* regional stories. Like the Scottish cottagers, Outalisso is a keeper and communicator of tradition. In contrast, the narrator's ignorance of these customs extends to the landscape itself. He is unable to navigate the forests, unaware of the signs of a thaw on a frozen lake, and continually at risk of death as he traverses the Canadian landscape. Without Outalisso's knowledge the protagonist is unlikely to make it back to his trading post. It is only with the assistance of a native informant figure that the colonist can survive the colony.

The relationship between coloniser and land is transformed and the landscape domesticated not through the capacity of that individual to claim *vacuum domicilium* but through the presence of other people who are native to the landscape. The careful rendering of Outalisso's burial practices is similar to the representation of the endangered customs of Scottish kirkyard characters. Simultaneously, in presenting Outalisso as the colonist's saviour, Howison co-opts traditional culture to the cause of colonial development. There is a value to the cultural knowledge and practices of colonised peoples which overrides liberal concepts of progressive civilisation and colonial conquest. Only a native person has the knowledge needed to survive in colonial space, and without this population the land is a site of terror.

As previous scholars have noted, the narrative pattern, where the knowledge of native peoples becomes essential to the survival of a colonist protagonist, can be traced across Howison's fiction.[49] We can see it even in stories which do not engage with what we might at first recognise as native or Indigenous knowledge. 'The Fatal Repast' is narrated by a passenger onboard a ship travelling through the Caribbean and describes an 'Ancient Mariner'-esque encounter with maritime folklore. His fellow travellers shoot two seabirds despite a warning from the captain not to do so. After the captain's ominous comment that 'we have not seen the end of it', the accidental consumption of poisonous fish leads to a terrifying night as crew members fall insensible and the ship veers wildly off course.[50] It is the maritime world here that provides the empty stage on which the tale of terror can be enacted. During this night the narrator's world contracts to one of solitary terror: 'all the people on board were to me the same as dead; and I was tossed about, in the vast waters, without a companion or fellow sufferer.'[51] This register continues as the narrator details the discovery of the bodies of many of the crew, their ship's burial, and the horrific discovery that the corpses are still visible in the water below the becalmed ship. The narrator describes in detail the horrific illusions that the rippling water creates as 'a hundred corpses seemed to start up and struggle wildly together'.[52] However, these Gothic terrors are made legible through the ship's mate's explanation of seafaring traditions and customs. The story again lapses into a different register when the narrator converses with him. The mate explains that the seabirds are believed to be the spirits of dead sailors who warn their past shipmates of coming trouble. The near catastrophe experienced by the crew and passengers, then, can, in one reading, be avoided through the full understanding of the environment, customs and supernatural lore of the seas.

'The Fatal Repast' presents the potential legitimacy of supernatural belief in a way that chimes with James Hogg's foundational Scottish short fiction.[53] In Hogg's rural stories logical explanations for supernatural phenomena are often revealed to be insufficient and, as Gerard McKeever notes, conclusions 'unravel stadialism and show that improvement can barely suppress, never mind eliminate, the 'facts' of traditional belief'.[54] Similarly, 'The Fatal Repast' leaves open the possibility that the sailors' traditional beliefs are not just local colour but a legitimate mode of understanding the nautical world. Rather than adhering to a universal empirical system, spaces like Howison's ship and Canadian forests offer alternative ways to structure and understand the world. Where the logic of colonialism is predicated on similarity and perfectibility, the regionalism of these tales acknowledges difference and the value of traditional belief systems.

However, this championing of the local does not counter colonial expansionism. Rather, the traditional knowledge gained from native informants in Howison's tales serves to support his characters' capacity to survive and thrive in these spaces. The value of the local here is not as a rebuke to globalisation, instead it is a tool in the arsenal of the heroic colonist. It is only by valuing Indigenous knowledge that the colonial servant is positioned to successfully navigate and build the expanding British world. The characterisation of empire through liberal universalism is countered by a Romantic understanding of the importance of regionality. This opposition between liberal and Romantic imperialism is one mirrored in John Galt's North American fiction, where Galt explores the collision between kirkyard Romanticism and imperial mobility in scenes of colonial homecoming.

'Evergreens in my Remembrance': Death and Migration in John Galt's North American Novels

Galt was himself a colonial sojourner who spent three years in Canada between 1826 and 1829 in the role of secretary of the Canada Company. After returning to Scotland, Galt published two North American novels,

Lawrie Todd and *Bogle Corbet*, in 1830 and 1831 respectively. Galt's earlier novels, as we have already seen in Chapter 2, often highlighted the influence of outside forces on the rural parish but display a marked ambivalence towards change. These two later novels go a step further, placing Galt's Scotland of ministers, lairds and kirkyards within the wider Atlantic world which he had experienced first-hand. In doing so they are able to interrogate the relationship between memory, identity and heritage at the heart of the kirkyard project in ways which were impossible within Galt's Scottish regional writing of the 1820s. As the kirkyard Romantics diffused and lost the intense, interdependent character which had given the fiction of the 1810s and 1820s its distinctive quality, Galt utilised his own expanded perspective to redraw the boundaries of Scottish regional fiction, looking back on the kirkyard from the deck of an emigrant ship.

Although Galt's two North American novels have often been examined in tandem, it is their contrasts that define them in these critical accounts. Both follow the adventures of a male emigrant to North America but the fates and experiences of their eponymous heroes vary between what Katie Trumpener terms 'the optimistic *Lawrie Todd* ... and the sober *Bogle Corbet*'.[55] The two protagonists' contrasting emigration destinations, the United States and Canada respectively, also situate them within different histories: Bogle Corbet remains within a British imperial sphere throughout the eponymous novel while Lawrie Todd travels beyond these borders to the independent settler state. R. P. Irvine notes that *Lawrie Todd* follows the conventions of Galt's existing Scottish fiction, 'as Lawrie tells the story of his rise from impoverished youth in Scotland to wealthy real-estate developer in upstate New York', offering a familiar 'protagonist type and narrative arc for readers of Galt's Scottish stories'.[56] The more melancholy and troubling *Bogle Corbet*, by contrast, describes a character with an uncertain relationship with national identity and success. Trumpener notes the novel's 'moral disconnection and psychic dislocation'.[57]

However, one feature that Galt's two novels share is a high death toll. While the reprise of the 'Buried Alive' reanimation scene in *Lawrie Todd* is striking to a reader of Galt's wider work, it is not out of keeping with the numerous instances of spectacular death and near-death through epidemic disease, natural disaster, exposure and fatal duel that surround it. Emigration in Galt's account is a dangerous undertaking that places his characters in intimate quarters with their mortality. The growth of the British world is not a disembodied and inevitable flow of civilisation in either novel but an individually fought struggle where success and survival are never guaranteed. These scenes of colonial peril feature alongside more sentimental scenes of loss and sorrow, and backward glances towards Scotland, and the kirkyard, are distributed throughout the novels. In these scenes Galt knowingly invokes the conventions and imagery, not just of his own Scottish fiction, but of the kirkyard more broadly, using death and memory to explore national identity in a globalising British world. When Galt's sojourning characters return to the kirkyards of Scotland, they bring the complexities of empire to bear on kirkyard Romanticism.

The opening chapters of Galt's *Lawrie Todd* clearly signal the novel's position within the kirkyard tradition:[58]

> I was born in the little village of Bonnytown, so cosily situated in one of the pleasantest holms of the sylvan Esk. – Many a day, both of cloud and sunshine, has passed over me since I bade it farewell; but the trees and hedges are still evergreens in my remembrance; and I never look at 'the pictures in the big Ha' Bible,' where the saints are seen crowned with Glory, but I think of the sanctified old church, surrounded, in the solemnity of the churchyard, with its halo of tomb-stones.[59]

Galt in these early sentences rapidly touches upon many of the conventional images and themes of the *Blackwood's* regional tale describing a specific Scottish pastoral location, engendering a tone of wistful nostalgia, quoting 'the Cotter', and then finally leading the reader to the kirkyard. The author places his text in a canon of regional fiction through these references before transporting both his conventional kirkyard narrator, and by extension this set of national values, to the colony. Memory in the passage serves to preserve, ensuring the scenes remain 'evergreen' in Todd's remembrance, and to idealise: winter may come to Bonnytown's sylvan holms but in Todd's memory 'trees and hedges' are always in full leaf. The migrant's memories of his home country are frozen, and perhaps distorted, even as history marches onward. The 'churchyard, with its halo of tomb-stones' continues to serve its nation-forming role when it is not a tangible local location but has been converted into a memory, or fantasy, by distance and time.

However, Todd's subsequent return journey to Scotland complicates this continued affinity with a remembered or imagined past. Although at first it seems that the intervening twenty years have 'wrought but few changes in the appearance of the village', the returning emigrant quickly becomes aware that the 'evergreen' vision he had carried with him of Bonnytown has withered.[60] The first warning of these changes comes when Todd notes on first re-entering the village by night that:

> the old church was a little altered in effect, by two of the church elms being cut down. I forgave the parish for that sacrilege, but not for having enclosed the

church yard with a high wall, which hid the grave-stones from the glimpses of the moon, though it was done to protect the dead from violation.[61]

The incursion of body snatching into rural space has led to the segregation of the graves from the village that surrounds them and thus disrupted the 'transmortal' kirkyard community.[62] Protecting the dead requires severing them from the living world and breaking the relationship that fundamentally underwrites kirkyard Romanticism. This glimpsed change to the kirkyard, along with the construction of a new public house, foreshadow the changes which have also taken place in Todd's home. He arrives only in time to superintend his father's funeral. Just as the kirkyard is now barred from view and segregated from the living community, Todd finds himself unexpectedly exiled from the home of his father.

Following this death Todd is struck by the many changes which appear to have been wrought by time. He attempts to enumerate the various alterations in the physical environment and customs of the village: the ageing of the population, and the way that the houses have 'shrunken with old age and decay'.[63] The village is not immune to the forces of time; in fact, it is seemingly particularly vulnerable to them. His description of the changes in agriculture and verdure in the local area indicates a fundamental tension in Todd's approach to local custom and historical development:

> the hills that I had left bloomy and pastoral were ploughed to the top and many of them bonneted with fir trees, and belted with plantings. It was impossible to view the improvements without satisfaction; but I wondered where the schoolboys would find nests, and allowed myself to fancy that for lack of the brave sports of their fathers, the next generation would, may be, show themselves, in the dangers of wars, a less venturesome race.[64]

Todd is an emigrant who has headed the charge to settle the Americas, overseeing deforestation to make way for settlement. The foundation of his new settlement, Judiville, has been marked by the symbolic felling of a great maple tree.[65] Yet here in Bonnytown he finds himself divided between his 'satisfaction' in witnessing the improvement of his own home soil, and a nagging anxiety about what may have been lost. The image of evergreen pastoral that he carried with him and treasured is overlaid by the sight of the productive evergreens of commercial forestry.

These ecological changes bring with them cultural change. Todd is acutely aware of ways that the 'improvement' of the environment will potentially lead to a deterioration in local life. If places like Bonnytown are the nurseries of the 'venturesome race' who have acted as the foot soldiers of empire, then the loss of these spaces risks their disappearance. The preservation of local culture and the unimproved landscape is presented as essential to continued colonial expansion. Only where pockets of the past survive can the men be nurtured who are capable of spearheading imperial modernisation. British imperial strength is revealed to be grounded in the traditions and environment of rural Scotland. When the landscape changes so too may Britain's geopolitical power.

In addition to potentially eradicating the foot soldiers of empire, these changes also erode the potential of the village and kirkyard to function as a symbol of conservative nationalism. Todd's memories seemingly lose their nation-building power in the face of local change. The village and its kirkyard can function as national monuments only through a geographically limited historical stasis which is impossible in the face of the forces of 'improving' modernity. Without the presence of his father, Todd is struck by the hollowness of his attachment to home, and quickly marries and returns to the United States: 'to return to Bonnytown seemed no longer desirable. The place to me had become empty; I had seen it after a long absence and was satisfied with the sight: my father was removed, and no living object was there to attract me back.'[66] At this point in the narrative, it is the living parent, rather than his grave or a memory, that roots Todd in a particular geographical location and to a particular cultural identity. The imagined or remembered kirkyard is perhaps not a strong enough talisman to bind the thousands of Scottish colonists who leave the country to Britain and British values. The dead lack the potency of a living connection.

This rejection of the old country is not final, though. Later in the novel, when Todd reflects on the possibility of political candidacy in the United States, we encounter Galt's clearest statement of this conflict between origin and colony:

> my conscience could not away with the thought of renouncing the right to claim paternity with William Wallace and the brave old bald-headed worthies of the Covenant; my father's household gods, on whose altar, our lowly hearth, the incense of a special thanksgiving was every Sabbath-evening offered to Heaven, for having sent them to redeem and sanctify 'our ancient and never-conquered Kingdom of Scotland.'[67]

Todd's vision of Scottishness assembles the key talismans of kirkyard Romanticism. He imagines the nation as an extended patriarchal lineage that flows from Wallace and the Covenanters to his own father and himself. By contrast, the United States contains the 'friends, and kin, and substance' that have peopled Todd's adult life. He imagines the relationship between the two spaces in temporal terms: 'on one side stood an aged matron, pointing to the churchyard where my forefathers lay at peace; on the other, a sturdy youth, with an axe upon his shoulder, bade me look where my family was spreading and prospering around.'[68] Despite America's allegiance with the sturdy youth of futurity, Todd eventually allies himself with the aged matron and the churchyard of his forefathers, choosing to return to Scotland in his old age. In contrast to his earlier response to the death of his father, Todd chooses the past over the future, history over development. The Calvinist fatalism of *Lights and Shadows* resurfaces in Todd's retreat from the North American forests to the churchyard of his forefathers. There is a peculiar vision of life here that prioritises the individual's relationship with the collective dead over that with the living. Correctly choosing where to die motivates Todd whereas contributing to a new community or society does not. Just as Wilson's regional tales converted the Calvinist focus on mortality into an argument for politicised stasis, Todd's decision is underwritten, not by a desire to live a good life, but to die a good death in the correct place.

The colonial death drive resurfaces in a different form in Galt's other North American novel, *Bogle Corbet*. While travelling in the north of Scotland Corbet encounters a Highland laird, Captain Campbell, who has recently returned to Scotland from fighting in Canada. Campbell presents a perspective which is critical of memory's capacity to accurately recall home or preserve connection. The conversation between Corbet and Campbell focuses on the relationship between location, memory and migration that also characterised Lawrie Todd's early ruminations on the beauties of Bonnytown. Like Todd, Campbell describes the experience of return and the breaking of the spell of memory. Change and his own travels have altered his perceptions of his ancestral lands:

> After an absence of many years, I came back to this old spot, which often was remembered in distant scenes as the pleasantest that the earth could contain; but on my return, all that had endeared it in recollection existed no more ... it is only by missing early friends that we discover how little the aspect of our native land contributes to the sentiment with which it is pictured on the memory. In truth, I am weary of this empty place.[69]

Following the sweeping changes of the Highland Clearances, Campbell's idealised memories and ancestral connections are insufficient in countering the historical forces of depopulation and mobility in the region. Interestingly, Campbell, unlike Todd, makes no mention of a graveyard or other space where he might memorialise his 'early friends', finding the Highlands to be a truly 'empty place'. He suggests that mobility has fundamentally changed his relationship to the local: 'all countries are alike to me: it is one of the advantages of a military life that we lose local attachments. Before my return, every place had something about it inferior to my own home, but the delusion is gone.'[70] Local attachment is here dismissed as delusion. The role of colonial soldier re-educates the Highlander's attachments. Campbell proceeds to suggest that it is now military community that underwrites his identity: 'I think, however, that Canada will have my bones; for several officers whom I knew in the army, have settled their families there. I have no comrades here, and it sweetens death to fall among companions.'[71] Unable to find 'early friends' in the sheep-filled glens of his ancestral lands, Campbell imagines instead burial in a new land peopled by 'comrades'. Like Todd's decision, Campbell's vision for his subsequent life is focused on where, and among whom, he would like to die.

Campbell's divorce from the bonds of local memory, and desire for colonial death, is underwritten by the social and economic changes being wrought in the Highlands, and the region's status in the cultural imagination as an ancient, empty space. If the Highlands are now extinct and desolate, then Campbell is an Ossianic last bard figure, returning to find himself a ghostly presence in an empty landscape. However, the similarly imaginatively emptied North American 'wilderness' offers an opportunity to transform from a forgotten ancestor to a pioneer. During the early decades of the nineteenth century the migration of Highlanders to the British colonies was increasingly advocated as a solution to Highland displacement. The problem of the Highlander's obsolescence could be solved through the settlement of land even more ancient and empty than the Highlands. 'Primitive' peoples are to be the foot soldiers in the modernisation of even more 'primitive' lands. In giving Canada his bones Campbell escapes his own obsolescence and ensures his own memorialisation and place in history.

The solution to Bogle Corbet's own rootlessness, however, is not so apparent. The earliest chapter of Galt's novel adheres to the conventions of the emigrant Bildungsroman by describing the events of the protagonist's early life, but also subverts these conventions through its hazy sense of time and self-conscious engagement with the subjectivity of the written account. Corbet is himself the child of colonial sojourners. He is not rooted in a place-based sense of identity, and there is no account of the loss of his parents or the location of their graves. The one thing that is recorded precisely is the removal of Corbet from his enslaved West Indian nurse Baba: 'it is just fifty years, a month, a week and a day, counting backward from this very night, that Baba left me.'[72] Consequently, the loss of Baba seems to take on a particular importance within the chapter. The reader's sense of the geography of Corbet's early travels is imprecise but they do know the childhood trauma of losing Baba. That this foundational relationship is interracial and underwritten by slavery further deranges any sense of the organic, local ties of the kirkyard world.

Later in the novel the death of Corbet's Scottish kinswoman and childhood guardian Mrs Busby further serves to disarray his sense of identity. Galt describes a similar scenario to the one deployed in *Lawrie Todd*: like Todd, Corbet returns to regional Scotland after time abroad to visit an ageing relative but arrives just in time for their death. For Corbet, Mrs Busby's death breaks his last, already weak, tie to Scotland:

> I trust, when I confess that, saving a filial reminiscence of Mrs Busby, then aged and infirm, my regret at the idea of seeking a new life in another world was not of an intense kind, I shall not be deemed insensible to the moral worth and political splendor of my native country. But even the tie in my remembrance of that venerable gentlewoman, the only parent I ever really knew, was destined to forego its hold.[73]

Despite the weakness of this connection, the loss of Mrs Busby has a profound impact on Corbet who, following this event, describes a period of ill health and a tendency 'to fall into an unaccountable mood of sadness' which has continued to affect him.[74] Galt depicts Corbet seeking solace in John Wilson's novel *Margaret Lyndsay* but struggling to read the book: 'after making several attempts to read a pious book called "Margaret Lindsay," I let down the curtains, and laid myself down on the bed.'[75] Although this comment may just be a small intertextual stab at Wilson, Corbet's selection and rejection of this novel can also have a deeper meaning in the context of his upcoming journey to Canada. That Wilson's novel of resignation, rootedness and reward is insufficient in the aftermath of the expiry of Corbet's last 'filial' connection to Scotland, and on the eve of his permanent emigration, indicates the limits of the kirkyard's capacity to cement national ties. Cobert's experience of loss and the one described in the book are at odds. He finds no comfort in the text and will afterwards decisively turn away from its world of local ties instead seeking 'a new life in another world'.

Where a return to the kirkyard is central to the resolution of *Lawrie Todd*, this mode of solving the conflict between origin and colonial settlement is contested in *Bogle Corbet*. Corbet's unsettled colonial upbringing makes any such retreat into the past impossible. The national vision of the kirkyard is brought into troubling conflict with the complexities of colonial identity. Can the emigrant remain a citizen of the kirkyard nation? And should he? Despite the disenchantment of Bonnytown, *Lawrie Todd* upholds the possibility of an ongoing imaginative connection to the Scotland of 'William Wallace' and the Covenanting 'worthies'. However, *Bogle Corbet* with its sojourning and unsettled narrator suggests that there is no talisman powerful enough to tie colonial Scots to their origin and little compensation in the cosmopolitanism of the expansive Atlantic world. The forward thrust of 'universal history' cannot be mitigated through the veneration of an imagined past or the foundation of a new history. In *Bogle Corbet* the Romantic imperialism of Moir and Howison rings hollow.

This chapter has explored the relationship between the lonely graves and empty spaces of the colonial and Celtic periphery, and the memory-rich, but endangered, kirkyards of the Scottish lowlands in the writing of kirkyard writers. Galt, Howison, Moir and Wilson adopt different perspectives on the relationship between these two categories of site, but their texts collectively avoid outright critique of the processes transforming them. Across their colonial and Highland poetry and fiction, the progressive logic of universal world history is submerged and postponed through the foregrounding of mourning and loss but never wholly rejected. The patina of pathos in many of these texts masks or softens their role in the building and legitimisation of empire and modernisation in a way that would have huge appeal for Victorian colonists. Their insistence on the regional offers an opportunity to imagine a proto-national identity for spaces within British imperial dominion. The pioneering, lonely grave can clear space for the writing of a new history.

The International National Dead: Thomas McCombie's 'The Bush-Graves of Australia'

The final section of this chapter returns to Thomas McCombie and his sketch 'The Bush-Graves of Australia' (1858), in light of both the kirkyard and its colonial applications. This book has argued for the kirkyard as a Romantic motif for engaging with and sometimes challenging liberal history and its emphasis on development, rationalism and mobility. This final chapter has described the ambivalent and complicated ways that kirkyard authors employed this motif in their responses to colonialism. The dead in their writing offer the opportunity to return emotion, history and stability to the faceless sweep of colonial expansion, often without critiquing its progress. In this coda I argue that Thomas McCombie's sketch, published a quarter of a century later in the liberal periodical *Tait's Edinburgh Magazine*, explicitly invokes the same literary precedent and again uses its pathos to combine the Romantic and the progressive.

Thomas McCombie was a Scottish-Australian writer and politician from near Tough, in Aberdeenshire. He migrated to Port Phillip in 1841, aged twenty-two. McCombie first attempted to establish himself as a squatter in rural New South Wales before taking an increasingly active role in the journalistic and political life of the colony. McCombie edited and shared proprietorship of the *Port Phillip Gazette* between 1844 and 1851 and set up the short-lived weekly *Reformer* in 1853. He was also an elected representative to the Melbourne Town Council and the Victoria Legislative Assembly.[76] Although not generally considered a canonical colonial Australian author, McCombie was prolific and through his journalistic work we might assume relatively widely read. McCombie's sketches are highly conventional, and even within the more circumscribed sphere of Scottish colonial writing there are many better-known texts. 'The Bush-Graves of Australia' is perhaps an unusual choice to start and end a book that engages with some of the most celebrated and canonised novels in Scottish literary history. However, it is this very conventionality, the normalness of this sketch, that makes it interesting, suggesting the penetration of kirkyard ideas far beyond the original sphere in which they were published.

Within his essay McCombie draws from the body of Australian bush burial writing, quoting the first two verses of Robert Lynd's 1845 poem 'Leichhardt's Grave'.[77] However, he also incorporates a much wider range of possible sources. As the opening to this book discussed, the kirkyard texts are particularly prominent among these points of reference, with McCombie explicitly invoking Scott's *Old Mortality*, Bowles's *Chapters on Churchyards* and Samuel Warren's *Diary of a Late Physician*. The early paragraphs, where McCombie sets forth a Scottish origin story for 'Bush Graves', also appear drawn straight from the pages of Bowles's sketches, and earlier Scottish rural writing that had appeared in the magazine's pages. McCombie describes 'a residence of some years with a near relative, who is the pastor of a country parish in Scotland, and whose residence is in close proximity to the churchyard', setting himself up as the interpreter narrator of a kirkyard sketch.[78] This churchyard articulates a, by now, familiar vision of Scottish life:

> Within a few feet of me lay the dust and bones of those who had tilled the land of the Parish for many generations, who, after 'life's fitful fever' of dear farms, bad crops, and other rustic grievances, now slept well. The part of the country was not remarkable for great natural attractions, but the people were kind, homely, honest, and unsophisticated.[79]

In this passage, the 'generations' of burials articulate a continuity between past and present. The starting point for McCombie's interest in graves is the cultural nationalism of kirkyard Romanticism.

McCombie's essay represents the Australian bush grave as a break with these British ideals:

> after an absence of many long years from Europe, I can still call up quiet nooks overhung with the drooping branches of sombre trees, where the dead sleep, under the shade of venerable Gothic churches, in whose silent, solemn aisles they had worshipped, one generation after another, for ages. How different in Australia.[80]

Like Moir's India and Wilson's Highlands, McCombie's Australia is a space defined by difference and absence. A large section of the sketch describes the narrator's pilgrimage through the remote bush seeking 'the last resting place of a talented man, who died young, and was interred in the forest'.[81] The narrator's description of this site emphasises the contrast between it and the idealised graveyards of the old world:

> there was no sign of civilization here to meet the eye; no hum of human life or ploughman's cheerful carol to fall on the ear; but as it was a fertile flat where I stood I doubted not but all these would one day be present.[82]

Like his progenitors, McCombie presents the lonely grave as both tragedy and founding monument. The 'erring youth's' dissipation and demise are tragic and place him beyond the bounds of the archetypal kirkyard. However, his lonely grave is also imagined as the foundation of a settler presence in the region – a first grave that will soon be incorporated into the productive and pastoral world of anglophone settlement. The sketch offers the reader the necromantic capacity to undertake a virtual pilgrimage and participate in the extension of British national memory into the 'fertile' but as yet untilled flat.

The obvious issue with this symbol is the prior presence of Indigenous graves in Australian soil. If the burial of a dead man represents a claim upon the soil, then generations of Aboriginal people have a superior claim to live on this land than European settlers. McCombie's essay confronts the status of Aboriginal burials early on when he asserts that: 'In most cases, the dead in Australia are laid in the primordial soil. The only graves previous to the era of British colonization being those of the poor aborigines.'[83] To discount these graves and make the soil primordial again McCombie emphasises Aboriginal death rituals which do not involve interment in the soil: cremation, exposure and the enclosure of human remains within hollow logs. He also claims that Aboriginal burial sites are disappearing from the Australian landscape, casting this as a neutral impersonal process rather than engaging with the active dispossession being enacted on Aboriginal cultural sites by British settlers: 'But those are only now to be seen in the far interior, as their tombs have long disappeared in the settled portions of the country.'[84] Like Wilson's nameless 'mouldering' ancients and Scott's 'vanishing race', the Aboriginal dead are relegated beyond the realms of human memory and history. The land is imaginatively cleared and prepared for re-inscription.

McCombie's sketch is then explicitly modelled on kirkyard precedents. That the author turns to this mode of writing in the early paragraphs of his Australian sketch, I suggest, is indicative of a desire to employ the bush grave in a similar cultural assertion of identity. Like the archetypal country graveyards of Caroline Bowles and John Wilson, the graves of Australia's bush dead are part of a culturally nationalist project. That these archetypes came from writers negotiating a type of national identity that existed within another overfolding nation makes them particularly effective in a colonial Australian setting where federation had not yet fully registered on the political agenda. As Trumpener has observed, 'cultural nationalism (as long as it separates cultural expression from political sovereignty) can be contained within an imperial framework.'[85] The kirkyard dead already articulate a type of imagined nation that through regionalism and temporality is safely removed from, and complimentary to, the British state. Examining McCombie's short, conventional sketch makes the same case for a modular and transportable kirkyard that I began to build in the first chapter of this book. The set of ideas and concerns that characterise the resistant Romantic writing of Scotland's second-wave Romanticists, and which survive to underwrite the projects of the Scottish cultural revivalists, are redeployed to articulate the parallel concerns of an emerging colonial nation.

Notes

1. Galt, *Lawrie Todd*, vol. I, p. 72.
2. This chapter connects the representation of Indigenous peoples in the British colonies to that of Indian colonial subjects and the Highlanders and Scottish 'peasants' of domestic regional fiction. I argue that there is a crosspollination in the literary strategies used to represent groups associated with what Trumpener and others term 'peripheral' contexts. This argument is not intended to downplay the important differences between the experiences of these groups during this period.
3. 'Noctes Ambrosianae', *Blackwood's Edinburgh Magazine*, 26 (September 1829), p. 393.
4. Qtd in Sassi, *Why Scottish Literature Matters*, p. 85.
5. Hyam, *Britain's Imperial Century*.
6. Wallace, *Scottish Presbyterianism and Settler Colonial Politics*, p. 1.
7. Baucom, *Out of Place*, p. 8.

8. Said, *Orientalism*; Colley, *Britons*.
9. Pratt 'Arts of the Contact Zone'; Bahbha 'Signs Taken for Wonders'.
10. Davis, *Acts of Union*, p. 11.
11. Makdisi, *Romantic Imperialism*, p. 1.
12. Ibid., p. 11.
13. As O'Brien notes: 'the vocabularies of savagery and barbarism, inherited from the Enlightenment and especially from Gibbon's epic accounts of mass migration in ancient Europe, were valuable instruments through which literary writers could link questions of intellectual and economic impoverishment to those of man's relationship to land.' O'Brien, 'Colonial Emigration, Public Policy and Tory Romanticism', p. 166.
14. Makdisi has noted Romanticism and modernisation experienced a 'mutual process of constitution' during the late eighteenth and early nineteenth century. *Romantic Imperialism*, p. 16.
15. Finkelstein, 'Imperial Self-Representation', p. 106.
16. Jarrells explores this idea, arguing that *Blackwood's* colonial tales are part of a wider effort to apply the tools of conservative regionalism to colonial issues. These arguments are foundational to my own claims about the exportation of kirkyard Romanticism. See Jarrells, 'Tales of the Colonies'.
17. See Chapter 4.
18. Wilson, *Lights and Shadows of Scottish Life*, p. 340.
19. Wilson, 'Lines Written ...', p. 295.
20. Ibid., p. 295.
21. Ibid., p. 295.
22. Ibid., p. 295.
23. Shields, 'Highland Emigration and the Transformation of Nostalgia in Romantic Poetry', p. 773.
24. Manning, 'That Exhumation Scene Again', p. 93.
25. MacKillop, 'For King, Country and Regiment', p.185.
26. H. B. de Groot discusses these accounts in his 'Introduction' to Hogg, *Highland Journeys*, p. xxiv.
27. A similar narrative was used to justify Indigenous dispossession in colonial spaces and will be discussed in the next section of this chapter.
28. Scott, *Waverley*, p. 340
29. Moir, 'Lines Written ...', p. 665.
30. Ibid., p. 665.
31. Ibid., p. 665.
32. Ibid., p. 667.
33. Ibid., p. 666.
34. Ibid., p. 666.
35. Makdisi, *Romantic Imperialism*, p. 2.
36. Moir, 'Lines Written ...', p. 666.
37. Wilson, 'Lines Written ...', p. 295.
38. Westover, *Necromanticism*, p. 77.
39. McMullen, 'Howison, John'.
40. See Sandrock, *Scottish Colonial Literature*, p. 96.
41. Armitage, *The Ideological Origins of the British Empire*, p. 97.
42. Moreton-Robinson, *The White Possessive*, p. 18.
43. Mehta, *Liberalism and Empire*, p. 12.

44. See Jarrells, 'Tales of the Colonies', p. 274. My arguments are indebted to his interpretation of the generic boundaries of Howison's tales.
45. Fulford, *Romantic Indians*, p. 42.
46. See McNeil, *Scottish Romanticism and Collective Memory in the British Atlantic*, p. 145.
47. Howison, 'Adventure in the North-West Territory', p. 144.
48. Ibid., p. 144.
49. Jarrells, 'Tales of the Colonies', p. 275.
50. Howison, 'The Fatal Repast', p. 408.
51. Ibid., p. 410.
52. Ibid., p. 411.
53. See Chapter 1 for a brief discussion of Hogg's stories' role in the development of kirkyard Romanticism.
54. McKeever, *Dialectics of Improvement*, p. 10.
55. Trumpener, *Bardic Nationalism*, p. 278.
56. Irvine, 'Canada, Class, and Colonization in John Galt's *Bogle Corbet*', p. 259.
57. Trumpener, *Bardic Nationalism*, p. 274. Readings of this novel have interpreted it as both anti- and pro-imperialist (see McDonagh, *Literature in a Time of Migration*, p.101). My own reading of *Bogle Corbet* is as an ambivalent and mournful text where both registers serve to complicate and mask the liberal logic of progressive civilisation.
58. Contemporary commentators noted the novel's invocation of this tradition. A writer for the *Westminster Review* highlighted that: 'In this early part of the work, there is much to be pleased with: humble domestic life in Scotland is so marked by strong affections, piety and principle that we never fail to be interested in the pictures of it: and how many, and how admirable are the painters of it – Galt, Wilson, the author of Mansie Wauch rise instantly to the recollection.' See 'Galt's *Lawrie Todd*', p. 406.
59. Galt, *Lawrie Todd*, vol. 1, p. 7.
60. Ibid., vol. 2, p. 71.
61. Ibid., vol. 2, p. 71.
62. McAllister, *Imagining the Dead*, p. 30.
63. Ibid., p. 75.
64. Ibid., p. 75.
65. As McDonagh highlights, this scene parallels Galt's description of the foundation of Geulph. McDonagh, *Literature in a Time of Migration*, p. 103.
66. Ibid., p. 85.
67. Ibid., p. 150.
68. Ibid., p. 150.
69. Galt, *Bogle Corbet*, vol. 2, p. 220.
70. Ibid., vol. 2, p. 221.
71. Ibid., vol. 2, p. 221.
72. Ibid., vol. 1, p. 14.
73. Ibid., vol. 2, p. 183.
74. Ibid., vol. 2, p. 187.
75. Ibid., vol. 2, p. 198.
76. See Innett, 'Thomas McCombie'.

77. McCombie, 'Australian Sketches. – No. V. The Bush-Graves of Australia', p. 10.
78. Ibid., p. 9.
79. Ibid., p. 9.
80. Ibid., p. 10.
81. Ibid., p. 11.
82. Ibid., p. 11.
83. Ibid., p. 10.
84. Ibid., p. 10.
85. Trumpener, *Bardic Nationalism*, p. xiii.

Bibliography

Ackerknecht, Erwin H. 'Anticontagionism between 1821 and 1837', *International Journal of Epidemiology*, 38, no. 1 (2009): 7–21.
Allen, Michael. *Reformed Theology*. London: Bloomsbury, 2010.
Alvarez, A. *The Savage God: A Study of Suicide*. London: Penguin, 1987.
Anderson, Benedict. *Imagined Communities: Reflections on the Origin and Spread of Nationalism*. London and New York: Verso, 2006.
Aries, Phillipe. *The Hour of Our Death*. Oxford: Oxford University Press, 1991.
Armitage, David. *The Ideological Origins of the British Empire*. Cambridge: Cambridge University Press, 2000.
Barrell, John. 'Putting down the Rising', in *Scotland and the Borders of Romanticism*, edited by Leith Davis, Ian Duncan and Janet Sorenson, 130–8. Cambridge: Cambridge University Press, 2004.
Barrie, J. M. *A Window in Thrums*. London: Hodder & Stoughton, 1889.
Bates, A. W. *The Anatomy of Robert Knox: Murder, Mad Science and Medical Regulation in Nineteenth-Century Edinburgh*. Brighton, Portland, OR, and Toronto: Sussex Academic Press, 2010.
Battles, Kelly E. 'Bad Taste, Gothic Bodies and Subversive Aesthetics in Hogg's Private Memoirs and Confessions of a Justified Sinner', *Essays in Romanticism*, 19, no. 19 (2012): 49–64.
Baucom, Ian. *Out of Place: Englishness, Empire and the Locations of Identity*. Princeton: Princeton University Press, 1999.
Benchimol, Alex and Gerard McKeever. 'Introduction', in *Cultures of Improvement in Scottish Romanticism, 1707–1840*, edited by Alex Benchimol and Gerard McKeever, 1–16. London: Routledge, 2018.
Bewell, Alan, *Romanticism and Colonial Disease*. Baltimore and London: Johns Hopkins University Press, 1999.
Bhabha, Homi K. 'Signs Taken for Wonders: Questions of Ambivalence and Authority under a Tree outside Delhi, May 1817', *Critical Inquiry*, 12, no. 1 (Autumn 1985): 144–65.
Blain, Virginia H. *Caroline Bowles Southey, 1786–1854: The Making of a Woman Writer*. Aldershot and Brookfield, VT: Ashgate, 1998.
Blair, Kirstie. *Working Verse in Victorian Scotland: Poetry, Press, Community*. Oxford: Oxford University Press, 2019.
Bohrer, Martha 'Thinking Locally: Novelistic Worlds in Provincial Fiction', in *The Cambridge Companion to Fiction in the Romantic Period*, edited by

Richard Maxwell and Katie Trumpener, 89–106. Cambridge: Cambridge University Press, 2008.

Bowler, Peter J. *The Invention of Progress: The Victorians and the Past*. Oxford: Basil Blackwell, 1989.

Bowles, Caroline Southey. *Chapters on Churchyards*. Edinburgh: William Blackwood & Sons, 1841.

Bromwich, David. *A Choice of Inheritance: Self and Community from Edmund Burke to Robert Frost*. Cambridge, MA, and London: Harvard University Press, 1989.

Brown, William A. F. *What asylums were, are and ought to be: Being the substance of five lectures delivered before the managers of the Montrose Royal Lunatic Asylum*. Edinburgh: Adam & Charles Black, 1837.

Buchan, James. *Witch Wood*. Edinburgh: Birlinn, 2008.

Burke, Edmund. *Letter to a Noble Lord*. Boston, MA: Athenaeum Press, 1898.

Burke, Edmund. *Reflections on the Revolution in France*, edited by L. G. Mitchell. Oxford: Oxford University Press. 2009.

Butterfield, Herbert. *The Whig Interpretation of History*. New York: W. W. Norton, 1965.

Camlot, Jason. *Style and the Nineteenth-Century British Critic: Sincere Mannerism*. Aldershot and Burlington: Ashgate, 2008.

Campbell, Ian. 'George Douglas Brown's Kailyard Novel', *Studies in Scottish Literature*, 12, no. 1 (1974): 62–73.

Campbell, Ian. 'Introduction', in J. G. Lockhart, *Adam Blair*, edited by Ian Campbell, i–xxii. Edinburgh: Saltire Society, 2007.

Carey, John. 'Introduction', in *The Private Memoirs and Confessions of a Justified Sinner*, James Hogg, ix–xxii. Oxford: Oxford University Press, 1969.

Carruthers, Gerard. *Edinburgh Critical Guide to Scottish Literature*. Edinburgh: Edinburgh University Press, 2009.

Chandler, James. *England in 1819: The Politics of Literary Culture and the Case of Romantic Historicism*. Chicago: Chicago University Press, 1998.

Cheyne, George. *The English Malady; or a Treatise of Nervous Diseases of all kinds, as spleen, vapours, lowness of spirits, hypochondria, and hysterical distempers, and c. in three parts*. London, 1733.

Christie, William. '"Where Personation Ends and Imposture Begins": John Wilson, Noctes Ambrosianæ, and the Tory Populism of Blackwood's Edinburgh Magazine', in *Politics and Emotions in Romantic Periodicals*, edited by J. Macleod, W. Christie, P. Denney, 175–94. Cham: Springer Nature, 2019.

Colley, Linda. *Britons: Forging the Nation, 1707–1837*. New Haven: University of Yale Press, 1992.

Costain, Keith M. 'Theoretical History and the Novel: The Scottish Fiction of John Galt', *ELH*, 43, no.4 (Autumn 1976): 342–65.

Coyer, Megan J. 'The Embodied Damnation of James Hogg's Justified Sinner', *Literature and Science*, 7, no. 1 (2014): 1–19.

Coyer, Megan J. *Literature and Medicine in the Nineteenth-Century Periodical Press: Blackwood's Edinburgh Magazine, 1817–1858*. Edinburgh: Edinburgh University Press, 2016.

Craig, Cairns. 'Introduction', in George Douglas Brown, *The House with the Green Shutters*, v–xiii. Edinburgh: Canongate, 2005.

Craig, Cairns. 'The Modern Scottish Novel', in *A Companion to British Literature: Victorian and Twentieth, 1837–2000*, edited by Robert Demaria Jnr, Heesok Chang and Samantha Zacher, 404–23. Chichester: Wiley Blackwell, 2014.

Craig, Craig. *Out of History: Narrative Paradigms in Scottish and English Culture*. Edinburgh: Polygon, 1996.

Craig, Cairns. 'Scotland and the Regional Novel', in *The Regional Novel in Britain and Ireland, 1800–1990*, edited by K. D. M. Snell, 221–56. Cambridge: Cambridge University Press, 1998.

Crawford, Catherine. 'A Scientific Profession: Medical Reform and Forensic Medicine in British Periodicals of the Early Nineteenth Century', in *British Medicine in an Age of Reform*, edited by Roger French and Andrew Wear, 204–24. London and New York: Routledge, 1991.

Cronin, Richard. *Paper Pellets: British Literary Culture after Waterloo*. Oxford: Oxford University Press, 2010.

Daniell, David. *The Interpreter's House: A Critical Assessment of John Buchan*. London: Nelson, 1975.

Davis, Leith. *Acts of Union: Scotland and the Negotiation of the British Nation*. Stanford: Stanford University Press, 1998.

De Quincey, Thomas. 'Professor Wilson: Sketch in 1850', in *The Collected Writings of Thomas De Quincey*, vol. 5, edited by David Masson, 289–302. Edinburgh: Adam & Charles Black, 1890.

Devine, T. M. *The Scottish Nation, 1700–2007*. London and New York: Penguin, 2006.

Dick, Alexander. '*Blackwood's* Pastoralism and the Highland Clearances', in *Romantic Periodicals in the Twenty-First Century: Eleven Case Studies from Blackwood's Edinburgh Magazine*, edited by Nicholas Mason and Tom Mole, 137–60. Edinburgh: Edinburgh University Press, 2020.

Divine, Anne Roberts. 'The Changing Village: Loss of Community in John Galt's *Annals of the Parish*', *Studies in Scottish Literature*, 25, no. 1 (1990): 121–33.

Douglas, George. *The 'Blackwood' Group*. Edinburgh and London: Oliphant, Anderson & Ferrier, 1897.

Duncan, Ian. *Scott's Shadow*. Princeton and Oxford: Princeton University Press, 2007.

Duncan, Ian and Douglas S. Mack. 'Hogg, Galt, Scott and Their Milieu', in *The Edinburgh History of Scottish Literature, Volume 2: Enlightenment, Britain and Empire (1707–1918)*, edited by Susan Manning, 211–20. Edinburgh: Edinburgh University Press, 2007.

Dundas, Phillip. 'John Wilson to William Wordsworth (1802): A New Text', *The Wordsworth Circle*, 34, no. 2 (Spring 2003): 111–15.

Dunlop, C. R. B. 'Samuel Warren: A Victorian Law and Literature Practitioner', *Cardozo Studies in Law and Literature*, 12, no. 2 (Autumn–Winter 2000): 265–91.

Dunlop, C. R. B. 'Warren, Samuel (1807–1877), Lawyer and Writer', in *Oxford Dictionary of National Biography*. Oxford: Oxford University Press, 2004, https://www.oxforddnb.com/view/10.1093/ref:odnb/9780198614128.001.0001/odnb-9780198614128-e-10316 (accessed 10 June 2023).

Egan, Joseph J. 'The Indebtedness of George Douglas Brown to *The Mayor of Casterbridge*', *Studies in Scottish Literature*, 2, no. 1 (1992): 203–17.

Evans, Tanya. 'Courtship, Sex and Marriage in Eighteenth-Century Popular Literature', in *Unfortunate Objects: Lone Mothers in Eighteenth Century London*, edited by Tanya Evans, 47–66. London: Palgrave Macmillan, 2005.

Finkelstein, David. 'Decent Company: Conrad, "Blackwood's", and the Literary Marketplace', *Conradiana*, 41, no.1 (Spring 2009): 29–47.

Finkelstein, David. *The House of Blackwood: Author–Publisher Relations in the Victorian Era*. University Park: Pennsylvania State University Press, 2002.

Finkelstein, David. 'Imperial Self-Representation: Constructions of Empire in Blackwood's Magazine, 1880–1900', in *Imperial Co-Histories: National Identities and the British and Colonial Press*, 95–108. Madison: Fairleigh Dickson University Press, 2003.

Finkelstein, David. 'Moir, David Macbeth [pseud. Delta] (1798–1851), Physician and Writer', *Oxford Dictionary of National Biography*. Oxford: Oxford University Press, 2004, https://www.oxforddnb.com/view/10.1093/ref:odnb/9780198614128.001.0001/odnb-9780198614128-e-18890 (accessed 1 July 2023).

Finkelstein, David. 'Periodicals, Encyclopedias and Nineteenth-Century Literary Production', in *The Edinburgh History of Scottish Literature: Volume Two: Enlightenment, Britain and Empire (1707–1918)*, edited by Susan Manning. Edinburgh: Edinburgh University Press, 2007.

Flynn, Phillip. 'Early "Blackwood's" and Scottish Identities', *Studies in Romanticism*, 46, vol. 1 (2007): 43–56.

Fosso, Kurt. *Buried Communities: Wordsworth and the Bonds of Mourning*. Albany: State of New York University Press, 2003.

Fry, Michael, *A New Race of Men: Scotland, 1815–1914*. Edinburgh: Birlinn, 2013.

Fulford, Tim. *Romantic Indians: Native Americans, British Literature, and Transatlantic Culture, 1756–1830*. Oxford: Oxford University Press, 2006.

Galt, John. 'Annals of the Parish', in *Annals of the Parish, The Ayrshire Legatees and The Provost*. Edinburgh: The Saltire Society, 2002.

Galt, John. *Bogle Corbet, or The Emigrants*, 3 vols. London: Henry Colburn and Richard Bentley, 1831.

Galt, John. 'The Buried Alive', *Blackwood's Edinburgh Magazine*, 10, vol. 56 (October 1821): 262–4.

Galt, John. *Lawrie Todd, or The Settlers in the Wood*, 3 vols. New York: J. & J. Harper, 1830.

Galt, John. *The Literary Life and Miscellanies of John Galt*, 3 vols. Edinburgh: W. Blackwood, 1834.

Garside, Peter. 'Hogg and the Book Trade', in *The Edinburgh Companion to James Hogg*, edited by Ian Duncan and Douglas Mack, 21–30. Edinburgh: Edinburgh University Press, 2012.

Gates, Barbara T. *Victorian Suicide: Mad Crimes and Sad Histories*. Princeton: Princeton University Press, 1988.

Gifford, Douglas. 'The Roots That Clutch: John Buchan, Scottish Fiction and Scotland', in *John Buchan and the Idea of Modernity*, edited by Kate MacDonald and Nathan Waddell. London and New York: Routledge, 2013.

Gilbert, Pamela K. *Cholera and Nation: Doctoring the Social Body in Victorian England*. Albany: State University of New York Press, 2008.

Goldsmith, Oliver. *The Deserted Village: A Poem*. London: W. Griffin, 1770.
Gordon, Ian. 'Galt's "The Ayrshire Legatees": Genesis and Development', *Scottish Literary Journal*, 16, no. 1 (1989): 35–43.
Groot, H. B. de. 'Introduction', in James Hogg, *Highland Journeys*, edited by H. B. de Groot, xi–lxvii. Edinburgh: Edinburgh University Press, 2010.
Haekel, Ralf. 'Romanticism and Theory: An Introduction', in *Handbook of British Romanticism*, edited by Ralf Haekel, 1–26. Berlin and Boston, MA: De Gruyter, 2017.
Halliday, Andrew. *A General View of the Present State of Lunatics and Lunatic Asylums in Great Britain and Ireland*. London: Thomas & George Underwood, 1828.
Hamline, Christopher and Kathleen Gallagher-Kamper, 'Malthus and the Doctors: Political Economy, Medicine, and the State in England, Ireland and Scotland, 1800–1840', in *Malthus, Medicine and Morality: 'Malthusianism' after 1798*, edited by Brian Dolan, 115–40. Amsterdam and Atlanta, GA: Rodopi, 2000.
Hart, Francis Russell. *Lockhart as Romantic Biographer*. Edinburgh: Edinburgh University Press, 1971.
Hart, Francis Russell. *The Scottish Novel: A Critical Survey*. London: John Murray, 1978.
Hasler, Antony. 'Introduction', in James Hogg, *The Three Perils of Woman*, edited David Groves, Anthony Hasler and Douglas S. Mack, xi–xliii. Edinburgh: Edinburgh University Press, 1995.
Hassell, Duncan Ingraham. 'Material Fictions: Readers and Textuality in the British Novel, 1814–1852', PhD diss., Rice University, Houston, 2009.
Hatfield, Edwin F. *The Poets of the Church: A Series of Biographical Sketches of Hymn Writers*. New York: Randolph & Co., 1884.
Hayden, John O. *The Romantic Reviewers, 1802–1824*. London: Routledge and Kegan Paul, 1969.
Henderson, T. F. 'Introduction', in D. M. Moir, *The Life of Mansie Wauch Tailor in Dalkeith Written by Himself*, v–xiv. London: Methuen & Co, n.d.
Herman, Arthur. *How the Scots Invented the Modern World*. New York: Broadway Press, 2001.
Heron, Robert. *A Memoir of the Life of the Late Robert Burns*. Edinburgh: T. Brown, 1797.
Hessell, Nikki. *Romantic Literature and the Colonised World: Lessons from Indigenous Translations*. Cham: Palgrave Macmillan, 2018.
Hewitt, David. 'Scott, Sir Walter (1771–1832), Poet and Novelist', in *Oxford Dictionary of National Biography*. Oxford: Oxford University Press, 2004, https://www.oxforddnb.com/view/10.1093/ref:odnb/9780198614128.001.0001/odnb-9780198614128-e-24928 (accessed 28 June 2023).
Hewitt, Regina. 'Introduction: Observations and Conjectures on John Galt's Place in Scottish Enlightenment and Romantic-Era Studies', in *John Galt: Observations and Conjectures on Literature, History and Society*, edited by Regina Hewitt, 1–32. Plymouth, MA: Bucknell University Press, 2012.
Higgins, David. 'Blackwood's Edinburgh Magazine and the Construction of Wordsworth's Genius', *Prose Studies*, 25, no. 1 (2008): 122–36.
Hogg, James. *Highland Journeys*, edited by H. B. de Groot. Edinburgh: Edinburgh University Press, 2010.

Hogg, James. 'One Thousand, Eight Hundred and Thirty-one', *Fraser's Magazine for Town and Country*, 25 (February 1832): 84.

Hogg, James. 'A Peasant's Funeral', in *Winter Evening Tales*, edited by Ian Duncan, 141–4. Edinburgh: Edinburgh University Press, 2002.

Hogg, James. *The Private Memoirs and Confessions of a Justified Sinner*. Oxford: Oxford University Press, 2010.

Hogg, James. 'A Scots Mummy', in James Hogg, *Contributions to Blackwood's Edinburgh Magazine, Vol 1. 1817–1828*, edited by Thomas Richardson, 139–43. Edinburgh: Edinburgh University Press, 2008.

Hogg, James. 'Some Terrible Letters from Scotland', in John Polidori [et al.], *The Vampyre and Other Tales of the Macabre*. Oxford: Oxford University Press, 2008.

Home, John. *Douglas*, edited by Gerald D. Parker. Edinburgh: Oliver & Boyd, 1972.

Hopfl, H. M. 'From Savage to Scotsman: Conjectural History in the Scottish Enlightenment', *Journal of British Studies*, 17, vol. 2 (Spring 1978): 19–40.

Houston, R. A. *Punishing the Dead? Suicide, Lordship and Community in Britain, 1500–1830*. Oxford: Oxford University Press, 2010.

Howison, John. 'Adventure in the North West Territory', *Blackwood's Edinburgh Magazine*, 10 (September 1821): 137–44.

Howison, John. 'The Fatal Repast', *Blackwood's Edinburgh Magazine*, 9 (July 1821): 407–13.

Hughes, Gillian. 'The Edinburgh of Blackwood's Edinburgh Magazine and James Hogg's Fiction', in *Romanticism and Blackwood's Magazine: 'An Unprecedented Phenomenon'*, edited by Robert Morrison and Daniel S. Roberts, 175–86. Houndmills, Basingstoke, and New York: Palgrave Macmillan, 2013.

Hughes, Gillian. 'Introduction', in James Hogg, *The Spy*, edited by Gillian Hughes. Edinburgh: Edinburgh University Press, 2000.

Hyam, Ronald. *Britain's Imperial Century, 1815–1914: A Study of Empire and Expansion*. London: B. T. Batsford, 1976.

Inglis, Katherine. 'Maternity, Madness and Mechanization: The Ghastly Automaton in James Hogg's The Three Perils of Woman', in *Minds, Bodies, Machines, 1770–1930*, edited by Deirdre Coleman and Hilary Fraser, 61–82. Houndmills, Basingstoke: Palgrave Macmillan, 2011.

Innett, Caroline. 'Thomas McCombie 1819–1869: An Early Australian Writer', *MARGIN: Life and Letters in Early Australia*, 62 (April 2004): 28–32.

Irvine, R. P. 'Canada, Class, and Colonization in John Galt's *Bogle Corbet*', *The Yearbook of English Studies*, 46 (2016): 259–76.

Irvine, R. P. 'Introduction', in John Galt, *Annals of the Parish*, edited by R. P. Irvine. Edinburgh: Edinburgh University Press, 2020.

Jack, R. D. S. 'Critical Introduction: Where Stands Scots Now?' *The Mercat Anthology of Early Scottish Literature, 1375–1707*, edited by R. D. S Jack and P. A. T. Rozendaal, vii–xxxix. Edinburgh: Mercat Press, 1997.

Jalland, Pat. *Death in the Victorian Family*. Oxford: Oxford University Press, 1996.

Jarrells, Anthony. 'Reading for Something Other Than Plot in Galt's Tales of the West', in *International Companion to John Galt*, edited by

Gerard Carruthers and Colin Kidd, 110–24. Glasgow: Scottish Literature International, 2017.
Jarrells, Anthony. 'Tales of the Colonies: Blackwood's, Provincialism, and British Interests Abroad', in *Romanticism and Blackwood's Magazine: 'An Unprecedented Phenomenon'*, edited by Robert Morrison and Daniel S. Roberts, 267–78. Houndmills, Basingstoke, and New York: Palgrave Macmillan, 2013.
Jeffrey, Francis. 'Secondary Scottish Novels', *Edinburgh Review*, 39 (1823): 158–79.
Kennedy, Meegan. 'The Ghost in the Clinic: Gothic Medicine and Curious Fiction in Samuel Warren's *Diary of a Late Physician*', *Victorian Literature and Culture*, 32, no. 2 (September 2004): 327–51.
Kennedy, Meegan. *Revising the Clinic: Vision and Representation in Victorian Medical Narrative and the Novel*. Columbus: Ohio State University Press, 2010.
Killick, Tim. *British Short Fiction in the Early Nineteenth Century: The Rise of the Tale*. Aldershot: Ashgate, 2008.
King, J. W. *James Montgomery: A Memoir Political and Poetical*. London: Artridge & Co. 1858.
Klancher, Jon. 'Reading the Social Text: Power, Signs and Audience in Early Nineteenth-Century Prose', *Studies in Romanticism*, 23, no. 2 (Summer 1984): 183–204.
Knowles, Thomas. 'Ideology, Art, and Commerce: Aspects of Literary Sociology in the Late Victorian Scottish Kailyard'. PhD diss., University of Gothenburg, 1983.
Kolhke, Marie-Luise. 'The Neo-Victorian Doctor and Resurrected Gothic Masculinities', *Victoriographies*, 5, no. 2 (July 2015): 122–42.
Kushner, Howard I. 'Suicide, Gender and the Fear of Modernity', in *Histories of Suicide: International Perspectives on Self-Destruction in the Modern World*, edited by John Weaver and David Wright, 19–52. Toronto: University of Toronto Press, 2009.
Laquer, Thomas W. *The Work of the Dead: A Cultural History of Mortal Remains*. Princeton: Princeton University Press, 2016.
Leask, Nigel. *Robert Burns and Pastoral: Poetry and Improvement in Late Eighteenth Century Scotland*. Oxford: Oxford University Press, 2010.
Lincoln, Andrew. *Walter Scott and Modernity*. Edinburgh: Edinburgh University Press, 2007.
Lochhead, Marion. *John Gibson Lockhart*. London: John Murray, 1954.
Lockhart, John Gibson. *Adam Blair*. Edinburgh: Saltire Society, 2007.
Lockhart, J. G. 'The Clydesdale Yeoman's Return', *Blackwood's Edinburgh Magazine*, 6 (December 1819): 321–2.
Lockhart, J. G. 'Remarks on Schlegel's History of Literature', *Blackwood's Edinburgh Magazine*, 3 (August 1818): 497–511.
Lockhart, J. G. *Peter's Letters to His Kinfolk*. Edinburgh: William Blackwood, 1819.
Löwy, Michael and Robert Sayre. *Romanticism against the Tide of Modernity*, translated by Catherine Porter. Durham, NC, and London: Duke University Press, 2001.
MacDonald, Helen. *Possessing the Dead: The Artful Science of Anatomy*. Melbourne: Melbourne University Press, 2010.

MacDonald, Michael and Terence R. Murphy. *Sleepless Souls: Suicide in Early Modern England*. Oxford: Clarendon Press, 1990.

Mack, Douglas S. 'The Body in the Opened Grave: Robert Burns and Robert Wringhim', *Studies in Hogg and His World*, 7 (1996): 70–9.

Mack, Douglas S. 'John Wilson, James Hogg, "Christopher North" and "The Ettrick Shepherd"', *Studies in Hogg and His World*, 12 (2001): 5–24.

Mack, Douglas S. 'Lights and Shadows of Scottish Life: James Hogg's The Three Perils of Woman', in *Studies in Scottish Fiction: Nineteenth Century*, edited by Horst W. Drescher and Joachim Schwend, 15–27. Johannes Gutenberg-Universität Mainz in Germersheim: Publications of the Scottish Studies Centre, 1985.

Mackenzie, Henry. 'Unsigned Essay in *Lounger*, 97 (9 December 1786)', in *Robert Burns: The Critical Heritage*, edited by Donald A. Low, 67–71. London and Boston, MA: Routledge and Kegan Paul, 1974.

Mackillop, Andrew. 'For King, Country and Regiment?: Motive and Identity within Highland Soldiering, 1746–1815', *Fighting for Identity: Scottish Military Experiences c.1550–1900*, edited by Steve Murdoch and Andrew Mackillop. Leiden: Brill, 2002.

Maclaren, Ian. *Beside the Bonnie Brier Bush*. Glasgow: Kennedy & Boyd, 2007.

Maclaren, Ian. *The Days of Auld Lang Syne*. Glasgow: Kennedy & Boyd, 2007.

Makdisi, Saree. *Romantic Imperialism: Universal Empire and the Culture of Modernity*. Cambridge: Cambridge University Press, 1998.

Malthus, T. M. *An Essay on the Principle of Population*, edited by Donald Winch. Cambridge: Cambridge University Press, 1992.

Manderson, David. 'The Hidden Highlander: The Noctes Ambrosianae and the Highlands', in *Gael and Lowlander in Scottish Literature: Cross-Currents in Nineteenth Century Scottish Literature*, edited by Christopher MacLachlan and Ronald W. Renton, 88–103. Glasgow: The Association for Scottish Literary Studies, 2015.

Mangham, Andrew. 'Buried Alive: The Gothic Awakening of Taphephobia', *Journal of Literature and Science*, 3, no. 1 (2010): 10–22.

Manning, Susan. 'That Exhumation Scene Again: Transatlantic Hogg', *Studies in Hogg and His World*, 16 (2005): 86–111.

Marshall, Tim. *Murdering to Dissect: Grave-robbing, Frankenstein and the Anatomy Literature*. Manchester and New York: Manchester University Press, 1995.

Massie, Allan. 'Introduction', in John Buchan, *Witch Wood*, vi–xiv. Edinburgh: Birlinn, 2008.

Mason, Michael York. 'The Three Burials in Hogg's Justified Sinner', *Studies in Scottish Literature*, 13, no. 1 (1978): 15–23.

Maxwell-Stuart, Peter. 'Witchcraft and Magic in Eighteenth-Century Scotland', in *Beyond the Witch Trials: Witchcraft and Magic in Enlightenment Europe*, edited by Owen Davies and Willem de Blécourt, 81–100. Manchester and New York: Manchester University Press, 2004.

McAllister, David. *Imagining the Dead in British Literature and Culture, 1790–1848*. Houndmills, Basingstoke, and New York: Palgrave Macmillan, 2018.

McCausland, Joan. 'James Hogg and the 1831–32 Cholera Epidemic', *Studies in Hogg and His World*, 10 (1999): 40–7.

McCombie, Thomas. 'Australian Sketches – No. V. The Bush-Graves of Australia', *Tait's Edinburgh Magazine*, 25 (January 1858): 9–13.

McCracken-Flesher, Caroline. *The Doctor Dissected: A Cultural Autopsy of the Burke and Hare Murders*. Oxford: Oxford University Press, 2012.

McCrone, David. *Understanding Scotland: The Sociology of a Stateless Nation*. London and New York: Routledge, 2001.

McGill, Martha. 'The Evolution of Haunted Space in Scotland', *Gothic Studies*, 24, no. 1 (2022): 18–30.

McGuire, Kelly. *Dying to be English: Suicide Narratives and National Identity, 1721–1814*. London and Brookfield, VT: Taylor & Francis, 2012.

McIlvanney, Liam. 'Mohowks: Review – *The House of Blackwood: Author-Publisher Relations in the Victorian Era* by David Finkelstein', *London Review of Books*, 25, no. 11 (June 2003): 6–7.

McKeever, Gerard. *Scotland and the Dialectics of Improvement*. Edinburgh: Edinburgh University Press, 2020.

McKeever, Gerard. '"With Wealth Comes Wants": Scottish Romanticism as Improvement in the Fiction of John Galt', *Studies in Romanticism*, 55, no. 1 (Spring 2016): 69–93.

McMullen, Bonnie Shannon. 'Howison, John (1797–1859), Writer and Surgeon', in *Oxford Dictionary of National Biography*. Oxford: Oxford University Press, 2004, https://www.oxforddnb.com/view/10.1093/ref:odnb/9780198614128.001.0001/odnb-9780198614128-e-49224 (accessed 15 June 2023).

McNeil, Kenneth. *Scottish Romanticism and Collective Memory in the British Atlantic*. Edinburgh: Edinburgh University Press, 2020.

Means, James. 'A Reading of the Grave', *Studies in Scottish Literature*, 12, no. 4 (1975): 270–81.

Mehta, Uday Singh. *Liberalism and Empire: A Study in Nineteenth-Century British Liberal Thought*. Chicago: Chicago University Press, 1999.

Millar, J. H. 'Literature of the Kailyard', *The New Review*, 12, no. 71 (April 1895): 384–94.

Millbank, Alison. 'The Victorian Gothic in English novels and stories, 1830–1880', in *The Cambridge Companion to Gothic Fiction*, edited by Jerrold E. Hogle, 145–66. Cambridge: Cambridge University Press, 2002.

Milne, Maurice. 'Archibald Alison: Conservative Controversialist', *Albion: A Quarterly Journal Concerned with British Studies*, 27, no. 3 (Autumn 1995): 419–43.

Moir, D. M. 'From the Autobiography of Mansie Wauch, Tailor', *Blackwood's Edinburgh Magazine*, 21 (January 1827): 39–44.

Moir, D. M. 'Lines Written in a British Burial Ground in India', *Blackwood's Edinburgh Magazine*, 8 (March 1821): 665–7.

Moir, D. M. 'Wonderful Passage in the Life of Mansie Wauch, Tailor', *Blackwood's Edinburgh Magazine*, 16 (October 1824): 456–9.

Mole, Tom. 'Blackwood's "Personalities"' in *Romanticism and Blackwood's Magazine: 'An Unprecedented Phenomenon'*, edited by Robert Morrison and Daniel S. Roberts, 89–100. Houndmills, Basingstoke, and New York: Palgrave Macmillan, 2013.

Montgomery, James. 'The Cholera Mount', *Blackwood's Edinburgh Magazine*, 32 (November 1832): 802–3.

Moreton-Robinson, Aileen. *The White Possessive: Property, Power and Indigenous Sovereignty*. Minneapolis: University of Minnesota Press, 2015.

Morris, R. J. *Cholera 1832: The Social Response to an Epidemic*. London: Croom Helm, 1976.

Morrison, Robert. 'Blackwood's Berserker: John Wilson and the Language of Extremity', *Romanticism on the Net*, 20 (November 2000).

Morrison, Robert. 'Camaraderie and Conflict: De Quincey and Wilson on Enemy Lines' in *Romanticism and Blackwood's Magazine: 'An Unprecedented Phenomenon'*, edited by Robert Morrison and Daniel S. Roberts, 57–68. Houndmills, Basingstoke, and New York: Palgrave Macmillan, 2013.

Morrison, Robert. 'John Galt's Angular Magazinity', in *John Galt: Observations and Conjectures on Literature, History and Society*, edited by Regina Hewitt, 257–82. Plymouth, MA: Bucknell University Press, 2012.

Morrison, Robert and Chris Baldick. 'Introduction', in *Tales of Terror from Blackwood's Edinburgh Magazine*, edited by Robert Morrison and Chris Baldick, vii–xviii. Oxford: Oxford World's Classics, 1995.

Morrison, Robert and Chris Baldick. 'Introduction', in John Polidori [et al.], *The Vampyre and Other Tales of the Macabre*, vii–xxii. Oxford: Oxford University Press, 2008.

Morrison, Robert and Chris Baldick. 'Notes', in John Polidori [et al.], *The Vampyre and Other Tales of the Macabre*: Oxford University Press. 2008.

Morrison, Robert and Daniel Sanjiv Roberts. '"A Character so various, and yet so indisputably its own": A Passage to Blackwood's Edinburgh Magazine', in *Romanticism and Blackwood's Magazine: 'An Unprecedented Phenomenon'*, edited by Robert Morrison and Daniel S. Roberts, 1–20. Houndmills, Basingstoke, and New York: Palgrave Macmillan, 2013.

Nash, Andrew. 'The Cotter's Kailyard', in *Robert Burns and Cultural Authority*, edited by Robert Crawford, 180–97. Edinburgh: Edinburgh University Press, 1996.

Nash, Andrew. 'Introduction', in *Beside the Bonnie Brier Bush*, Ian Maclaren, ix–xvi. Glasgow: Kennedy & Boyd, 2007.

Nash, Andrew. *Kailyard and Scottish Literature*, Amsterdam and New York: Rodopi, 2007.

Nash, Andrew. 'Victorian Scottish Literature', in *The Cambridge Companion to Scottish Literature*, edited by Gerard Carruthers and Liam McIlvanney, 145–58. Cambridge: Cambridge University Press, 2012.

Noble, Andrew. 'John Wilson (Christopher North) and the Tory Hegemony', in *The History of Scottish Literature. Volume 3: Nineteenth Century*, edited by Douglas Gifford, 125–52. Aberdeen: Aberdeen University Press, 1988.

O'Brien, Karen. 'Colonial Emigration, Public Policy and Tory Romanticism, 1783–1830', in *Lineages of Empire: The Historical Roots of British Imperial Thought*, edited by Duncan Kelly, 161–80. Oxford: Oxford University Press/ British Academy, 2009.

Otis, Laura. *Membranes: Metaphors of Invasion in the Nineteenth-Century Literature, Science and Politics*. Baltimore and London: The John Hopkins University Press, 1999.

Parisot, Eric. *Graveyard Poetry: Religion, Aesthetics and the Mid-Eighteenth Century Poetic Condition*. Farnham and Burlington, VT: Ashgate, 2013.

Parker, Mark. *Literary Magazines and British Romanticism*. Cambridge: Cambridge University Press, 2006.
Pfau, Thomas and Robin Mitchell. 'Romanticism and Modernity', *European Romantic Review*, 21, no. 3 (2010): 267–73.
Pittock, Murray. 'Introduction: What is Scottish Romanticism?', in *The Edinburgh Companion to Scottish Romanticism*, edited by Murray Pittock, 1–12. Edinburgh: Edinburgh University Press, 2011.
Pottinger, George. *Heirs of Enlightenment: Edinburgh Reviewers and Writers, 1800–1830*. Edinburgh: Scottish Academic Press, 1992.
Pratt, Mary Louise. 'Arts of the Contact Zone', *Profession* (1991): 33–40,
Radcliffe, Daniel Hill. 'Imitation, Popular Literacy and "The Cotter's Saturday Night"', in *Critical Essays on Robert Burns*, edited by Donald A. Low, 251–80. New York: C. K. Hall & Company, 1998.
Richardson, Ruth. *Death, Dissection and the Destitute*. London and New York: Routledge and Kegan Paul, 1987.
Richardson, Ruth. '"Trading Assassins" and the Licensing of Anatomy', in *British Medicine in an Age of Reform*, edited by Roger French and Andrew Wear, 74–91. London and New York: Routledge, 1991.
Richardson, Thomas. 'John Gibson Lockhart and Blackwood's: Shaping the Romantic Periodical Press', in *Romanticism and Blackwood's Magazine: 'An Unprecedented Phenomenon'*, edited by Robert Morrison and Daniel S. Roberts. Houndmills, Basingstoke, and New York: Palgrave Macmillan, 2013.
Roberts, Jessica. 'Medicine and the Body in Romantic Periodical Press', PhD diss., University of Salford, 2014.
Royle, Nicholas. 'The Ghost of Hamlet in *The House with the Green Shutters*', *Studies in Scottish Literature*, 27, no. 1 (1992): 105–12.
Ruddick, William 'Introduction', in J. G. Lockhart, *Peter's Letters to His Kinfolk*, vii–xxiii. Edinburgh: Scottish Academic Press, 1977.
Rudy, Jason. *Imagined Homelands: British Poetry in the Colonies*. Baltimore: Johns Hopkins Press, 2017.
Said, Edward. *Orientalism*. London: Penguin, 2003.
Salyer, Matt. '"Nae mortal man should be entrusted wi' sic an ingine": *Blackwood's Edinburgh Magazine* and the Tory Problem of Romantic Genius', *Victorian Periodicals Review*, 46, no. 1 (Spring 2013): 92–115.
Sanders, Andrew. *Charles Dickens Resurrectionist*. London: Macmillan Press, 1982.
Sappol, Michael. *A Traffic in Dead Bodies: Anatomy and Social Identity in Nineteenth-Century America*. Princeton: Princeton University Press, 2002.
Schoenfield, Mark. *British Periodicals and Romantic Identity: The 'Literary Lower Empire'*. Houndmills, Basingstoke, and New York: Palgrave Macmillan, 2009.
Schor, Esther. *Bearing the Dead*. Princeton: Princeton University Press, 1994.
Scott, Paul Henderson. 'Galt, John (1779–1839), Novelist', in *Oxford Dictionary of National Biography*, Oxford: Oxford University Press, 2004, https://www.oxforddnb.com/view/10.1093/ref:odnb/9780198614128.001.0001/odnb-9780198614128-e-10316 (accessed 10 June 2023).
Scott, Walter. *The Journal of Sir Walter Scott: From the Original Manuscript at Abbotsford*, 2 vols, edited by David Douglas. Cambridge: Cambridge

University Press, 2013.
Scott, Walter. *The Lay of the Last Minstrel*. London and Edinburgh: Ballantyne & Co, 1810.
Scott, Walter. *Old Mortality*. Oxford: Oxford University Press, 1993.
Scott, Walter. *Waverley*. Oxford: Oxford University Press, 1998.
Segerblad, Hege R. 'Transcending the Gothic: "The Extravagancies of Blackwood"', MPhil thesis, University of Glasgow, 2010.
Shapira, Yael. *Inventing the Gothic Corpse: The Thrill of Human Remains in the Eighteenth-Century Novel*. Houndmills, Basingstoke, and New York: Palgrave Macmillan, 2018.
Sharp, Sarah. 'A Club of "murder-fanciers": Thomas De Quincey's Essays "On Murder" and Consuming Violence in *Blackwood's Edinburgh Magazine*', *Nineteenth-Century Contexts*, 46, no. 1 (2023): 1–18.
Sharp, Sarah. 'A Death in the Cottage: Spiritual and Economic Improvement in Romantic-Era Scottish Death Narratives', in *Cultures of Improvement in Scottish Romanticism 1707–1840*, edited by Alex Benchimol and Gerard McKeever, 213–32. London: Routledge, 2018.
Sharp, Sarah. 'Exporting the Cotter's Saturday Night: Robert Burns, Scottish Romantic Nationalism and Colonial Settler Identity', *Romanticism*, 25, no. 1 (2019): 81–9.
Sharp, Sarah. 'Hogg's Murder of Ravens: Storytelling, Community and Posthumous Mutilation', *Studies in Hogg and His World*, 23 (2013): 31–40.
Shattock, Joanne. 'George Eliot, G. H. Lewes, and the House of Blackwood, 1856–60', *19: Interdisciplinary Studies in the Long Nineteenth Century*, 29 (2020), doi: 10.16995/ntn.1920.
Shattock, Joanne. 'The Sense of Place and Blackwood's (Edinburgh) Magazine', *Victorian Periodicals Review*, 49, no. 3 (2016): 431–42.
Shaw, Michael. *The Fin-de-Siècle Scottish Revival: Romance, Decadence and Celtic Identity*. Edinburgh: Edinburgh University Press, 2020.
Shields, Juliet. 'From Family Roots to the Routes of Empire: National Tales and the Domestication of the Scottish Highlands', *ELH*, 72, no. 4 (2005): 919–40.
Shields, Juliet. 'Highland Emigration and the Transformation of Nostalgia in Romantic Poetry', *European Romantic Review*, 23, no. 6 (December 2012): 765–84.
Shields, Juliet. 'Margaret Oliphant at the Margins of Maga', *The Bottle Imp*, 4 (2017).
Shields, Juliet. *Nation and Migration: The Making of British Atlantic Literature, 1765–1835*. Oxford: Oxford University Press, 2015.
Shields, Juliet. 'Oliphant and Co.', *The Bottle Imp*, 5 (2018).
Siek, Thomas. '"A Rose by Any Other Name": Types of Cholera in the 19th Century', in *Cholera: Hamilton's Forgotten Epidemics*, edited by D. Ann Herring and Heather T Battles. Hamilton, Ont.: Department of Anthropology, McMaster University, 2012.
Smith, Adam. *The Theory of Moral Sentiments*. Edited by D. D. Raphael and A. L. Macfie. Indianapolis: Liberty Fund, 1982.
Smollett, Tobias. *The Expedition of Humphry Clinker*. Oxford: Oxford University Press, 2009.

St Clair, William. *The Reading Nation in the Romantic Period*. Cambridge: Cambridge University Press, 2005.

Stevenson, Robert Louis. 'The Body Snatcher', in Robert Louis Stevenson, *Strange Case of Dr Jekyll and Mr Hyde and Other Tales*, edited by Roger Luckhurst, 67–84 .Oxford: Oxford University Press, 2006.

Stevenson, Robert Louis. 'A Gossip on Romance', in *R.L. Stevenson on Fiction*, edited by Glenda Norquay, 57–63. Edinburgh: Edinburgh University Press, 1999.

Stevenson, Robert Louis. 'Review: The Noctes Ambrosianae: The Comedy of the Noctes Ambrosianae', *The Works of Robert Louis Stevenson*, vol. 9, 230–1. London: Forgotten Books, 2013.

Strout, Alan Lang. *A Bibliography of Articles in Blackwood's Magazine*. Lubbock: Texas Technical College Library, 1959.

Sucksmith, Peter. 'The Secret of Immediacy: Dickens' Debt to the Tale of Terror in Blackwood's', *Nineteenth-Century Fiction*, 26, no. 2 (1971): 145–57.

Sullivan, Alvin. *British Literary Magazines: The Romantic Age, 1786–1836*. Westport, CT, and London: Greenwood Press, 1983.

Trumpener, Katie. *Bardic Nationalism: The Romantic Novel and the British Empire*. Princeton: Princeton University Press, 1997.

Veitch, James. *George Douglas Brown*. London: Herbert Jenkins, 1952.

Verdery, Katherine. *The Political Lives of Dead Bodies*. New York: Columbia Press, 2000.

Waddell, Nathan. *Modern John Buchan: A Critical Introduction*. Newcastle: Cambridge Scholars, 2020.

Wall, Dan. 'Looking for Literary Scotland: J. G. Lockhart and the "Horae Germanicae"', in *What rough beasts?: Irish and Scottish Studies in the New Millennium*, edited by S. Alcobia-Murphy, 207–17. Newcastle upon Tyne: Cambridge Scholars, 2008.

Wallace, Valerie. *Scottish Presbyterianism and Settler Colonial Politics* (Cham: Palgrave Macmillan, 2018).

Walton, Samantha. 'Scottish Modernism, Kailyard Fiction and the Woman at Home', in *Transitions in Middlebrow Writing, 1880–1930*, edited by Kate Macdonald and Christopher Singer, 141–60. London: Palgrave Macmillan, 2015.

Warren, Samuel. 'Passages from the Diary of a Late Physician – Chap X – A Slight Cold, Rich and Poor and Gravedoings', *Blackwood's Edinburgh Magazine*, 29 (June 1831): 946–67.

Webby, Elizabeth. 'The Grave in the Bush', in *Tilting at Matilda: Literature, Women, Aborigines and the Church in Contemporary Australia*, edited by Dennis Haskell, 30–38. Fremantle: Fremantle Arts Centre Press, 1994.

Westover, Paul. 'At Home in the Churchyard: Graves, Localism and Literary Heritage in the Prose Pastoral', in *Representing Place in British Literature and Culture, 1660–1830*, edited by Evan Gottlieb and Juliet Shields, 70–88. London: Routledge, 2013.

Westover, Paul. *Necromanticism: Travelling to Meet the Dead, 1750–1860*. Houndmills, Basingstoke, and New York: Palgrave Macmillan, 2012.

Wheatley, Kim. 'Introduction', in *Romantic Periodicals and Print Culture*, edited by Kim Wheatley, 1–20. London: Taylor & Francis, 2003.

Williams, J. C. 'Deathly Sentimentalism: Sarah Fielding, Henry Mackenzie', *Eighteenth Century Fiction*, 30, no. 2 (Winter 2017–18): 175–93.
Wilson, John. 'The Desolate Village. A Reverie', *Blackwood's Edinburgh Magazine*, 1 (April 1817): 70–1.
Wilson, John. *The Foresters*. Edinburgh and London: William Blackwood and T. Cadell, 1825.
Wilson, John. 'An Hour's Talk about Poetry', *Blackwood's Edinburgh Magazine*, 30 (September 1831): 475–90.
Wilson, John. 'Is the Edinburgh Review a Religious and Patriotic Work?', *Blackwood's Edinburgh Magazine*, 20 (October 1818): 228–33.
Wilson, John. 'Letters from the Lakes. Written during the Summer of 1818', *Blackwood's Edinburgh Magazine*, 4 (March 1819): 735–44.
Wilson, John. *Lights and Shadows of Scottish Life*. Boston, MA: Saxton & Kelt: 1846.
Wilson, John. 'Lines Written in a Lonely Burial Ground on the Northern Coast of the Highlands', *Blackwood's Edinburgh Magazine*, 2 (December 1817): 295–6.
Wilson, John. 'The Radical's Saturday Night', *Blackwood's Edinburgh Magazine*, 6 (December 1819): 257–62.
Wilson, John. 'Some Observations on the Poetry of the Agricultural and that of the Pastoral Districts of Scotland, Illustrated by a Comparative View of the Genius of Burns and the Ettrick Shepherd', *Blackwood's Edinburgh Magazine*, 4 (February 1819): 521–9.
Wilson, John. *The Trials of Margaret Lyndsay*. Edinburgh and London: William Blackwood and T. Cadell, 1823.
Wood, Nigel. 'Goldsmith's English Malady', *Studies in the Literary Imagination*, 44, no. 1 (Spring 2011): 63–83.
Wu, Duncan. 'Introduction' in *Romanticism: An Anthology*, edited by Duncan Wu, xxxii–xlv. Chichester: Wiley-Blackwell, 2012.
Wu, Duncan. *William Hazlitt: The First Modern Man*. Oxford: Oxford University Press, 2008.

Unattributed Articles and Broadsides

'Galt's *Lawrie Todd*', *Westminster Review* (April 1830): 405–16.
'The Nature and the Cure of the Indian Cholera', *The Englishman's Magazine* (London), 1 (June 1831): 146–58.
'Noctes Ambrosianae', *Blackwood's Edinburgh Magazine*, 18 (December 1825): 751–65.
'Noctes Ambrosianae', *Blackwood's Edinburgh Magazine*, 25 (March 1829): 371–400.
'Noctes Ambrosianae', *Blackwood's Edinburgh Magazine*, 26 (September 1829): 389–404.
Resurrection. Edinburgh: John Campbell, 1830–9.
'Review: Observation on the Nature and Treatment of Cholera and on the Pathology of Mucous Membranes', *The Eclectic Review*, 5 (March 1831): 244–7.

'A Scots Resurrectionist', *The Saturday Review of Politics, Literature, Science and Art*, 84 (17 October 1897): 403–4.

'Scottish Novels of the Second Class', *The Edinburgh Magazine and Literary Miscellany* (July 1823): 1–9.

'Some Passages in the Life of Mr Adam Blair, Minister of the Gospel at Cross Meikle', *London Magazine*, 5 (May 1822): 385–400.

Index

References to notes are indicated by n.

Aboriginal peoples, 174–5
Ackerknecht, Edwin H., 132
adultery, 61
afterlife, 57, 81–2, 156
Alison, Archibald, 132–3, 148n25
Alvarez, A., 76
ambition, 109–11
anatomy, 106–7, 108–9, 112, 114–19
Anderson, Benedict, *Imagined Communities*, 8, 9, 10
anonymous dead, 9–10
Aries, Phillipe, 8
Australia, 1, 21, 152–3, 161, 173–5

Barrell, John, 4, 138
Barrie, J. M., 3, 19, 53, 65
 A Window in Thrums, 66–9
Bates, A. W., 109
Baucom, Ian, 153
Benchimol, Alex, 10
bereavement, 56
Bewell, Alan, 130, 131
Bhabha, Homi K., 154
Blackwood, William, 2, 15, 35, 79
 and Lockhart/Wilson, 28, 29, 30
Blackwood's Edinburgh Magazine, 2, 13–14
 and body snatching, 23, 103–4, 105–6
 and cholera epidemic, 128–9
 and colonies, 130, 152, 155
 and Galt, 79
 and Hogg, 90–1, 94
 and Howison, 160–4
 and Lockhart/Wilson, 28–9
 and Montgomery, 135–6
 and novels, 17–18
 and politics, 15–17
 and Stevenson, 121
 see also Burke, Edmund; *Chapters on Churchyards*; *Noctes Ambrosianae*
Blair, Kirstie, 20
Blair, Robert, 'The Grave', 158
body snatching, 23, 103–4, 107–9, 112, 118
 and Stevenson, 119–23
Bowler, Peter J., 11
Bowles, Caroline Southey, 1, 2, 3, 13; *see also Chapters on Churchyards*
Britain *see* Great Britain
British Empire, 3, 21, 151–2, 153–5, 157–9
Bromwich, David, 6
Brown, W. A. F., 78
Buchan, John, 3, 21
 Witch Wood, 129, 144–7
Burial Act (1823), 77, 79
burials, 2
 and Buchan, 146
 and bush graves, 1, 173–5
 and cholera epidemic, 128, 132–4
 and colonies, 162–3
 and the Highlands, 156
 and India, 157–9

and kailyard, 66
and living beings, 115
and suicides, 76, 77, 81, 83–4, 86
Burke, Edmund, 4, 5–6, 8, 45, 46
Letter to a Noble Lord, 6–7
Reflections on the Revolution in France, 5
Burke, William, 104, 108, 110–11, 120
Burns, Robert, 22, 38, 39, 42–3
'Holy Willie's Prayer', 40
'The Cotter's Saturday Night', 28, 38, 39, 40–1, 43–4
'The Holy Fair', 43
Byron, Lord, 76
'English Bards and Scotch Reviewers', 135

cadavers, 104, 106–8, 114–15
Calvinism, 57, 169
Campbell, Ian, 53, 59, 95
Canada, 161–3, 170
Carlyle, Thomas, 20
Past and Present, 141
catacombs, 1
Chadwick, Edwin, 135
Chaldee Manuscript, 30
Chandler, James, 74
Chapters on Churchyards (Bowles), 52, 62–3, 64–5, 173
'Broad Summerford', 63–4
Cheyne, George, *The English Malady; or, a treatise of Nervous Diseases of all kinds*, 78
cholera epidemic, 23, 127–9, 131–3
and colonialism, 130–1
and conspiracy theories, 136–7
and Hogg, 138–43
and Montgomery, 133–6
Christie, William, 104
Clearances, 142, 157, 169
Cockney School, 15, 17–18, 30, 64
Coleridge, Samuel Taylor, 42
collective identity, 7–8, 9
Colley, Linda, 8, 154
colonialism, 23, 152–3
and cholera, 130–1
and the dead, 155–6
and Galt, 164–72

and Howison, 160–4
see also British Empire
Constable, Archibald, 2, 14–15, 35
corpses, 4–5, 60, 73
and brides, 100n55
and Hogg, 89, 91–2, 93, 94, 138–9
see also cadavers
cottage life, 44–5
Covenanters, 34, 61, 81
Coyer, Megan, 21, 92, 106, 133
Craig, Cairns, 97, 98
Crawford, Catherine, 110
Crockett, S. R., 65
Cronin, Richard, 33
cultural nationalism, 9, 12, 21, 35, 173–4, 175
and *Blackwood's*, 14, 16, 18
and England, 62
and Lockhart, 37
cyclicality, 54, 67–8

Daniell, David, 145
Davidson, John, 20
Davis, Leith, 12
De Groot, H. B., 142
De Quincey, Thomas, 31, 47n5
dead, the, 2–3, 4–10
and Barrie, 66–7
and colonialism, 165–6
and tales of terror, 113
and Wilson, 51–2, 53–5
see also national dead
deathbed, 2, 4, 5, 56, 66
and *Adam Blair*, 59–60
dissection, 106–8
Divine, Ann Roberts, 84
doctors, 106, 108–12, 118–19
Douglas, Sir George, 105
The 'Blackwood' Group, 65–6
Douglas Brown, George, *The House with the Green Shutters*, 76, 95–8
Duncan, Ian, 4, 13, 39
and *Edinburgh Review*, 15
and history, 98n12
and regional novels, 17
and Scott, 32, 35
Scott's Shadow, 80
and upright corpse, 138

economics, 104
Edinburgh Review, The, 13, 14–16, 20–1
emigration, 165–72
emotion, 54, 104–5, 110
English churchyards, 62–4
English Malady, 77–8
Enlightenment, 4, 8, 74, 80, 154; *see also* Scottish Enlightenment
epidemic disease, 36; *see also* cholera epidemic
exhumation, 73, 88–9, 90, 91–2, 93; *see also* body snatching
exile, 58, 64, 69, 155, 167

family, 28, 60, 63–4, 68–9, 93, 96–7
  and cholera epidemic, 134, 140, 142
  and Moir, 103, 105–6, 158
  and Wilson, 41–2, 44–6, 53–7
famous dead, 9
Flynn, Phillip, 37
forefathers, 22, 28, 36, 41–2, 52
  and Bowles, 62
  and Galt, 81, 169
  and kailyard, 65, 66
foreshadowing, 97
forgotten graves, 152, 155–60, 173–5
Fosso, Kurt, 41
French Revolution, 5, 6–7
Fry, Michael, 19
Fulford, Tim, 162
funerals, 54, 59, 60, 67, 128

Galt, John, 13–14, 17, 18, 98n12, 164–72
  Annals of the Parish, 22, 23, 60, 75, 79–87
  Bogle Corbet, 152, 165–6, 169–72
  'The Buried Alive', 2, 113, 114–16, 121, 139, 151
  The Entail, 84
  Lawrie Todd, 151, 152, 165–9, 171–2
ghost stories, 4
Gifford, Douglas, 5, 147
Godwin, William, 4
Goethe, Johann Wolfgang von, 76

Goldsmith, Oliver, 'Deserted Village', 36, 37
good death, 52, 54, 55, 56, 169
Gothic novels, 4, 109
graveyards, 1, 4
  and *Adam Blair*, 60–2
  and *Annals of the Parish*, 82–3, 87
  and body snatchers, 103–4
  and Bowles, 63–4
  and empire, 152
  and French Revolution, 6–7
  and *Old Mortality*, 33–4, 35
  and suicide, 91–2
  and Wilson, 51–2, 54, 58–9
  see also forgotten graves
Gray, Thomas, Elegy Written in a Country Churchyard, 43, 62
Great Britain, 8
  and cholera epidemic, 130–3, 136–7
  and suicides, 76–8
  and Victorian period, 19–20
  see also British Empire
Great Reform Bill (1832), 23, 127, 128
Greek tragedy, 97
Green, Sarah, *Scotch Novel Reading; or, Modern Quackery, by a Cockney*, 17–18
grief, 4, 59, 60; *see also* mourning

Hallam, Henry, 20
Halliday, Andrew, *A General View of the Present State of Lunatics and Lunatic Asylums in Great Britain and Ireland*, 78
Hamilton, Elizabeth, *The Cottagers of Glenburnie*, 56
Hardy, Thomas, *The Mayor of Casterbridge*, 97
Hare, William, 104, 108–9, 110–11, 120
Hart, Francis, 31
Hasler, Anthony, 5, 55
Hayden, John O., 29
Hazlitt, William, 30
Henderson, T. F., 105–6
Herman, Arthur, 10
Heron, Robert, 38

Hessell, Nikki, 21
Hewitt, Regina, 80
Higgins, David, 41, 42
Highlands, 4, 141–2, 143, 152, 162
 and emptiness, 156–7, 169–70
historical narrative, 75
historical romance, 19
Hogg, James, 2, 3, 4–5, 13–14, 18, 98n12
 'A Scots Mummy', 73, 75–6, 87–90, 91, 92
 'Description of a Peasant's Funeral', 38
 Highland Journeys, 142
 'One Thousand, Eight Hundred and Thirty One', 127
 The Private Memoirs and Confessions of a Justified Sinner, 22, 23, 73, 75, 90–5
 'Some Terrible Letters from Scotland', 121, 128–9, 138–43
 The Three Perils of Woman, 142
 and Wilson, 38–9, 47n5, 100n77
Home, John, *Douglas*, 34
Howison, John, 18, 23, 160–4
 'Adventure in the North West Territory', 152, 161–3
 'The Fatal Repast', 163–4
Hughes, Gillian, 17
Hyam, Ronald, 153

imagination, 36–7
immortality, 9, 54
India, 130, 133, 154, 161
 and burials, 157–9
 and Scotland, 153
Indigenous peoples, 152, 161–3, 174–5
industrialisation, 78, 85–6
Ireland, 8
Irvine, R. P., 79, 165
Italian Boy murders, 108

Jack, Ronnie, 30
Jacobite Rebellion, 4, 157
Jarrells, Anthony, 5, 17, 80, 129
 and colonies, 130, 155
Jeffrey, Francis, 15, 17, 31–2, 59, 79

kailyard, 3, 19, 53, 65–70, 95
Keats, John, 15
Kennedy, Meegan, 110, 119
Killick, Tim, 53, 113
King, J. W., 135
kirkyard, 2, 3, 22–4
 and afterlives, 52
 and Buchan, 144–5, 146–7
 and colonialism, 151–2
 and empire, 155
 and English literature, 63
 and fiction, 13–18
 and kailyard, 69
 and lonely graves, 159
 and McCombie, 173–5
 and migrants, 165–8
 and stasis, 129–30
 and Stevenson, 120–1, 123
 and time, 74–5
 and Whig influence, 20–1
 and Wilson, 28, 45–7
 see also graveyards
Knowles, Thomas, 69
Knox, Dr Robert, 108–9, 120
Kohlke, Marie-Louise, 109–10

Lake School, 41
Laquer, Thomas W., 8
Lights and Shadows of Scottish Life (Wilson), 2, 44, 51–2, 53, 65
 'Consumption', 155
 'The Elder's Death-Bed', 55
 'The Elder's Funeral', 54, 55, 58, 129–30
 "The Headstone', 54–5
 'The Minister's Widow', 55
 "The Twins', 53, 55
Lincoln, Andrew, 8, 12
Lockhart, J. G., 13–14, 28–31
 Adam Blair, 59–62, 74, 146
 and graveyards, 35–6
 and kirkyard, 22, 52
 and nation, 104–5
 and novels, 17, 18–19
 Peter's Letters to His Kinfolk, 31, 42–3
 'Remarks on Schlegel's History of Literature', 37
 and Scott, 15

Lockhart, J. G. (*cont.*)
    'The Clydesdale Yeoman's Return', 50n92
London Magazine, The, 15, 59
lonely graves *see* forgotten graves
Löwy, Michael, 11
Lynd, Robert, 'Leichhardt's Grave', 173

McAllister, David, 9
McCausland, Joan, 138, 139
McCombie, Thomas
    'Australian Sketch', 1–2, 3–4, 21, 152–3
    'The Bush-Graves of Australia', 172–5
McCracken-Flesher, Caroline, 107, 110–11
McCrone, David, 12
MacDonald, George, 20
McGuire, Kelly, 78
McIlvanney, Liam, 121
Mack, Douglas S., 39, 58
McKeever, Gerard Lee, 10, 164
    Dialectics of Improvement, 13
Mackenzie, Henry, 38, 55
Mackillop, Andrew, 157
Maclaren, Ian, 19, 21, 53, 65, 66
    'A Scholar's Funeral', 67
    Beside the Bonnie Brier Bush, 66, 68
    The Days of Auld Lang Syne, 66, 68, 69
McNeil, Kenneth, 13
Macnish, Robert, 133
    'An Execution in Paris', 113
Macpherson, James, 4, 156
Makdisi, Saree, 2, 11, 74, 154, 158–9
Malthus, T. M., *Essay on the Principles of Population*, 137, 148n42
Manderson, David, 14, 15, 141
Mangham, Andrew, 115
Manning, Susan, 90
Marshall, Tim, 109
Mason, Michael York, 91
Massie, Alan, 145
Maxwell-Stuart, Peter, 83
medicine, 106–7, 113

Mehta, Uday Singh, 154, 161
memory, 36–7, 54, 64
    and cholera epidemic, 134
    and graveyards, 58–9
    and migrants, 166–7
    and native burial, 155–6
mental health, 78–9
Metropolitan Magazine, The, 138, 148n47
Mill, James, *History of British India*, 154
Millar, J. H., 'The Literature of the Kailyard', 65, 66
Mitchell, Robert, 11–12
mobility, 129–30
modernity, 10–12, 54, 95–8
    and kailyard, 68
    and suicides, 76–8, 84
Moir, D. M., 18, 23, 113, 117, 133
    'Benjie on the Curtain', 111–12
    The Life of Mansie Wauch Tailor in Dalkeith, 105–6
    'Lines Written in a British Burial Ground in India', 157–9
    'Wonderful Passage in the Life of Mansie Wauch', 103–4
monarchy, 45
Montgomery, James, 23
    'The Cholera Mount', 128, 133–6
    The Wanderer of Switzerland, 135
morality, 56
Morris, R. J., 137
Moreton-Robinson, Aileen, 161
mourning, 8, 41, 128
Murder Act (1752), 107

Napoleonic Wars, 16
Nash, Andrew, 19, 20, 38, 44
    and kailyard, 65, 66
national dead, 1, 7, 8, 9, 36
    and *Blackwood's*, 22, 23
    and Bowles, 62–3, 64
national memorials, 1, 9, 134, 136
nationalism, 21, 52, 168–9
nationhood, 5–6, 7, 8, 9–10
Noble, Andrew, 31, 47n5
Noctes Ambrosianae, 14, 87–90, 117, 135

and Burke and Hare, 108–9
and Highlands, 141–2
North America, 151, 152, 162, 164–72; *see also* Canada; United States of America
nostalgia, 67, 78

Oliphant, Margaret, 20
Ossian poems, 4, 156
Otis, Laura, 132

paganism, 145
Paine, Thomas, 46, 57
pastoralism, 36–7, 52, 58, 62, 174
and Galt, 166, 167
and Hogg, 88, 90, 92, 138–9
patriarchy, 45, 46
patriotism, 6, 15–16
peasantry, 39–40, 44, 129
and Highlands, 141
and mental health, 78–9
and politics, 58
periodicals, 29–30
Peterloo Massacre, 40
Pfau, Thomas, 11–12
physicians *see* doctors
piety, 28, 40
Pittock, Murray, 12–13
plague, 129, 144–7
politics, 4, 8, 9, 134–6
and cholera epidemic, 128, 132–3, 137
and rival magazines, 14–16
and working classes, 58
see also Burke, Edmund
poor, the, 136–7, 143
Poor Law Act (1834), 137
Pratt, Mary Louise, 154
predestination, 57
Presbyterianism, 40, 47, 57, 65, 66; *see also* Covenanters
Price, Richard, *A Discourse on the Love of Our Country*, 5
Pringle (Thomas) and Cleghorn (James), 29, 36
professionalism, 110–11, 113–14
provincial fiction, 69–70

Quarterly Review, 19

radicalism, 28
realism, 19, 20
regional novels, 17–18
religion, 15–16, 45, 55–6, 93
and cholera epidemic, 132–3
see also piety; Presbyterianism
resignation, 54, 55–7, 64
resurrection, 66, 139
resurrectionists, 104, 107, 112, 118
Richardson, Ruth, 107
rising corpses, 4–5
Roberts, Jessica, 133
Robertson, William, 10
romance revival, 20
Romanticism, 3, 11–13
and Europe, 37
and periodicals, 29–30
and Stevenson, 122, 123
Ruddick, William, 42–3
Rudy, Jason, 21
rural scenes, 19, 30
and *Adam Blair*, 60–2
and *Annals of the Parish*, 82–3
and Barrie, 66–8
and Buchan, 144–5
and Douglas Brown, 95–6
and Hogg, 38–9
and Lockhart, 42–3
and mental health, 78–9
and *The Private Memoirs and Confessions of a Justified Sinner*, 92–3
and Wilson, 36–7, 44–5, 53–9

Said, Edward, 154
Salyer, Matt, 5, 7
Sandford, Daniel Keyte, 'A Night in the Catacombs', 113, 117
Sappol, Michael, 107
Sayre, Robert, 11
Schlegel, August Wilhelm, 42
Schlegel, Friedrich, 22, 42
Lectures on the History of Literature, Ancient and Modern, 37
Schoenfield, Mark, 16, 90–1, 94
Schor, Esther, *Bearing the Dead*, 8–9
science, 104

Index

Scotland, 3, 8, 43, 44
  and *Blackwood's*, 16–17
  and cholera epidemic, 138
  and colonialism, 152, 153–5
  and *Old Mortality*, 32–3, 34, 35
  and Poor Relief, 137
  and provincial fiction, 69–70
  see also Highlands
Scots Magazine, The, 15
Scott, John, 15, 30
Scott, Walter, 1, 2, 3, 13, 22
  The Black Dwarf, 35
  and Burke and Hare, 110–11
  and death, 18
  Heart of Midlothian, 84
  Lay of the Last Minstrel, 34
  Old Mortality, 4, 32–5, 173
  Paul's Letters to His Kinfolk, 42
  and regional novels, 17
  Tales of my Landlord, 17, 33, 35
  Waverley, 32, 37, 157
Scottish Enlightenment, 10–11, 12–13
self-murder *see* suicide
sentimental fiction, 4, 105
sentimentality, 55
separation, 55
Shakespeare, William, 97
Shapira, Yael, 113, 117
Shattock, Joanne, 14
Shaw, Michael, 20
Shelley, Percy Bysshe, 15
Shields, Juliet, 18, 19, 20, 21, 156
Siek, Thomas, 130
Smith, Adam, 10, 74, 115
  The Theory of Moral Sentiments, 110
Smollett, Tobias, *The Expedition of Humphry Clinker*, 42
Southey, Robert, 2, 41, 62
Spy, The (newspaper), 38
stadial history, 74, 80, 154
Staël, Germaine de, 37
Stevenson, Robert Louis, 19, 21, 105
  'The Body Snatcher', 119–23
Stewart, Dugald, 74
suicide, 23, 75–9
  and ballads, 100n55
  and Douglas Brown, 95–8

  and Galt, 79–87
  and grave scene, 73–4
  and Hogg, 88–95
supernatural, 34, 83, 109, 120
  and Buchan, 144, 146
  and Hogg, 73, 138, 164
surgeons *see* doctors

Tait's Edinburgh Magazine, 1, 172
terror, tales of, 105, 112–17, 122
  and colonialism, 152, 161, 163–4
Thomson, Henry, 'Le Revenant', 113, 121
Thomson, James, 20
time, 74–5, 95–6; *see also* cyclicality; nostalgia
Toryism, 7, 15, 43
Trumpener, Katie, 10–11, 12, 21, 165, 175
Tuke, William, 79

uncanny, 4–5
Union of Parliaments (1707), 12, 40
United States of America (USA), 69, 151, 161, 168–9
unknown soldier, 9, 10
'upright corpse', 4–5, 138
urbanisation, 78

Verdery, Katherine, 9
Victoria of Great Britain, Queen, 19

Walton, Samantha, 65
Warburton Anatomy Act (1832), 106
Warren, Samuel, 1, 2, 13, 18
  Diary of a Late Physician, 173
  'Gravedoings', 116–17, 118–19
West Port murders, 108–9, 120, 139
Westover, Paul, 9, 62
Wheatley, Kim, 29
Whigs, 14–16, 20–1, 131
Wilson, John, 3, 5, 13–14, 28–31
  and Burke and Hare, 109
  and colonialism, 23
  and *Edinburgh Review*, 15–16
  and Edinburgh University, 19
  and graveyards, 35–6
  and Hogg, 100n77
  and kirkyard, 22

and Montgomery, 136
and nation, 104
and novels, 17, 18
and reviews, 47n5
and rural fiction, 53–9
Wilson, John (works)
'The Desolate Village', 36–7, 58, 74
The Foresters, 53, 56, 60
'Letters from the Lakes', 41–2
'Lines Written in a Lonely Burial Ground on the Northern Coast of the Highlands', 156–7, 159
'The Radical's Saturday Night', 28, 43–7
'Some Observations on the Poetry of the Agricultural and that of the Pastoral Districts of Scotland, Illustrated by a Comparative View of the Genius of Burns and the Ettick Shepherd', 37–8, 39–41
The Trials of Margaret Lyndsay, 53–4, 55–6, 57, 171
see also *Lights and Shadows of Scottish Life*
witchcraft, 83
women, 84–5
Wordsworth, William, 22, 41, 47n5, 74
Excursion, 62
'Letters from the Lakes', 63
working classes *see* peasantry
Wu, Duncan, 11, 30

www.ingramcontent.com/pod-product-compliance
Lightning Source LLC
LaVergne TN
LVHW011724070225
803225LV00004B/375